Alternative Leadership Strategies in the Prehispanic Southwest

Alternative Leadership Strategies in the Prehispanic Southwest

EDITED BY BARBARA J. MILLS

The University of Arizona Press   *Tucson*

The University of Arizona Press
© 2000 The Arizona Board of Regents

First Printing

05   04   03   02   01   00   6   5   4   3   2   1

Library of Congress Cataloging-in-Publication Data

Alternative leadership strategies in the prehispanic Southwest /
edited by Barbara J. Mills
    p. cm.
Includes bibliographical references and index.
    ISBN 0-8165-2028-3 (cloth : alk. paper)
    1. Indians of North America—Southwest, New—Antiquities.
2. Indians of North America—Southwest, New—Politics and
government.   3. Pueblo Indians—Politics and government.
4. Southwest, New—Antiquities.   I. Mills, Barbara J., 1955–.
    E78.S7 .A4757 2000   99-050694
    303.3'4'09790902—dc21   CIP

British Library Cataloguing-in-Publication Data
A catalogue record for this book is available from the British Library.

Publication of this book is made possible in part by the proceeds of a
permanent endowment created with assistance of a Challenge Grant
from the National Endowment for the Humanities, a federal agency.

To my parents,
Joan A. Mills and William F. Mills, Jr.

Contents

Preface

THE INITIAL INSPIRATION for this volume was a graduate seminar that I taught at the University of Arizona in the spring of 1997 on the "Roots of Inequality." Like other archaeologists working in small-scale societies, I had been disappointed with political models based solely on hierarchical, highly centralized societies. I was also excited by a burgeoning anthropological literature on inequality and the prospect of reading it with a fine group of graduate students. I thank Dale Breneman, Sarah Herr, Eric Kaldahl, Matthew Littler, A. Rene Muñoz, Elizabeth Perry, Susan Stinson, and Scott Van Keuren for their critical reading and lively discussions.

During the seminar, it became evident that the new literature had important implications for the interpretation of inequality in Southwestern societies. It seemed time for a pan-Southwestern look at political organization and especially its intersection with social, ritual, and economic organization. New questions could be asked of Southwestern data, and Southwestern case studies clearly had potential for interesting worldwide comparisons of trajectories through time. Therefore, I decided to organize a Society for American Archaeology (SAA) symposium to look at case studies of leadership strategies across the Southwest.

The symposium was held at the 1998 SAA annual meetings in Seattle. The symposium was entitled "Network or Corporate?: Alternative Leadership Strategies in the Greater Southwest." I specifically asked the participants to focus on one of the recent models, dual-processual theory, that was currently being used to address leadership. The papers in this volume were all originally presented at that SAA symposium. However, in making revisions, I asked the participants to consider the implications of other theoretical approaches that could be used to model leadership development in Southwestern societies. It is to all the authors' credit that they not only were up to the task but did so in such varied and interesting ways.

I particularly thank the contributors to this volume for their unflagging enthusiasm. With short notice, they quickly responded to my initial queries regarding the original SAA symposium. The authors devoted precious time before the commencement of their field seasons to paper revisions and again, right before the 1999 SAA meetings, to the reviewers' comments.

Two anonymous reviewers provided cogent comments for manuscript revisions. I also thank Kerstin Reinschmidt, a graduate student at the University of Arizona, who ably merged the references cited and helped with the final manuscript checking and preparation, and Sarah Herr for her insightful comments on chapter 1. Evelyn VandenDolder, formerly of the University of Arizona Press, provided essential guidelines for the manuscript revision, and Mary M. Hill carefully copyedited the final manuscript. Christine Szuter, director of the University of Arizona Press, is to be profusely thanked for her initial encouragement and excellent advice for manuscript revision. Finally, I thank T. J. Ferguson for his unflagging encouragement and support.

Alternative Leadership Strategies in the Prehispanic Southwest

1

Alternative Models, Alternative Strategies

Leadership in the Prehispanic Southwest

BARBARA J. MILLS

WHAT IS THE basis of leadership in middle-range societies? How are differences in leadership strategies manifested in the archaeological record? What do differences in leadership strategies in middle-range societies tell us about the institutionalization of inequality? These questions form the chrysalis of a new direction in archaeological research on the evolution of complexity (e.g., Arnold 1996b; Price and Feinman 1995) yet have not been systematically asked of Southwestern data. The goal of this volume is to use these new models to look at leadership strategies in the Greater Southwest to understand the different trajectories that characterized the diverse social formations in this large geographic area. The case studies illustrate complementary approaches that may be taken in studying political organization in middle-range societies. They also provide a basis for comparative analyses between areas of the Southwest and with other regions.

The study of leadership strategies is embedded within four major changes that have influenced recent archaeological practice. First, there is reconsideration of models used to interpret social and political change. Instead of a single, dictatorial, neo-evolutionary process, models incorporating alternative, multiple trajectories are now being used (e.g., Gilman 1991; Yoffee 1993). The recognition of multiple trajectories between and within regions need not be a return to anthropological particularism. Instead, it offers the opportunity to strike a balance between historical contingency and more general processes through comparative analysis.

The second major change influencing current archaeological research on leadership is the recognition that inequality is pervasive and can be expressed in many ways (Brumfiel 1992; Flanagan 1989; Paynter 1989). Reinterpretations of the ethnographic record of middle-range societies provide a foundation for investigating the various sources and expressions of inequality (e.g., Strathern 1982). Recent ethnographic research has been particularly influential in changing the traditional view of Southwestern societies as the epitome of egalitarianism (Brandt 1994; Levy 1992; Plog 1995; Reyman 1987; Whiteley 1988). Although agreement among these studies is not always present, they urge re-evaluation of the definition of equality and the roles of situational versus institutional inequality. These studies also reinforce earlier questions about the suitability of using traditional interpretations of Southwestern ethnographic accounts to interpret the organization of archaeological polities (Upham 1982; Wilcox 1981).

Because inequalities can be manifested along many different dimensions, a third change in studies of leadership strategies has been to unpack the different domains of economy, kinship, politics, and ritual (Feinman and Neitzel 1984; McGuire and Saitta 1996; Netting 1990; Upham 1990). Once separated, each dimension can be re-evaluated and linkages constructed depending on the contexts of analysis. While some domains are hierarchically organized, it is becoming clear that in some contexts, heterarchically organized domains are also present (Crumley 1979, 1995; Crumley and Marquardt 1987). In fact, the concept of heterarchy depends on separate consideration of organizational dimensions and provides an alternative way of looking at organizational structure(s) (Rautman 1998).

The fourth change is a widening of the social scale at which analyses are focused. The behavior of individual actors provides a microlevel scale of analysis that is complementary to analyses at the regional or macrolevel. A focus on microscale analyses parallels the more widespread use of practice theory in anthropology (Bourdieu 1977; Giddens 1984; Ortner 1984). An emphasis on social action, reproduced through daily life, provides a stage for looking at how inequalities are formed and re-formed, manipulated, and maintained. In archaeological theory an actor-based approach offers archaeologists the opportunity to look at the factors that influence and are influenced by individuals (human agency) and their decisions from the ground up, rather than on factors that are imposed from the top down. Actor-based approaches to the evolution of social complexity can be found in dual-processual theory (Blanton et al. 1996a) and complex adaptive systems theory (Dean et al. 1999; Gumerman, Gell-Mann, and Cordell 1994; Wills et al. 1994).

Leadership Strategies in the Southwest

Given the above trends, it is no surprise that there is currently an interest in leaders and their strategies for obtaining and maintaining power. As subject matter, leaders allow archaeologists to focus on individuals and their social interactions. Leaders control different kinds of resources through variable social networks, illustrating inequalities along a number of dimensions. Finally, cross-cultural patterning in the way that leadership strategies are expressed can be used to identify and contrast different trajectories in social complexity.

In no other area should this new turn of events be more welcome than in the Greater Southwest. The models used by Southwestern archaeologists for many years have assumed causal linkages between centralized political control, social hierarchy, and prestige economies (e.g., Upham 1982; Lightfoot 1984; McGuire 1986; Reid and Whittlesey 1990; Wilcox 1993). Debates became unproductive largely because they concerned an unsolvable problem, given the assumption of linked dimensions of inquiry.

Calls for restructuring past assumptions (e.g., Feinman 1994; McGuire and Saitta 1996; Mills 1995; Nelson 1995; Upham 1990) and the use of alternative perspectives based in political (Sebastian 1992a), neo-Darwinian (Kantner 1996), neo-Marxist (Saitta 1994, 1997), and complexity theory (Wills et al. 1994) illustrate many of the trends in the general archaeological literature discussed above, albeit in different ways. Today, a diversity of lines of evidence and new models is being marshaled that collectively emphasizes organizational variation across the Southwest. However, these models have not been widely applied using a comparative framework (but see Nelson 1995 for an interesting exception). More comparison using a common set of assumptions is clearly needed. The chapters in this volume were included with that goal in mind. Rather than seeing one area of the Southwest as more or less complex than another or lacking in particular hallmarks of complexity, the authors were asked to view political variation across the Southwest as the expression of different trajectories in leadership development. They were specifically asked to consider alternative models of leadership development, including dual-processual, heterarchical, and complex adaptive systems theory in the analysis of their specific case studies.

Of central importance to the case studies in this volume is that there are different sources of power that can be used by leaders to acquire and maintain their authority. Some authors in this volume emphasize differences in the political economy or funds of power. Others emphasize a less tangible but no less important ideological basis for leadership roles. All of the chapters challenge traditional notions about the linkages between prestige goods, political centralization, and social hierarchy in productive ways.

In the remainder of this introduction, I discuss the sources of power that have been identified in the emerging literature on leadership strategies in the Southwest. These sources are used in the following essays to varying degrees. I then summarize three overarching models that have been formulated outside the Southwest that are most commonly used in this volume. Last, I contrast the areas of the Southwest discussed in the case studies and suggest that fundamental differences in the way that leaders constructed power can be identified across this broad geographic area.

Sources of Inequality in Prehispanic Southwestern Societies

Leaders drew upon many sources of power in the ancient Southwest. Analytically, we can identify economic, ritual, kinship, and factional sources, but it is apparent that these dimensions are highly interdependent and were drawn upon by leaders in multiple ways.

In the arid Southwest, environmental variation has been at the heart of economic models. Past research suggests that leaders managed risk (Kohler and Van West 1996). Both the control over surplus (e.g., Feinman 1997a; Saitta 1997; Sebastian 1992a) and the control over scarcity (Crown and Judge 1991; McGuire and Saitta 1996) have been argued to be important means of constructing economic inequality. Simulations suggest that economic inequality between households can be created from environmental variation and that households could use this variation for their own interests (Hegmon 1996; Kohler and Van West 1996; Sebastian 1992a). However, as simulations based on non-Southwestern data indicate (e.g., Pauketat 1996), random factors may also keep the transferal of leadership positions across multiple generations in check as different households are variably rewarded and penalized.

Simulations thus suggest that the multigenerational transmission of economic benefits within agricultural societies can only be maintained under certain conditions. Settlement stability combined with the investment of labor in such facilities as drainage systems, reservoirs, and irrigation networks may have provided one such context. For most of the archaeological record, households in the Southwest moved frequently. Exceptions include many sites in the Hohokam area that were tethered to irrigation works. In the northern Southwest, durations of occupation appear to have been shorter, at least until the protohistoric period, when "deep sedentism" occurred (Lekson 1990).

Interest in migration, a logical outgrowth of research on mobility, has been renewed in the Southwest. Levy's (1992) influential ethnographic work provides one window into the interaction of migration and inequality in a pueblo context. Cross-culturally, migrants often do not have access to the best land, creating and reinforcing inequalities in subsistence production (Stinson 1996). However, frequent movement also held this source of power in check as newcomers became potential first-comers. Only long-term sedentism may have allowed individual households and other kinship groups to maintain differential access to land across several generations. Thus, for contact period Pueblo, Hohokam, and Casas Grandes communities, first-comer status as a basis for inequality as well as leadership itself may have been more similar than for other communities.

Control over the products of craft producers, or attached specialization, is often assumed to be a source of economic inequality. In the general archaeological literature these models, too, are being rethought (Ames 1995; Feinman 1999). Craft specialization was present in the prehistoric Southwest, including shell working, ground stone, and ceramics, but intensified production was largely confined to the household (Mills and Crown 1995). Embedded specialization (Ames 1995), in which high status families overproduced to construct and maintain exchange networks, and the activities of caching and hoarding illustrate the intersection of craft production and inequality in the Greater Southwest. Embedded specialization may be most clearly seen in Classic period Hohokam and Paquimé households (Mills 1997; see also Whalen and Minnis, this volume), but other communities may show evidence for this kind of economic inequality in future examinations.

Another example of specialization was the late prehistoric production of textiles by Pueblo men in suprahousehold ritual contexts. Production of these "inalienable possessions" (Weiner 1994) for use within ritually proscribed contexts underscores an alternative relationship between economy, ritual, ideology, and status in the northern Southwest (Mills 1997; Webster 1997). Production in household versus suprahousehold contexts provides an additional means by which to contrast and compare the structure of leadership and the basis of inequality.

Economics, ritual, and leadership intersect within the contexts of food consumption. Food and status are clearly linked, especially when consumption is in public settings (Hayden 1995; Wiessner and Schiefenhövel 1996). In the northern Southwest, larger vessels are associated with refuse closer to ritual structures (Blinman 1989), and serving vessel sizes show clear increases commensurate with the increased importance of crosscutting integrative societies between A.D. 1100 and 1300 (Mills 1999). Hayden's (1995) work underscores the fact that feasting was used in different ways and by different kinds of leaders, both coercively and cooperatively. Differences in the scale and structure of public architecture are key to understanding the context of feasting across the Southwest and how leaders may have used these contexts to elicit particular results.

Ethnographic and archaeological evidence from the Puebloan Southwest indicates that religious and political leadership is often the same thing. For example, Pandey (1994:330) notes that "the Hopis make no sharp distinction between religious and political domains," because village leadership was often isomorphic with religious office. Howell's analysis of prehispanic leaders at the contact period Zuni site of "Hawikku" also suggests that the basis of their power was ritual but not economic (see also Kintigh, this volume). Turquoise and shell were not the primary items associated with these interments, nor were these leaders characterized by better health (Howell 1996:79–80).

Ritual may have been one of the most important ways in which late prehispanic leadership was defined, but it varied in its correspondence with economic inequality. In their essay on the relationship between ritual and social power, Burns and Laughlin (1979) argue that ritual constitutes a major power resource, different from social power derived from material resources such as goods, land, and so on. They identify three different kinds of social power: constraint power, persuasive power, and sanctioning power. The latter two are more indirect forms of power and are frequently used by leaders in the context of ritual. Ritual organized as collective or corporate action is a particularly effective context for the use of persuasive power. However, collective action may take the form of competitive rituals or sets of rituals as other actors emerge who wish to use rituals for their own power construction. Ritual thus becomes a locus of social change, where it once was used to maintain the status quo. The Burns and Laughlin model is fundamental to many current archaeological analyses in the Greater Southwest, particularly the essays in this volume by Graves and Spielmann, Van Keuren, and Potter and Perry.

How leaders act in the context of ritual is an important means of distinguishing among different kinds of leadership strategies. Steiner's (1990:437–

40) discussion of the relationship between leadership and masking has important implications for understanding variation in the strategies of leaders. Masks are useful in defusing factional competition and outright conflict in that they symbolically disguise the identity of executives who must exact punishment but whose actions would be interpreted quite differently if they were not protected behind the mask. Masking, like clowning, simultaneously allows leaders to symbolically express conflict and cooperation as well as factionalism and group integration. Ritual leaders who do not use masking illustrate a different strategy of ritual authority and tend to use other symbols of authority. Based on the contrasts discussed by Steiner, different interpretations of the Kachina Cult (Adams 1991; Plog and Solemeto 1996) may be less significant than is the very use of masking by religious leaders across the Southwest. In addition, the use of masks can be seen as a particular strategy of leaders, not necessarily the hallmark of a particular religious society, as Feinman (1997a; see also this volume) has recently suggested for the Southwest.

Kinship networks are additional sources of inequality, whether for agricultural labor, construction of communal architecture, or as the basis of exchange networks. Labor estimates for large sites in the Southwest often strike archaeologists as low given overall site population (e.g., Lekson 1984a; but see Wills, this volume), suggesting selective recruitment below the level of the entire community. Yet these networks clearly drew upon the labor of multiple households; kinship networks and sodality memberships were likely sources for this labor. The internal frontier model recently applied by Herr (1999) to the dispersed frontier communities of the Mogollon Rim area posits that leadership was based on "wealth-in-people" (Nyerges 1992) recruited along lineage lines.

Control of and access to labor as a source of building inequality is clearly part of neo-Marxist models, including the model of class processes and the communal formation presented by Saitta (1994). In terms of the scale of kinship networks, Douglas (1995:250) suggests that "expansive kinship linkages" are better sources of power in small-scale societies than the surplus food production, specialization, and conflict sources of larger-scale societies, which have high transaction costs. Moreover, he suggests that kinship linkages over wider spatial scales may be more stable and more reliable than linkages over shorter distances because distant kin are less likely to defect to local leaders (Douglas 1995:251–52).

Besides the scale of kinship and sodality networks, variation in patterns of descent undoubtedly presented alternative sources of power in prehistoric

Southwestern societies. Bilateral kin networks were likely sources of labor recruitment in Classic period Hohokam communities (Fish and Yoffee 1996; see Fish and Fish, this volume) and Eastern Pueblos, whereas kin networks in Western Pueblos were more unilateral (Ware and Blinman 1996). These differences have implications for how communities were factionalized and integrated, how labor was recruited and allocated, and how goods were distributed among kin.

The above examples illustrate the variation in sources of inequality present across the Southwestern political landscape. Some strategies were clearly used more often than others in different areas. However, controlled comparisons across the Southwest have not been made, nor has a general model been applied that does not rely on traditional neo-evolutionary assumptions. In the following section, three general models are summarized that provide a basis for making such comparisons.

Alternative Models

Several general models have been proposed in recent years that provide alternative frameworks for looking at leadership trajectories. These models include dual-processual theory (Blanton et al. 1996a; Feinman 1995), heterarchy (Crumley 1979, 1995; Crumley and Marquardt 1987), and complex adaptive systems (CAS) theory (Gumerman and Gell-Mann 1994; Wills et al. 1994). Two of these are discussed extensively in the final two chapters of this volume by Kohler and his colleagues (CAS) and Feinman (dual-processual theory).

The network/corporate model of leadership strategies outlined by Blanton and his colleagues (1996a; Feinman 1995, this volume) provides a particularly useful way of considering alternative strategies expressed across the prehistoric Southwest. However, this model has not been extensively applied to middle-range societies outside of central Mexico. The dual-processual model has at its core two forms of leadership strategies: corporate- and network-based. Leaders using one strategy over the other draw upon different funds or sources of power, both objective and symbolic (Blanton et al. 1996a:2–3). A corporate strategy is one in which power is derived from a local group and individual prestige is deemphasized. Hence, corporate or communal architecture is more important and legitimization of authority more ecumenical. Lineage organization is often an important source of labor, knowledge a more important source of authority, and membership in corporate organization more important than personal status distinctions. By contrast, the network strategy derives power from individual networks of leaders. Greater value is placed on portable wealth that can be held by leaders and used to build alliances. Communal architecture is less important than in corporate leadership, and authority is legitimized through ritual centered on the common ancestors of a smaller descent group. The network strategy is therefore more exclusionary.

The two strategies are not mutually exclusive within any particular society, but one mode tends to dominate. Indeed, they may even be regarded as variation along multidimensional continua in the way that power is gained, manipulated, and expressed. Support for the distinctions made in the network/corporate model can be found in ethnographic and archaeological contrasts, such as Strathern's home production versus finance production, Earle and D'Altroy's staple finance versus wealth finance (Blanton et al. 1996a:6), and Renfrew's individualizing and group-oriented chiefdoms (Feinman 1995:266). In addition, the sequential and simultaneous decision-making hierarchies of Johnson (1989) are superficially similar but are more functionally based.

The proponents of the network/corporate model are quick to point out that none of the previous distinctions captures the full range of variation that the two leadership strategies encompass. They also stress that these are not relative degrees of complexity; neither of the two strategies can be regarded as more complex than the other (see Feinman, this volume). For example, corporate-based leadership may be found at such diverse scales as Early/Middle Formative Mexico and Teotihuacan, while examples of network-based leadership are present in the Late/Terminal Formative in Mexico and Classic Maya. In fact, cycles of corporate- and network-based leadership strategies have been suggested in all of the above geographic areas (Blanton et al. 1996a:7), forming an interesting problem for future research (Brumfiel 1996).

The descriptions of individualizing versus collective power underlying the model of network/corporate leadership strategies are ideal modes that provide a framework for interpreting and comparing strategies. Although Gary Feinman (1997) has already suggested its usefulness in understanding late prehispanic Pueblo leadership strategies in east-central Arizona, the full implications of the model for placing the diversity of societies in the Southwest in comparative perspective have not been explored.

Another model with potential for understanding leadership strategies in middle-range societies relies on the concept of heterarchy. First proposed by the cognitive theorist Warren McCulloch (1945), its use in anthropology has been forefronted by Carole Crumley (Crumley 1979, 1995; Crumley and Marquardt 1987). As defined by Crumley (1995:3), heterarchy is "the relation of elements to one another when they are unranked or when they possess the potential for being ranked in a number of different ways." Explicitly rejecting the idea of uniformitarian notions of hierarchy, heterarchy embraces simultaneous but different sources of social power depending on the dimensions or "elements" being considered.

Rautman makes a compelling case for the applicability of heterarchy to Southwestern societies. As she points out, Southwestern societies have a "mix" of egalitarian and nonegalitarian organizations, a situation that is well described by heterarchical theory. By differentiating among variables of scale from those of control, Rautman (1998:329) suggests that archaeologists might be able to differentiate groups that "simultaneously occupy positions of power that may be variously defined." Her formulation fits well with the assumptions behind alternative leadership strategies and the different sources of power drawn upon by leaders to construct their authority, however small in scale or fleeting in duration.

Crumley (1995) has made an important connection between heterarchical theory and CAS theory in that both rely on the principles of order without assumptions of hierarchical organization. Like heterarchy, CAS theory recognizes that regularities or structure may occur along different dimensions, resulting in what is known as "schemata" (Gumerman, Gell-Mann, and Cordell 1994:3). CAS theory is explicitly concerned with the adaptation, evolution, or change in schemata. As Kohler and his colleagues (this volume) discuss, individual agents gather information on a local basis that often results in patterned decisions or outcomes. Kohler and his colleagues use random Boolean networks to better understand the conditions under which economic interactions shift from reciprocal to nonreciprocal exchanges.

None of the above models are necessarily contradictory, and each holds potential for looking at leadership strategies in different ways. Heterarchy allows that these strategies may be based on a number of different sources; CAS emphasizes the evolution of new strategies (or schemata); and dual-processual theory provides comparative evidence for two generalized trajectories in leadership strategies. The models are highly complementary, and it is useful to consider how each model may add to the interpretation of variation in leadership strategies in any case study, as do many of the contributors to this volume.

All of the chapters in this volume provide alternative perspectives on leadership strategies in the Greater Southwest. They are alternative in two distinct ways. First, they veer significantly from previous models used in the Southwest that assume that all differences in complexity are underlain by differences in hierarchy. Whether they explicitly use dual-processual theory, heterarchy, or complex adaptive systems theory, the contributors in this volume emphasize approaches to the construction of inequality that do not clearly correlate with arrangements along a single dimension ranging from egalitarianism to hierarchy (see Feinman, this volume). Second, the contributors to this volume provide alternative perspectives on leadership itself through their case studies. These case studies are rich sources for understanding similarities and differences in the way that leadership was structured in the Greater Southwest.

Alternative Trajectories: Case Studies from the Greater Southwest

Five of the chapters in this volume address leadership strategies in the northern (plateau) Southwest (chapters by Wills, Graves and Spielmann, Van Keuren, Potter and Perry, and Kintigh), while four chapters are devoted to the southern Southwest (Elson and Abbott, Harry and Bayman, Fish and Fish, and Whalen and Minnis). The case studies look at communities within the Chaco, Eastern and Western Pueblos, Tonto Basin, Phoenix Basin, Tucson Basin, and Casas Grandes areas. Each case study draws upon recent work conducted in each area to illustrate the trajectories of change in leadership strategies.

Wills's analysis of leadership in Chaco Canyon uses several converging lines of evidence to demonstrate that the process of great house construction was itself an important means of establishing leadership. In contrast to many of the other previous analyses of Chaco Canyon political organization, he argues that ritual was not the primary source of power for leaders in these communities and that the production of monumental architecture was not to promote the exclusionary rituals of leaders. Instead, he suggests that a corporate-based system of collective allocation of labor was present, organized at the household level. Following Vivian (1992, 1997), Wills agrees that land tenure and water rights were fundamental sources of building political power, which provided a calendrical cycle to the construction activity. Ritual specialists may indeed have been present at

Chaco, but these specialists were counterpointal to other leaders and may not have been responsible for the production of the most dramatic edifices of Chaco society—the great houses.

Graves and Spielmann discuss the role of exchange of subsistence and nonsubsistence goods in fostering inequalities within the protohistoric Rio Grande pueblos. They point out that those goods that were widely traded were either consumed during feasts or used as serving vessels during feasting activities. The demand for those goods must have been high and likely enhanced prestige, even if the material items were not prestige goods themselves. The use of specialized vessels may have set the stage for institutionalized inequalities when specific groups or institutions controlled critical rituals.

Potter and Perry focus on the use of ritual as an "authoritative" power resource by Zuni leaders in the late prehistoric period. They point out that association of ritual leaders with hunting was widespread among ethnographic (historic) Pueblos and likely was the case in prehistory. Potter and Perry argue that the uneven distribution of allocative resources created by environmental deterioration and population aggregation would have reinforced the power of those leaders associated with the communal hunting of certain highly valued food animals. The differential distribution of subsistence and ritual fauna at sites in the region indicates that all communities did not have equal access to all types of animals and that specific ritual societies may have had limited distribution within the community. They take a dialectical approach in arguing for the simultaneity of inclusive and exclusive features of membership in ritual societies within each community.

In a highly complementary essay that also focuses on the late prehispanic Pueblo IV period, Van Keuren shows how differences in ritual participation and leadership construction may be indicated by stylistic variation. Rather than concentrating on material bases for power, like Potter and Perry he views leaders as drawing upon knowledge as a power resource. Van Keuren takes a recognized shift from the panregional Pinedale style to the more spatially restricted Fourmile style in eastern Arizona to suggest that there was a change from a widespread belief system to one in which differential access to social information prevailed. Leadership strategies were based on enhanced control over the information conveyed in public ceremonies yet did not indicate a change to a prestige goods economy or a network-based leadership strategy. Instead, the greater restriction in accessibility reflected by the style shift is seen as enhancing the prominence of certain households or other corporate groups within the community.

Kintigh's long-term research in the Zuni area approaches leadership through analyses of materials recovered from the protohistoric site of Kechipawan. Previous analyses by Howell (1994) of collections from the contemporaneous site of Hawikuh are used for comparison. Although the two sites are approximately equal in size, Kintigh finds that Hawikuh burials showed greater variety (richness) than those from Kechipawan and that some burials were extraordinarily rich in ritual objects. The analysis supports an interpretation of restricted access to some forms of communal ritual by residents of the two sites. At least in part, the differences are attributable to differences in the occupational histories of each site and the contribution of migrant populations. Kintigh suggests that unequal ritual and political power reflects a mother–daughter village relationship within a corporate model of political leadership. His analysis underscores the variation that may be present in leadership strategies within a single region at the same time.

Four case studies in the southern Southwest illustrate a greater range of leadership strategies than in the northern Southwest. Elson and Abbott join forces to compare leadership in the Tonto and Phoenix Basins, focusing on platform mound communities. They begin with a summary of ethnographically documented use of platform mounds. This research indicates that although these architectural constructions have diverse functions, they are usually associated with lineages and descent groups with higher status than other groups in their communities (see also Elson 1998). However, they consider that variation through time and across the region suggests diverse means by which this power was constructed. For example, the distribution of red ware and polychrome ceramics indicates greater social differentiation and increased territoriality that probably reflect a shift in the construction of leadership strategies within the Phoenix Basin, possibly to a system more characteristic of a network-based model. By contrast, smaller mounds in the Tonto Basin do not show the same differential distribution of high valued materials and were probably occupied by a single descent group within a corporate leadership strategy. The temporal priority of Phoenix Basin mounds suggests to the authors that emulation may also have been a strategy of leaders in the Tonto Basin communities.

Harry and Bayman use a political economic approach in their analysis of a Tucson Basin Hohokam platform mound community. The authors compare the distribution of nonlocal ceramics, obsidian, shell, and turquoise within and between sites of the Marana community. They find that networks of exchange crosscut sites and features of similar forms. Like

Kintigh's Zuni study, they rely on community history to explain how differences in the distribution of wealth items occurred. In the Marana case, they suggest that leaders at established sites excluded newcomers from trade networks to maintain their power. The exclusive access to the platform mound was balanced by both exclusionary and inclusionary economic participation.

Fish and Fish argue persuasively that kinship is not the only way that leaders recruited followers in the prehistoric Southwest. Instead, participation in civic-territorial units included individual village membership, councils of elders for units of different scales, and broader regional territorial affiliations. Each of these social units necessitated leaders of different kinds and structured social dynamics in different ways. Among Hohokam irrigators, participation in canal construction was one particularly effective means of establishing rights that formed the basis of economic power but was not necessarily kin-based. Heads of kin groups and performers of ritual were other kinds of leaders, and there is evidence for greater political centralization and diversification of these roles through time. However, an exclusionary or network strategy was not manifested; wealth accumulation and symbols of personalized authority remained rare.

By contrast, Whalen and Minnis offer a perspective on Casas Grandes that argues for the development of exclusionary wealth and authority during the Medio phase. However, the influence of Casas Grandes leaders does not appear to have been spatially extensive, and centralization was relatively low. Mortuary evidence does not indicate that hereditary ranking was present, and the authors suggest that traditional notions of centralization and ranking are not as useful for defining variation in leadership in the Casas Grandes polity. Prestige goods acquisition, the manipulation of kinship networks, and factional rivalry were alternative pathways of leadership development, more fitting with a heterarchically organized network strategy.

Conclusion

Taken as a group, the case studies in this volume provide ample evidence for alternative models of leadership in middle-range societies. The different trajectories discussed in each chapter reveal many common strategies of leaders and common avenues of exploring these strategies among Southwestern archaeologists. Nonetheless, differences in the way that leadership was constructed in various areas of the Greater Southwest are quite striking. The two summary chapters by Kohler and his colleagues and Feinman bring out many of the commonalities and contrasts. Here, I close with two observations on the topics of similarities in the sources of power and cyclic changes in the structure of leadership within particular areas.

Commonalities in the sources of power used by leaders in different parts of the Greater Southwest are clearly evident from the essays in this volume. In the northern Southwest, relatively little emphasis was placed on the control of prestige goods production. In fact, prestige goods are relatively few in Pueblo assemblages, an argument that has erroneously fostered interpretations of egalitarianism. Other sources of power *were* present in the northern Southwest. Wills's interpretation of Chacoan leadership suggests that labor mobilization was one of the most important sources of power, perhaps even running counter to the power of ritual specialists in the same society. By contrast, the chapters addressing later Eastern and Western Pueblos of the northern Southwest more explicitly advocate ritual as the most significant power resource. Most of these contributions emphasize a corporate basis for ritual.

Ritual is also cited in the southern Southwest, but the basis of power appears to be more economically and kinship-based. Those papers addressing the Tonto, Phoenix, and Tucson Basin societies more frequently cite differences in access to irrigation networks, other forms of productive lands, and agricultural labor. As Elson and Abbott argue, platform mounds are evidence for the importance of descent groups and their claims on lands. Fish and Fish point out that civic-territorial units and the kinship networks that constitute them are key to understanding the Hohokam political landscape. These units are physically defined by concentrations of monumental architecture and their associated irrigated and nonirrigated agricultural areas. Harry and Bayman cite economic power as the most significant power resource in their analyses of the Tucson Basin Hohokam community of Marana and provide hints of an exclusionary economy. Economic power was clearly the way that leadership was constructed at Paquimé (Casas Grandes), described by Whalen and Minnis. Of all the case studies in the volume, a network strategy entailing exclusionary, rather than cooperative, economic processes was present in this community.

All of the essays in this volume address changes through time in the way that leadership strategies are constructed. It is this level of analysis that is particularly instructive for understanding the internal tensions that led to shifts in power. Although some of these shifts were subtle and did not extend to changes in the overall structure of leadership, other shifts were more profound. That the balance of power was upset is evident in the fact that most of the communities described in this volume were not continuously occupied. What archaeologists have termed abandonments or even "collapses" is evidence for cyclic changes that went awry.

But just how did these leadership strategies shift through time? Wills suggests that different kinds of leaders are present in all societies, and at Chaco, ritual specialists may have been in competition with other leaders. Competition between leaders played out in the context of feasting is suggested to be an important process of change in the late prehistoric Rio Grande (Graves and Spielmann, this volume) and Zuni areas (Potter and Perry, this volume). Rather than causing changes in the basis or source of leadership, however, both of these cases suggest that ritual feasting reinforced existing inequalities within the same kind of leadership strategy. Increasing heterogeneity in ritual organizations is evident from the papers by Van Keuren, Kintigh, and Potter and Perry. Underlying all three analyses is the theme that this ritual diversity provided a foundation for competition.

Several case studies in both the northern and southern Southwest emphasize the importance of first-comer status in establishing authority. Multigenerational communities have constantly shifting statuses of first- and latecomers. The case studies from the Tonto Basin (Elson and Abbott), the contact period Zuni (Kintigh), and the Tucson Basin Hohokam (Harry and Bayman) are most explicit in how cyclic changes in leadership are instituted by fluctuating demographic processes such as migration.

The contributions to this volume are based on long-term research projects in relatively well studied areas of the Greater Southwest. The authors marshal substantive data to illustrate their points and provide significant new syntheses. However, the most significant contribution of these essays is how they combine careful assessments of the archaeological data with more general models of leadership trajectories. Without this balance of data and models, the sources and cycles of power outlined so briefly here would not be so evident.

2

Political Leadership and the Construction of Chacoan Great Houses, A.D. 1020–1140

W. H. WILLS

BETWEEN A.D. 900 and 1100, a dramatic transformation in human settlements occurred in Chaco Canyon, New Mexico. Widely and famously known as the "Chaco Phenomenon," this change involved the construction of massive communal structures containing hundreds of rooms in locations where only small aggregates of household settlements had previously existed. Tree-ring dates from excavated sites indicate two major construction episodes for these structures, which archaeologists call "great houses," the first between A.D. 850 and 925 and a second, much more intensive period between A.D. 1020 and 1140. Great houses built during the eleventh century were unprecedented in their architectural elaboration, which included dressed masonry, design patterns in wall facings, dressed wooden beams, selective use of different woods for particular architectural features, repetitive remodeling of floors and wall surfaces, corner doorways, balconies, stairs, and interior room platforms (Judd 1925, 1959, 1964; Lekson 1984a; Pepper 1920; Vivian 1990; Windes and Ford 1996). It is not clear to what extent or manner the Chaco Phenomenon incorporated populations from outside the canyon proper, but great houses undoubtedly reflect the power to deploy large amounts of labor in construction work. In recognition of these labor costs, researchers view great houses as the most direct materialization of the Chacoan political economy.

Chacoan great houses are routinely described as "monumental" in scale compared to other kinds of contemporaneous vernacular architecture. Current archaeological models associate this monumentality with ritual functions and assume that the power of the Chacoan religious system is reflected in the size of these buildings (e.g., Fowler and Stein 1992; Judge

1989; Kantner 1996; Saitta 1997; Sebastian 1992a; Stein and Lekson 1992).
Yet the relationship between great houses, ritual, and political economy is
surprisingly vague in current Chaco Phenomenon models. Prevailing constructs propose that great houses were the product of aggrandizing behavior
by leaders whose power was based in control of agricultural land but whose
authority was legitimized by control of religious office. In other words,
religious leaders competed for followers by financing and directing the
construction of great houses (Saitta 1997:17–18; Sebastian 1992a:120–38).
However, except for a general suggestion that construction labor could
have been obtained by ritual specialists in exchange for sponsoring ceremonies, current models do not attempt to connect the actual construction
process to political organization.

This seems an astonishing omission, since the production of architecture
offers an excellent entry point into the dynamics of decision making and
managerial control in prehistoric political economies. In the remainder of
this chapter I suggest an initial approach to utilizing the processual features
of great house construction to delineate the nature of political leadership at
Chaco during the intensive building projects characteristic of the eleventh
and early twelfth centuries A.D. This approach is limited to the issue of
architecture, but I think the results have implications for current perceptions of the entire Chaco Phenomenon.[1] In particular, I believe that current models of the political economy overestimate the significance of religious ritual as the context within which great houses were built. Indeed, it
may be that the conceptualization of great houses as markers of religious
power is incompatible with the construction process.

Background

Many reconstructions of Chacoan political organization have been developed by different scholars over the past three decades (Altschul 1978;
Breternitz and Doyel 1987; Breternitz, Doyel, and Marshall 1982; Doyel
and Lekson 1992; Doyel, Breternitz, and Marshall 1984; Grebinger 1973;
Irwin-Williams and Shelley 1980; Judge 1989, 1993; Judge et al. 1981;
Kantner 1996; Lekson 1983, 1984a, 1997; Lekson et al. 1988; Mahoney
1998; Marshall et al. 1979; Neitzel 1989; Nelson 1995; Powers, Gillespie,
and Lekson 1983; Saitta 1997; Schelberg 1984, 1992; Sebastian 1991, 1992a,
1992b; Tainter and Gillio 1980; Toll 1985; Vivian 1970, 1974, 1989, 1990,
1991, 1992, 1997; Windes 1987; and others). At least one envisions the
Chaco Phenomenon as a state-level polity extracting tribute from a subor-

dinate regional population (Wilcox 1993), but most suppose a less elaborate political system based on power sharing among a variety of hierarchically organized coresidential groups. The main point of contention within this latter group is the degree to which decision making was invested in ranked kin groups, with some researchers favoring relatively little ranking (e.g., Toll 1985; Vivian 1990) and others positing a system of highly structured status differentiation (e.g., Grebinger 1973; Sebastian 1992a). However, none of these models projects a single paramount leader or lineage, and therefore Feinman (1997a) has argued that for the most part these latter reconstructions fit the concept of a "corporate hierarchy" wherein leadership is invested in social segments or groups rather than contested by prominent individuals (see also Blanton et al. 1996a).

Collectively, these various attempts to delineate the organizational structure of the Chaco Phenomenon probably touch on every facet of the known archaeological record, and so it is extremely interesting that with one exception (Wilcox 1993) they converge on a view of leadership that is indistinguishable from ethnological descriptions of political organization in historical Puebloan societies. As understood from ethnographic research, Puebloan political power resides in a complicated network of interdependent ritual organizations and offices but is not consolidated in a single individual or kin group. Cultural anthropologists have recognized the complex character of power sharing in Pueblo society at least since Titiev's (1944) study of Hopi factionalism. Sahlins (1968:43–44) attributed the lack of political centralization in Pueblo communities to the independence of discrete segments such as clans in economic production (see Dozier 1966, 1970; Eggan 1950), while Ortiz's (1969) detailed analysis of Tewa social organization provided in-depth explication of the hierarchical control of economic and religious power through ritual offices (see also Brandt 1994; Levy 1992; Upham 1982). Some recent archaeological models of Chaco political organization are so similar to these ethnographic perspectives, particularly in identifying the source of political power as control of ritual knowledge (McGuire and Saitta 1996; Saitta 1997), that they could be direct analogues.

Despite the fact that so many researchers have arrived at the same basic understanding of Chacoan political organization, it seems paradoxical that archaeologists should find in Chacoan great houses evidence for a ritual organization indistinct from modern Pueblos. For one thing, there are no ethnographic examples of communal production in Pueblo communities involving large and protracted labor allocations. Among some Pueblos there is corporate control of irrigation that might affect household surplus, but this finances ritual only indirectly through household contributions to feasting (Ford 1972). Nor is there any evidence that ritual leaders actually manipulate agricultural production to benefit segments of the ritual system. In fact, among the Eastern Pueblos the ritual system is severely constrained by its inability to make excessive demands on surplus production, and many households can be excluded from participation by their lack of resources (Ford 1972; Ortiz 1969; Snow 1981). Hopi clans control agricultural land and use that control to assert power in ceremonial affairs, but clan leaders do not control agricultural surplus. According to Levy (1992:156), the Hopi "system of social stratification worked to manage scarcity, not abundance." At Hopi, as in other Pueblos, the economic power associated with ritual leaders is the ability to exclude community members from the means of production, not the authority to command surplus production.

Why then does the impressive record of massive labor mobilization at Chaco during the eleventh and twelfth centuries provide archaeologists with a model of a political system based on ritual power that is notable for its weak capacity to extract social labor for communal production? Perhaps it is because Chaco is often described as a "ceremonial center" in the Anasazi world. Chaco Canyon does have more examples of architecture that archaeologists attribute to ritual or esoteric functions than are found in modern Pueblo villages, especially small kivas, and I suspect researchers are therefore inclined to assume that the people of Chaco were more involved in ritual activity than their descendants. Hence, if political power in modern Pueblos is inseparable from ritual office, then it must have been even more so in prehistoric Chaco. For instance, Feinman (1997a) argued that "corporate Pueblo power was rooted in the creation of (and restricted access to) ceremonial space, and so ultimately ritual performance and the control of sacred knowledge, as well as food production and consequently land." Similarly, in discussing great houses outside of Chaco Canyon proper, Kantner (1996:60) maintained that since competition among aspiring leaders in tribal societies is spatially focused on architecture where ceremonies occur, the "amount of authority and power that a leader possesses should be reflected in the size and elaboration" of such places (see also Lightfoot and Feinman 1982; Potter 1997a).

Still, there is no evidence that leadership power in modern Pueblos is expressed this way in architecture. The ethnographic record does not reveal much emphasis on the construction of sacred space generally or competition between leaders through sponsorship of such work. Consequently, despite having generated organizational models that reproduce the structure of modern Puebloan ritual organization, archaeologists have had to connect great house construction to ritual power in specific ways other than those found in historic Pueblo societies. For example, Sebastian (1992a, 1992b) argued that prior to A.D. 1020, great house construction was financed by ambitious leaders who controlled enough agricultural surplus to attract followers through sponsorship of ritual performances. After A.D. 1020, lineages used their religious monopoly and the metaphor of ritual to legitimize their ranked status. Agricultural success reinforced the elites' claim to be supernatural mediators, drawing yet more followers. Sebastian posited that competitive displays gained importance throughout the eleventh century as various power holders in Chaco began to vie not only for local followers but also for regional alliances, using construction projects as a medium for display competition (1992a:126).

Competitive leadership models are currently popular among Chaco scholars, but they present a puzzling mechanism for great house construction. Debt payment to ritual specialists for sponsoring performances is an unlikely source of sustained labor investment in tribal societies generally (see Earle 1997:154), and it is especially difficult to envision at Chaco if the poor souls who were chronic failures at food production were the ones who additionally provided labor service. Even Sebastian (1992a:123) allows that religious leaders would actually have had to contribute the food and resources required for both ritual events and construction efforts. This model actually seems to assert that wealthy communities hired poorer neighbors to build great houses in a relatively straightforward exchange of food for work and therefore is more akin to the sort of staple finance found in institutionalized political systems that require obligatory payments to the system rather than the wealth finance typical of competing leaders (Blanton et al. 1996a; Earle 1997). In patron-client and other "agency" models for the Chaco Phenomenon, ritual is actually not given a direct role in the process of building great houses, it is merely the instrument by which elites solicited labor to construct such buildings.

Competition models emphasize an extremely structured political world at Chaco, as illustrated by Saitta's (1997:18) assertion that ritual leaders were engaged in "exploiting labor and manipulating mass psychology in the interests of creating and sustaining tributary class relationships." Ritual leaders held institutionalized offices, were accorded status, prestige, and authority in deference to their roles as mediators with the supernatural, engaged in alliance building and exchange with other ritual leaders outside

Chaco, and controlled the allocation and use of economic resources (Judge 1989; Kantner 1996; Sebastian 1992a). Leaders were also the managers of a complex "ritual landscape," deliberately reproducing the political world in great house architecture by creating "an excessively formal and massive fabric to dramatize an obsessively formal and massive geometric order" (Stein and Lekson 1992:93; see also Morrow and Price 1997).

Although competition theorists apparently envision a straightforward linear relationship between construction and ritual organization, with escalating building investments matched by increases in institutional religious complexity, no researcher has yet proposed an explicit mechanism by which households sustained increasing demands on their production. This is a crucial issue in understanding the political economy, since the various reconstructions that emphasize elaborate religious complexes controlled by highly structured ritual systems imply a very expensive political organization. Marginal returns for household production in the Anasazi world were probably never high in general (e.g., Kohler 1992; Winter 1983), and the period during which the most construction occurred in Chaco was one of unusually poor conditions for food production (Sebastian 1992a). How then did ritual specialists extract the rapidly increasing amount of surplus needed to support the projected political system from an economically stressed populace?

It seems ironic that leadership models based on ritual power raise a number of questions about the efficacy of religious specialists as the agents of architectural production. In part, this is probably due to the reliance on structural-functional approaches, in which researchers begin by assigning a social or political meaning to these buildings based on their form and size. This approach provides plausible and provocative reconstructions but lacks any means to evaluate the accuracy of the initial inference. I think some of this ambiguity can be avoided by adopting a processual approach to understanding great houses, especially one that links labor and communication complexity to the organization of production.

Construction Sequencing and Energy Expenditure

Despite the importance that scholars have given to great houses as the products of labor mobilization, there has been little study of the production process itself. There are excellent reconstructions of the construction *histories* at several great houses for which excavation and dendrochronological data (Dean and Warren 1983; Lekson 1983, 1984a; Windes 1987; Windes and Ford 1996) and detailed knowledge about building techniques exist (Durand 1992; Judd 1964; Vivian 1990; Vivian and Matthews 1964), but the organizational framework within which building projects were conceived and executed remains very poorly understood.

The limited state of knowledge about the organization of great house construction is well illustrated by current labor estimates for building these structures. In an extremely influential study, Lekson (1984a, 1984b) calculated labor *rates* (in person-hours) and concluded that construction labor could have been drawn from the canyon population alone. Some scholars have dismissed labor as a significant factor in Chacoan politics on the basis of this analysis (e.g., Judge 1989; Lekson et al. 1988), while others have suggested that construction costs were higher than Lekson estimated (e.g., Durand 1992; Sebastian 1992a:117).

Some of the controversy on this point may stem from the fact that inferences about the significance of labor estimates have been impressionistic and without reference to any particular standard regarding what the amount of labor per se indicates about political organization. As an example, labor rates for monumental temple construction in complex Hawaiian chiefdoms are *less* than those Lekson calculated for great houses (Earle 1997; Kolb 1994). The important point is simply that labor alone is not a straightforward indication of organization. Any production process has fixed costs, such as the amount of material needed to complete a product, that cannot be altered but variable costs, such as labor and technology, that can be manipulated. It is in the management of variable costs that the working of the political economy is most clearly revealed, and thus, as Plog (1995) noted, the pivotal issue in understanding political organization through great house construction is in the *way* that labor was mobilized.

Consider the building sequence at Chetro Ketl, the second largest Chacoan great house after Pueblo Bonito with at least 550 rooms rising 3 or more stories and covering about 3 acres (Figure 2.1). Extensive excavation and sampling have generated an exceptionally large array of tree-ring dates, especially cutting dates, that allow for a detailed architectural chronology.[2] Construction was initiated between A.D. 1020 and 1030 according to a prepared ground plan, and by A.D. 1070 more than 60 percent of the final form had been completed. Building proceeded sequentially, from major ground-level room blocks to second-story room additions to plaza features such as kivas, and incorporated approximately 53 million sandstone blocks. Fifteen distinctive building stages can be grouped into two parts; between A.D. 1020 and 1075 there were at least seven stages devoted to room-block

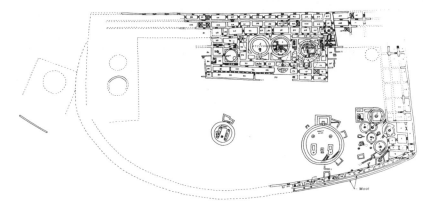

FIGURE 2.1. Ground plan for Chetro Ketl showing portions of the building excavated by the School of American Research (1916–21), the University of New Mexico (1929–34), and the National Park Service (1949–50). Courtesy of the National Park Service.

construction, while between A.D. 1075 and 1105 there were six stages involving additions and modifications to the plaza (Lekson 1983).

Dean and Warren (1983:206) estimate that approximately 24,000 trees were harvested prior to A.D. 1070 for building Chetro Ketl, or nearly 93 percent of all construction beams for the entire occupation span of the structure (Figure 2.2). Astonishingly, over 5,000 beams are projected between the years A.D. 1037 and 1039 and more than 4,000 between A.D. 1051 and 1052 (or 36 percent of the total in just five years). Assuming a six-person work crew per beam (Betancourt, Dean, and Hull 1986), the caloric expenditure in walking to and from the timber collection areas would have exceeded 54 million kilocalories between A.D. 1037 and 1039 at 54,000 person-days per year.

Energy invested in tree harvesting declined precipitously after A.D. 1070 as room-block construction was completed. In the two decades between A.D. 1050 and 1070 over 8,000 beams were used at Chetro Ketl, but from A.D. 1070 to 1090 the number dropped 1,000 percent to 800 trees. Similarly, labor for building diminished 63 percent in this same interval, from an estimated 110,093 to 41,175 person-hours (Lekson 1984a). This drop in person-hours closely tracks the decline in wall volume associated with the cessation of room-block construction (Figure 2.3). A recent mathematical study of the Chetro Ketl cutting dates by Marinakis (1995) found a statistical equivalency between the shift to annual tree harvesting at A.D. 1032 and phase transitions in thermodynamics. Phase transitions occur when there is a rapid change from one energy state to another, as from a liquid to a gas,

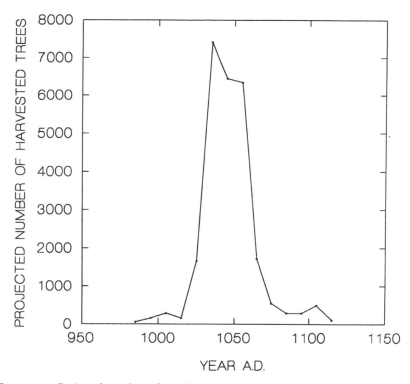

FIGURE 2.2. Projected number of trees harvested for construction of Chetro Ketl (data from Dean and Warren 1983).

and the similarity of the Chetro Ketl pattern to these sorts of threshold phenomena suggests that the organization of wood procurement experienced a sudden increase in production efficiency in the early A.D. 1030s.

Indications of plunging energy investment in architecture after A.D. 1070 are consistent with the shift from the logistical requirements of building room blocks to those of other, smaller kinds of construction. Room blocks were composed of freestanding matrices of rectangular rooms, with shared load-bearing walls to support additional layers of rooms. Great houses were masonry structures, but the walls had an earth and rubble core, so that there were three distinct components: the two exterior facings and the interior core. Unlike true core-veneer construction, the facings and the core had to be built as a unit. Consequently, while the stone and earth components could be assembled over prolonged periods, walls had to be erected rapidly and a roof constructed to protect them. The erection process demanded plumb lines, consistent floor and ceiling levels between

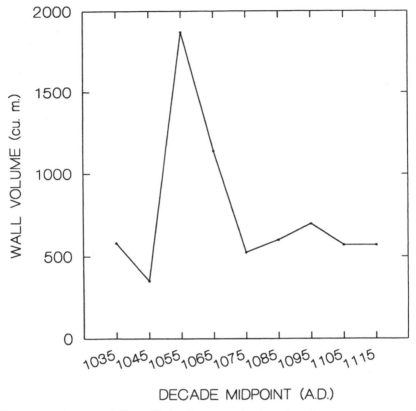

FIGURE 2.3. Amount of Chetro Ketl wall construction by volume between A.D. 1035 and 1115 (data from Lekson 1983).

rooms, and falsework (scaffolding). Simply raising these buildings posed significant engineering problems that could not have been resolved without close coordination between workers.

Climate constraints were critical in scheduling building tasks. For instance, wall construction required huge amounts of water, approximately 130 liters for every cubic meter of wall volume, but large quantities were probably only available seasonally. Vivian (1992:54) argued that the acquisition of water for construction probably required "some measure of management and decision making inasmuch as it called for collecting as much water as possible during a short period of time for relative immediate use." The largest room-block construction at Pueblo Bonito required over 361,000 liters of water, or more than 40,000 transport events given the average 9-liter volume of Chacoan ceramic jars. Considering that liquid transport vessels have extremely high breakage rates in ethnographic contexts (Varien and Mills 1997:153), construction must have been a major consumer of pots. Ceramic import is one of the defining characteristics of the Chaco Phenomenon (Toll 1985; Toll and McKenna 1987, 1997), and therefore it is likely that construction projects incorporated exchange relations as part of the overall production process.

None of the structures built at Chetro Ketl after the completion of room blocks—including large kivas—presented problems as large or complex. Kivas in great houses are isolated subterranean cylinders that required only moderate engineering skill and much less labor and material than room blocks. With the exception of two large plaza kivas, the ten excavated kivas at Chetro Ketl were smaller than the average *single* room within the room blocks (see Lekson and McKenna 1983:33–45). Most of these probably were built and used by small segments of the community (see Lipe and Hegmon 1989a; Lekson 1988).

In contrast, the Great Kiva at Chetro Ketl was indeed an immense structure, nearly 17 meters in diameter, with roof posts almost a meter in diameter supporting a weight in excess of 200,000 kilograms (cf. Lightfoot 1988), and the construction of this building must have involved a large workforce. However, despite the obvious costs in excavating the Great Kiva and roofing it, the overall cost, including wall construction, was less than 29,000 person-hours (Lekson 1984a; cf. Lightfoot 1988). Of the 32 large room blocks constructed in Chacoan great houses between A.D. 1025 and 1130, 21 required between 55,000 and 117,000 person-hours (Lekson 1984a:259).[3] Great Kivas were expensive to build, but kivas as an architectural *class* were a minor component in the production of architecture at Chaco.

Data on labor investment for Chaco Canyon great house construction developed by Lekson (1984a, 1984b) show that the sequencing of residential and nonresidential architecture at Chetro Ketl was characteristic of great houses in general. Throughout the canyon, room-block construction was negatively correlated with other types of building activities, which reflects the construction of room blocks before most kivas and other features at individual pueblos (Figure 2.4). In other words, when room blocks were being built, little energy was expended on other types of building, and when room blocks were finished, labor allocated to other construction projects increased. At no time, however, did labor expended on nonresidential constructions exceed the labor invested in room blocks.

Labor expenditure on great house construction after A.D. 1020 exhibits periodicity. Between approximately A.D. 1040 and 1100 there were at least

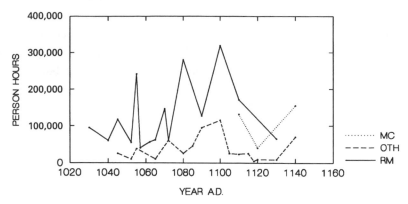

FIGURE 2.4. Labor rates for types of great house construction through time; RM=room block, MC=McElmo phase room block, OTH=non-room-block structures (data from Lekson 1983).

eight "pulses" of labor expenditure exceeding 100,000 person-hours, including three massive peaks at 300,000 (Figure 2.5). These three huge labor spikes correspond to the construction of new pueblos around A.D. 1050 (Chetro Ketl, Hungo Pavi, and Alto), massive additions to room blocks at Pueblo Bonito, Peñasco Blanco, and Pueblo del Arroyo in the A.D. 1080s, and a huge enlargement of room blocks at Pueblo Bonito around A.D. 1100. Smaller peaks all represent room-block construction of some sort, including the McElmo phase high point at A.D. 1140, while the low points correspond to an emphasis on non-room-block building efforts. Periodicity in labor allocation through the eleventh century suggests that labor mobilization for room-block construction was cyclic, with large task forces marshaled for building or enlarging residential portions of great houses, then reduced in size as construction shifted to smaller projects, then assembled again in a new round of room-block building. As these cycles are evident in the combined labor estimates for multiple great houses, it seems likely that labor mobilization was coordinated among these various construction projects.

Construction after A.D. 1050 was largely concentrated around Pueblo Bonito, and other portions of the canyon may have experienced population declines. For example, Mathien and Windes (1988:93) note that ceramic assemblages dating between A.D. 1050 and 1100 are absent at the great house of Una Vida, located 6 kilometers east of Bonito, which may indicate a "major reduction in occupation" and a transfer of population to the area around Pueblo Bonito. A similar paucity of ceramics at the Wijiji great house, 4 kilometers east of Una Vida and built in the early twelfth century,

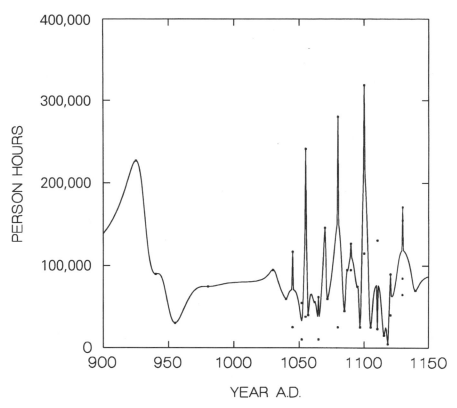

FIGURE 2.5. Total construction rates for great houses through time. The solid line is the inverse squared distance of the X and Y values.

led Durand (1992) to argue it was never occupied at all. These interpretations are clearly tentative, but if correct they could mean that the canyon population was increasingly aggregated in the vicinity of Pueblo Bonito during the heaviest outlay of construction labor. Parenthetically, many of the Chacoan Great Kivas were built in the eastern portion of the canyon away from great houses (e.g., Kin Nahasbas and 29SJ 1254); that is, some of the largest labor projects in the nonresidential or "integrative" category were spatially distinct from the great houses proper and perhaps outside the main population areas. In any case, the huge labor projects of the late A.D. 1000s and early A.D. 1100s were located in close proximity to one another, a situation that would have both necessitated coordination and facilitated communication among builders.

I believe these patterns indicate that the intended product in the construction of great house architecture was a residential complex. I use the term *residential* carefully because many archaeologists have posited that great houses, especially prior to A.D. 1100, were not primarily habitations and that most of the built space was created as specialized expressions of the Chacoan political economy rather than for more mundane domestic activities (e.g., Kantner 1996; Lekson 1984a; Lekson et al. 1988; Sebastian 1992a; Windes 1984, 1987). However, the main argument for assigning great houses a nonresidential function is the inference that large rooms lacking hearths were not part of the domestic sphere or that interior rooms were too dark for habitation. Great house rooms were very large, but while many excavated rooms lack features that archaeologists use to identify domestic functions such as cooking, domestic features are *not* absent from great houses. Food preparation would not have taken place in every room, just as plazas were not the exclusive locations for ritual or ceremony; the plaza at Pueblo Alto, for instance, had dense concentrations of roasting pits and other domestic features. Excavated rooms at Pueblo Alto exhibit more remodeling and higher densities of domestic floor features than any other archaeological site studied in Chaco (Windes 1987), and the vast majority of artifacts recovered from great houses are identical to those found at small sites (Mathien 1997; McKenna and Truell 1986). In fact, great houses did not even have exclusive access to the more esoteric material that archaeologists associate with ritual activity (Toll and McKenna 1987, 1997; Vivian, Dodgen, and Hartmann 1978:63; Windes 1992). In their detailed analysis of wood use at Chetro Ketl, Dean and Warren (1983:239) argued that evidence for nearly continual repair and modification of rooms seems "more typical of a permanent residential occupation of the pueblo in which wear and tear of daily use coupled with population growth required frequent additions and alterations to the structure." No one understands the exact function of large, featureless rooms in great houses, but perhaps the focus should be less on inferring individual room function and more on the builders' intention to create large residential-like space (cf. Vivian 1990:445).

The drop in energy expenditure that marks the shift from room-block to plaza feature construction at Chetro Ketl and other great houses reflects the lower costs associated with kivas and other nonresidential features. Although kivas are conventionally associated with activities that fostered "social integration," such as ceremonies and religious ritual (Adler 1989; Hegmon 1989), it was room-block construction that clearly commanded a sustained, community-wide (or greater) plan and investment. Some kivas were contemporaneous with the initial room blocks in great houses, but most integrative architecture was not built until after the completion of residential architecture and therefore could not have had a direct role—if any—in the huge energy input that produced the bulk of great house architectural mass. Moreover, although caches of symbolic objects such as turquoise ornaments have been recovered from Great Kivas, the vast majority of presumed ritual material at Chaco has come from rooms, including all evidence for mortuary ritual (Akins 1986; Judd 1964; Kovacik 1996; Pepper 1920; Vivian, Dodgen, and Hartmann 1978). Although these rooms obviously lost whatever domestic function they might have had originally, they might have represented a fundamental connection between ritual and the domestic sphere. Kivas and other nonresidential space surely were integral parts of Chacoan society, and they almost certainly were associated with religious functions (Plog 1989; Wilshusen 1989), but there is currently no substantive evidence that power derived from the creation and control of presumed ritual or sacred architecture can explain the construction of great houses.

Ritual and Great House Construction

Although the evidence for coordination and synchronization of construction between individual great houses and the huge amount of labor invested in these projects does not conform to expectations for competition between ritual leaders or for integrative architecture as the raison d'être of great house construction, ritual may nevertheless have been critical to the production process. Blanton and his colleagues (1996a) argue that corporate leadership strategies are characterized by efforts to suppress competition, at least openly, through the development of an ethos of reciprocity between community subgroups. Ritual systems may have a central role in promoting community solidarity by emphasizing cyclical, repetitive obligations to the community as a whole and by removing wealth from the control of individuals.

Several aspects of the great house construction process are consistent with collective ritual, especially tree harvesting. Beams had to be obtained outside the canyon from distinctly different montane ecological zones and at distances requiring extended trips of several or more days. Such journeys were likely made by men only and may have been hazardous, literally in the sense of entering the territories of other groups or encountering dangerous animals and culturally in the exposure of workers to exotic or proscribed places (see Ferguson and Hart 1986; Ortiz 1969). Once workers entered tree-harvesting locales, they initiated a standardized and labor-intensive

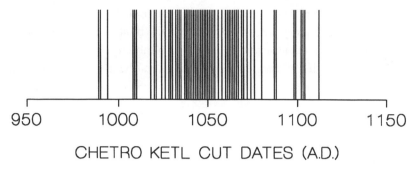

FIGURE 2.6. Density plot of cutting dates from Chetro Ketl. Each bar represents a single year in which one or more cutting dates occur.

processing sequence, using stone axes to fell trees and trim off limbs, then immediately stripping the bark and cutting logs to predetermined lengths (Dean and Warren 1983). Individual beams were carried back to the canyon in such a way as to avoid any surface damage from dragging or rolling. According to Dean and Warren (1983:228), the amount of secondary modification to Chacoan beams after cutting was unprecedented in the Anasazi region.

By the middle of the eleventh century, these tree-harvesting journeys had become an annual event for the Chaco Canyon population. Tree-ring cutting dates from Chetro Ketl indicate a shift from an episodic to an annual or nearly annual harvesting regime at A.D. 1032 that lasted until A.D. 1075 (Figure 2.6) and was part of a canyon-wide development between about A.D. 1030 and 1080 (Figure 2.7). Eighmy (1979:210) pointed out that the cumulative distribution of cutting dates from Chetro Ketl fit a logistical growth curve, which he attributed to "a potent underlying density-dependent growth process," most likely population increase among the pueblo residents because the number of beams is a good proxy for the amount of roofed space. Population growth is difficult to evaluate at Chaco, but the increasing returns curve that Eighmy demonstrated may indicate that between A.D. 1020 and 1070, wood harvesting for Chetro Ketl construction experienced very strong positive feedback effects. Among the common positive feedback mechanisms in economics are coordination effects from multiple individuals or groups pursuing similar activities and "adaptive expectation," where economic agents believe that the activity will persist in the future (Arthur 1988:10). Both these mechanisms are inherent in collective ritual predicated on regular schedules.

The annual or repetitive nature of tree harvesting at Chaco during the

CHACO GREAT HOUSE CUT DATES (A.D.)

FIGURE 2.7. Density plot of cutting dates for all great houses in Chaco Canyon for which dendrochronological data are available, including the most recently obtained dates from Pueblo Bonito (Windes and Ford 1996).

eleventh century probably had a seasonal characteristic as well, since it appears that trees were cut primarily in the late spring or early fall (Dean and Warren 1983; Windes 1987), and therefore tree harvesting was very likely part of a calendric cycle of community activity. Researchers have identified astronomical alignments in great house architecture that are consistent with seasonal calendars, particularly lunar cycles (Sofaer 1997), suggesting that scheduling functions were incorporated into some parts of some buildings. The duration of annual tree harvesting in Chaco exceeded the lifetime of any community member and, indeed, probably continued through multiple generations, indicating that the organization and conduct of this activity were not linked to any particular person or leader but rather were ingrained in Chacoan social structure.

Over 250,000 trees were imported to Chaco from distances between 40 and 100 kilometers to build just 13 great houses (Betancourt, Dean, and Hull 1986; Dean and Warren 1983:204). Wood use for smaller Chacoan buildings (and some great houses), fuel, and other domestic functions is not included in this figure. The high cost of wood use in general must have given this resource tremendous value, and the examples of excessive wood consumption found in many Chacoan contexts very likely reflect some sort of display behavior (Cordell 1997; Plog 1997). Consequently, it seems probable that trees and tree harvesting were symbolic of a connection between distant montane collection areas and great house architecture, perhaps one that expressed some degree of corporate affiliation by association with upland zones.

Various other features of great house construction suggest that collective production was achieved through the coordination of discrete social segments. For example, the serial construction of room blocks in vertical layers certainly points to a "barn-raising" approach by large work parties, particularly since it would have been disastrous to leave incomplete walls or partially roofed rooms exposed to the winter climate. Akins (1987:644) argued that concentrations of animal bone associated with construction debris at Pueblo Alto might be the remains of meals for such workers. The highly stylized veneer patterns that vary among rooms within single construction stages may indicate different groups of workers with distinctive "signatures." Windes and Ford (1996:302) made a similar argument from dendrochronological data at Pueblo Bonito, positing that "clusters of re-used wood at the site suggest that specific areas of the site were controlled by different social or political groups" (see also Stuart 1997:50).

Two extensive studies of architectural form and structure in great houses by Cooper (1995) and Bustard (1996) also identified within-structure variability that may be linked to distinctive sociopolitical groups. Both analyses employed space syntax analyses developed by Hillier and Hanson (1984; see also Ferguson 1996) to evaluate standardization of spatial organization between room blocks within great houses. Instead of redundant modules of rooms, Bustard (1996:263) found that room blocks "differ dramatically in terms of spatial organization." Individual room blocks were similar in overall form, with adjacent rows of large rectangular rooms, but designs were different in the degree to which there was access between rooms, a pattern that may reflect interaction patterns unique to different residential groups within individual great houses.

I believe these various inferences fit a pattern of calendrical collective commitment involving large numbers of participants that was most pronounced during the construction of residential room blocks. The formal characteristics of tree harvesting and construction are certainly ritual-like (see Bell 1997) and reflect a predictable, stable pattern of corporate activity. Construction during the eleventh century was an ongoing concern in Chaco (Lekson 1984a; Vivian 1990), but the continuous allocation of social labor to building efforts was broken down into many discrete projects that might be indicative of diverse social units.

Discussion

Building a great house presented complex scheduling problems, from obtaining construction material to assembling work parties, in which effective task coordination was critical to construction success. As labor expenditure on construction grew through the eleventh century, the overall number of tasks and the amount of information that builders had to control increased as well. Additionally, construction took labor and possibly resources (e.g., water) away from the subsistence economy or had to have been scheduled around farming and foraging commitments. Either scenario implies an increased division of labor and specialized roles for workers. Although there were changes in building technique, there was no technological innovation that accompanied the construction of great houses, no known development of tools or instruments that made the process more efficient. Consequently, the production of great houses was heavily information-dependent, and if innovations were part of the rapid transformation of canyon settlements in the eleventh century, they must have involved communication and decision making.

The large amount of information and complex task coordination inherent in great house construction was probably a good example of what Kauffman (1995) described as a "hard combinational optimization problem," or one where there are many possible combinations of factors that have to be evaluated in order to determine the best or most efficient solution. Centralized control is one way to solve coordination problems, but it may not produce the best solution because it reduces flexibility and the capacity to respond quickly to change. Archaeologists are familiar with the evidence that increases in communication load quickly lead to degraded performance in task-oriented groups unless some hierarchical decision-making mechanism emerges, but such coordinating structures need not be very complex (Johnson 1982; Kohler and Van West 1996). In fact, highly centralized control systems that attempt to process too much information can lose their capacity to coordinate at all. Kauffman (1995:253) argued that dividing a decision-making process into nonoverlapping "patches" and allowing each patch to pursue its own optimizing strategies tends to produce the most effective solution for all patches collectively. As long as patches share information with a few patches and do not attempt to coordinate with all others, the overall system will converge on an optimal solution without direction from a centralized authority (see also Gordon 1995). Such "small-world networks" may be especially good at coordinating spatially dispersed or distinct groups and can potentially generate extremely rapid and profound organizational change by finding efficient structures quickly (Watts and Strogatz 1998).

Patching suggests how collective ritual might have allowed a nonliterate society to handle the complex coordination problems in great house construction so successfully. Say that the construction process was broken into relatively autonomous production units, either specialized with respect to different tasks, such as wall construction or tree harvesting, or redundant in terms of linked tasks. If the construction process was conceptualized by the participants as a ritual activity, predictable in time and space, its purpose sanctified and symbolic of corporate obligation, then those production roles could have been identified with roles in the ritual system. A calendrical cycle of group participation in predictable, standardized activities would have at least reduced the coordination complexity and may have enhanced its efficiency through learning effects (see Arthur 1988). Concentrating the production process in a single location would likewise have improved coordination and perhaps in the case of Pueblo Bonito provided a symbolic or "traditional" focal point for the ritual activity (cf. Stein, Suiter, and Ford 1997). The result of such a collective process could be quite impressive but need not have involved very much institutionalized structure or an elaborate political organization.

What if the construction of Chacoan great houses was a ritual process? If so, then the organizational properties of the ritual system may have driven new construction projects, utilizing available labor in service to the system rather than to any individuals or even segments of the society. Analogous models have been proposed to explain labor mobilization for monumental construction in Neolithic Europe (Renfrew 1974; Whittle 1985). Mendelssohn's (1971) argument that Egyptian pyramid building was motivated by the existence of an organization for deploying a large labor force rather than political expediency parallels the model for great house construction that I am suggesting here. In other words, once the organization for producing great houses was in place, it continued to generate these buildings or enlargements of them for as long as labor (or energy) was available.

Current political models for Chaco assume that construction labor was attracted through the expenditure of agricultural surplus, but the lack of *consistent fit* between measures of agricultural production and building episodes is notorious (see especially Vivian 1990, 1992; also Sebastian 1991, 1992a; Windes and Ford 1996). In fact, the empirical record presents no obvious positive or negative correlation through time between construction and food production. However, great house construction in Chaco Canyon did occur during a period of very dramatic regional demographic change. Beginning in the late ninth century and continuing through the eleventh century, the San Juan Basin experienced a huge influx of population from surrounding regions, especially the montane zones of the San Juan River drainage to the north (Schlanger, Lipe, and Robinson 1993;

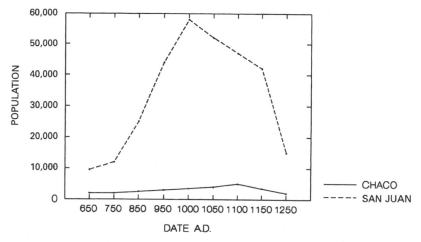

FIGURE 2.8. San Juan Basin population estimates (after Dean 1993). Recent fieldwork indicates that the San Juan population peak was probably greater than 60,000 (Chapman, Daniel, and Schutt 1997). Chaco population estimates have not changed since the early 1980s.

Schlanger and Wilshusen 1993; Wilshusen and Schlanger 1993). Survey data indicate that the number of sites in the San Juan Basin may have increased by a factor of thirteen (Cordell 1982) during the A.D. 1000s, accompanied by the expansion of habitation sites into previously unoc- cupied or low density areas (Chapman, Daniel, and Schutt 1997; Hogan and Winter 1983; Powers, Gillespie, and Lekson 1983; Stuart and Gauthier 1981; Winter 1988, 1994). Population estimates for Chaco proper do not vary much through the exponential growth of the tenth century but peak between A.D. 1050 and 1100 *after* the overall San Juan Basin population had begun to decline from its A.D. 1000 apex, perhaps reflecting some canyon immigration (Figure 2.8).

The close parallel between labor expenditure on Chaco great houses and the burgeoning regional population almost certainly indicates a connection between them. A causal relationship would be consistent with several as- pects of great house construction, particularly the trend of increasing labor investment through time, the possible symbolic connection between tree harvesting and mountains, and the indications of distinct social groups. Although recent competition models imply a labor scarcity, perhaps the critical problems faced by the Chaco population during this period of demographic change involved accommodation rather than expropriation. Only five great houses existed in the tenth century, and just three in Chaco Canyon proper with a combined estimated population of fewer than four hundred residents. These three communities (Pueblo Bonito, Una Vida, and Peñasco Blanco) were situated in agriculturally good settings (Vivian 1970, 1990, 1991, 1992) and so were probably attractive to newcomers, but perhaps great house residents were not powerful enough (or willing) to exclude immigrants. Such a context might have fostered the emergence of a collective ritual system that provided well-defined participatory roles for new members while allowing older residents to exert some control over a rapidly changing demographic situation. It could also help explain why labor input for construction continued to grow through sustained periods of agricultural stress (Sebastian 1992a), since good agricultural locations presumably were even more attractive under these conditions (cf. Leonard and Reed 1993).

A demographic "push-pull" model might also offer some insight regarding the abrupt initiation of planned construction projects between A.D. 1020 and 1030. Tree-ring data clearly indicate a hiatus in construction from the mid–tenth century to the early eleventh century, a pattern evident in records from individual great houses such as Pueblo Bonito (Figure 2.9). Therefore, the organizational capability to design, finance, and conduct major construction projects existed *before* these projects began. The only obvious economic realm in which collective production might have existed at Chaco was agriculture, which is also where the impact of immigrant populations would have been felt most immediately. I think Vivian (1970, 1990, 1992, 1997) is almost certainly correct that land tenure and water rights at Chaco were the focal points of political power in that agrarian society, and therefore it would not be surprising if the ability to build great houses was predicated on an organizational structure that had already developed around the management of food production. A rapid infusion of new residents in the form of small, independent family or clan groups might have been enough to expand the production potential of this organization into nonagricultural realms.

Crown (1994) has posited that widespread population movements in the Southwest during the A.D. 1300s were facilitated by the development of a regional cult. Economic disruption prompted migrations and created a situation "ideal for the acceptance of a cult that emphasized the well-being of a community larger than the village, stressed peaceful relations, and promoted the flow of goods, information, and people across existing ethnic boundaries. Such a regional cult would deemphasize the ancestor and the specific interests of the kin group or villages" (Crown 1994:215). The construction process associated with Chacoan great houses appears to have

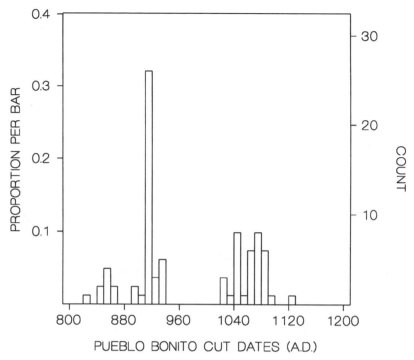

FIGURE 2.9. Histogram of cutting dates from Pueblo Bonito.

been predicated on a remarkably similar set of relations, from the extraordinary influx of material goods to the striking absence of mortuary programs. While not suggesting that the Chaco Phenomenon was a cult, I do think the construction of great houses indicates an inclusionary rather than an exclusionary social process.

An inclusionary ritual system emphasizing a corporate social enterprise is precisely what competitive models of ritual power are not. Competition models propose a highly regulated, very structured political world characterized by tension and underlying factionalism. Great house construction throughout the eleventh and twelfth centuries appears much more consistent with the kind of social endeavor that Turner (1974) defines as *communitas,* or antistructure. If structure "is all that holds people apart, defines their differences, and constrains their actions" (Turner 1974:47), then communitas is its opposite. It would make a great deal of sense with respect to the coordination in the building process if the creation of architecture and ritual were inseparable elements of a "universe of work, in which the whole community participates, as of obligation not optation" (Turner 1977:38). This general idea is clearly evident in Saitta's (1997) discussion of a Chacoan "communal mode of production," but he attributes community participation to the intentional efforts of ritual specialists to exploit corporate labor in their own interests through deceit. I am suggesting instead that the power evident in great house construction may have been the result of a secular ritual system that suppressed or eliminated much of the divisive dynamics of competition among religious leaders.

Secular or nonreligious ritual often does not have very complex or marked ideological features but may actually be more elaborate in expression than religious ritual for just that reason, since it must be more explicit in communicating its meaning (Moore and Myerhoff 1977:11). Similarly, secular ritual may be closely connected to a specific community context because it is not concerned with universal truths or knowledge. Great houses are notable for their scale and elaboration, and they represent a collective enterprise that produced hugely expensive and expressive communal dwellings. There were features and structures built into the overall architecture of great houses that undoubtedly had religious importance, but these constitute just one relatively inexpensive part of the entire structure. If great houses were metaphors for Chacoan society, as has been argued (Stein and Lekson 1992), I think the archaeological record indicates that their meaning was more closely tied to a house than to a religious edifice (cf. Ferguson 1989). Even in modern Pueblos, where religious ritual is so impressive and pervasive, the underlying economic and political structure is built around the household (Ford 1972; Levy 1992; Ortiz 1969; Watts 1997).

Recent models of Chacoan political economy utilize a structural approach that assumes great houses were the product of religious power and therefore focus almost exclusively on the role of religious leaders as agents producing a cosmological universe in architecture that matched their strategies for acquiring social power. However, the production process underlying the construction of great houses suggests a different sort of cosmology, one reflecting communitas, the central place of domestic life, and probably the suppression of competitive ritual. The materialization of ideological power does not have to be religious in nature, nor does monumental architecture need to be sacred (DeMarrais, Castillo, and Earle 1996). Religious rites and ceremonies may well have taken on profound and fundamental roles for the people of Chaco after great houses were built, but the capacity to deploy social labor was greatest when religious ritual was least evident.

Conclusion

Obviously the Chaco Phenomenon involved leaders, and undoubtedly those leaders competed with one another for prestige, influence, and power. In what segmentary society would we fail to find leaders behaving this way? The issue I have tried to raise in this chapter is whether competition between religious leaders is a likely model for the production of great house architecture between A.D. 1000 and 1140. In much the way that Blanton and his colleagues (1996a) suggest that leadership strategies can shift from one dominant but not exclusive mode to another through time, I think the Chaco case indicates the coexistence of two kinds of leaders. Ritual specialists were certainly one kind, but evidence for religious expression in the archaeological record is not associated with the most powerful examples of labor mobilization. The hypothetical public performances and elaborate but speculative cosmology that many researchers attribute to the consolidation of social power by religious leaders at Chaco might just as well indicate the loss of real community integration and the emergence of internal conflict and factionalism. In contrast, the massive labor mobilization in the eleventh century appears to have been associated with discrete social segments united through participation in corporate production of residential structures, their motivation perhaps a matter of simple entitlement, the right of access, rather than payment to an elite priestly class for services rendered. The ability of participants to produce great houses in a context of limited surplus production may reflect the power of relatively little leadership complexity, rather than the existence of an elaborate and expensive structure of religious specialists vying for followers.

NOTES

1. The scholarship regarding Chaco Canyon is immensely complex, and I apologize to anyone whose work I have unintentionally slighted, overlooked, or misinterpreted. I am grateful to Gwinn Vivian, Barbara Mills, Tim Kohler, Gary Feinman, and Patty Crown for their helpful comments and advice. Special thanks to Tom Windes for sharing his encyclopedic knowledge of Chaco and his new tree-ring dates from Pueblo Bonito. I regret that I cannot thank the dozen or more Chacoan scholars who declined my request for comments and advice.

2. Architectural history data used here are found mostly in Lekson (1983, 1984a), Dean and Warren (1983), Vivian (1990, 1992), and Windes and Ford (1996).

3. Lekson's construction data do not include estimates for all known architecture in Chaco dating between A.D. 1000 and 1140. Among the large excluded structures are Hillside Ruin adjacent to Pueblo Bonito, the Great Kivas at Kin Nahasbas, 29SJ 1253, 29SJ 1642, and the recently discovered East Community great house near Shabik'eschee Village. Small residential sites such as 29SJ 627, other buildings throughout the canyon, various features such as walls and staircases, and agricultural field systems were also not included.

3

Leadership, Long-Distance Exchange, and Feasting in the Protohistoric Rio Grande

WILLIAM M. GRAVES AND KATHERINE A. SPIELMANN

IN THIS CHAPTER, we discuss the potential sources of power and the bases of inequality that may have structured leadership strategies in protohistoric period (ca. A.D. 1400 to ca. A.D. 1600) Puebloan society in the northern and central Rio Grande region. Regional settlement pattern data and data from excavated sites in the Salinas area of central New Mexico suggest that an increasing intensity of long-distance exchange and intercommunity relations marks a fundamental transformation in the scale and scope of social interactions throughout the region during the protohistoric period. We argue that such interactions may have provided the foundations for the emergence of unequal sociopolitical relations during the protohistoric period.

The Protohistoric Social Landscape

The beginning of the protohistoric period in the northern and central Rio Grande region witnessed marked changes in settlement size and distribution. The size of Pueblo settlements increased substantially during this period, ranging from roughly three hundred to more than a thousand rooms (Creamer 1996; Spielmann 1996; Wilcox 1981, 1991). In addition, the protohistoric period is characterized by a dramatic shift in the distribution of pueblos, from a dispersed pattern to a pattern of settlement clustering (Mera 1934, 1940; Wilcox 1981, 1991). Pueblos within clusters are likely to have housed hundreds of people, whereas a few thousand people are expected to have inhabited individual clusters. Settlement clustering created a much more structured social landscape during the protohistoric period, one in which the scale and scope of interactions among pueblos within clusters became more intense, providing the context for increasing social inequality. It is relations both within and between clusters that we consider in this chapter.

In recent years, various models of social and political organization have been proposed for these settlement clusters (Creamer 1996; Graves 1996; Habicht-Mauche 1988; Spielmann 1994; Upham and Reed 1989; Wilcox 1981, 1991). These models all focus on the kinds of sociopolitical interactions that may have characterized relations among pueblos within individual clusters but differ in their interpretations of the organization and complexity of political relations. One model is based on complex, vertically differentiated decision-making hierarchies (Wilcox 1981, 1991), whereas another postulates less complex confederacy organizations (Spielmann 1994). Leadership per se remains poorly understood for the protohistoric period.

The Archaeological Record

The archaeological record for the protohistoric Rio Grande up to this point has been fairly ambiguous with regard to the nature of leadership. On the one hand, there is little evidence for individual prestige and wealth accumulation, and the mortuary record evidences little or no status differences among groups or individuals. Neither do there appear to be any differences in lifestyles, concentrations of wealth, or control over labor (Spielmann 1994:46) that would serve as material indicators of social inequality. Prestige goods, such as shell and turquoise ornaments, are extremely limited in quantity at protohistoric Rio Grande sites. In addition, although there is some variability in settlement size among protohistoric pueblos (see Wilcox 1991), no architectural or settlement pattern evidence exists that suggests hierarchical differentiation among villages (Creamer 1996; Spielmann 1994:46). Moreover, public works (largely kivas) are fairly modest in scale.

On the other hand, there are data that strongly suggest that variation in individual power and prestige would have characterized the protohistoric Rio Grande. Demographically, the population sizes of pueblo clusters approach the threshold at which cross-cultural research indicates that permanent leadership tends to develop (e.g., Kosse 1990, 1996). Leadership at this demographic scale tends to be based on personal persuasion and influence, rather than on the authority of an office (Kosse 1996). It is thus likely that the scale and nature of aggregation in the protohistoric period provided the opportunity for certain individuals to enhance their political position by seeking positions of leadership.

The marked increase in the intensity of long-distance exchange of decorated ceramics, obsidian, and cotton that occurred in the protohistoric period suggests an avenue through which individuals could acquire such prestige and power. Sourcing studies, for example, have documented the existence of several major production loci that exported large quantities of pottery throughout the entire central Rio Grande region (Allison 1993; Garrett 1992; Shepard 1936, 1942:185–90; Warren 1969, 1970, 1981a, 1981b). In particular, Tonque Pueblo and the Galisteo Basin pueblos, especially San Marcos, emerged as the major exporters of glaze ware vessels, from about A.D. 1400 until the mid-1500s (Snow 1981:363). Galisteo Basin and Tonque glaze ware vessels would have been readily identifiable to the residents of the pueblos to which they were imported due to their light-colored slips (Mobley-Tanaka 1998; Warren 1979).

Models of Leadership in Middle-Range Societies

Over a decade ago, Feinman and Neitzel (1984) established that leadership, power, and prestige in middle-range societies were highly variable and likely to produce the ambiguous kind of archaeological record we have outlined for the Rio Grande. They emphasized the importance of understanding particular cases rather than developing normative models for social inequality in middle-range societies. Here we elaborate on just such a case, the Salinas area of central New Mexico, which is discussed below.

More recently, models have been developed that highlight multiple pathways to social inequality and define certain variables that are useful in understanding the different ways in which individuals may acquire power and prestige. These include dual-processual theory (Blanton et al. 1996a; Feinman 1995) and heterarchy models (e.g., Crumley 1979, 1995; Ehrenreich, Crumley, and Levy 1995; Rautman 1998). In addition, archaeologists have begun to focus on the importance of communal feasting as a context in which prestige is often acquired in middle-range societies (Hayden 1995; Potter 1997b; Wiessner and Schiefenhövel 1996).

Briefly, dual-processual theory defines two alternate ways in which hierarchy can develop: network-based and corporate-based strategies. Network strategies characterize "political-economic pattern[s] in which preeminence is an outcome of the development and maintenance of individual-centered exchange relations established primarily outside one's local group"

(Blanton et al. 1996a:4). Individuals who manipulate long-distance social connections through which prestige goods and perhaps marriage partners are obtained may acquire prestige, power, and leadership authority within the local group. By controlling the acquisition of exotics, emerging leaders have an important political tool for establishing social and economic obligations with other individuals and groups in their local community. Because any individual or household within the group may establish network ties, this strategy may be characterized by a considerable degree of competition and rather volatile leadership (Blanton et al. 1996a:4).

Corporate-based strategies lack prestige goods systems and emphasize ideologies that stress corporate solidarity (Blanton et al. 1996a:5–7). Societies with corporate-based political economies are characterized by comparatively egalitarian ideologies and a "lack of evidence for domination by particular powerful rulers" (Blanton et al. 1996a:6). Aspiring leaders mobilize locally available resources to build local factions, serve central roles in ceremonial functions and other communal activities, and rely on their powers of personal persuasion to build a following (Feinman 1995).

Feasting is one of the more central strategies used by aspiring leaders in many middle-range societies to acquire prestige and power (Hayden 1995:25). The ability to successfully host feasts is indicative of one's access to and control of the substantial economic resources necessary for sponsoring a communal feast (Chowning 1979; Clark and Blake 1994; Hayden 1995; Johnson and Earle 1987; Potter 1997b; Sahlins 1972). Feasts are also social contexts in which public displays of economic wealth and surplus may occur (Hayden 1995). By displaying wealth and surplus, the feast organizer, and the group or community as well, seeks to impress invited guests. Thus, ceremonies and feasts are a means of attracting followers and their labor and resources as well as establishing and maintaining important social relationships with other groups or communities.

Heterarchy models recently have been proposed as an alternative to hierarchical models of sociopolitical complexity (e.g., Crumley 1979, 1995; Ehrenreich, Crumley, and Levy 1995). Heterarchical models disengage social, political, and economic behaviors, positing that they may operate more or less independently of one another (Brumfiel 1995:125; Rautman 1998:328). Heterarchy can be seen as a conceptual framework, one that acknowledges the potential range of variation that may exist in the ways in which individuals may achieve prestige and authority. As Rautman (1998:329) has stated, "A heterarchical perspective would imply that different groups might simultaneously occupy positions of power that may be variously defined."

Prestige, Power, and Leadership in the Protohistoric Rio Grande

The protohistoric Rio Grande archaeological record is exactly the kind that one would expect from a corporate-based system as described by Blanton and his colleagues (1996a). The absence of site hierarchies, the lack of material evidence for status differences, and the lack of prestige goods strongly suggest that sociopolitical relations both within and among proto-historic villages could be characterized as "corporate." A careful consideration of the protohistoric archaeological record, however, indicates that more "network-like" strategies, such as long-distance exchange and inter-community feasting, were prominent as well.

In the remainder of this chapter, we focus on examining strategies of prestige enhancement that may have been employed by aspiring leaders. The data we consider here are derived from archaeological excavations at two sites in the Salinas district in central New Mexico, Gran Quivira and Pueblo Colorado (Figure 3.1). Excavations at these sites focused primarily on recovering materials from trash midden deposits. Materials from contexts dating to the protohistoric period were recovered at both pueblos (Spielmann 1991a, 1992, 1998a). These data indicate that pueblos within a cluster may have differed in their emphasis on intercommunity interactions, specifically long-distance exchange and the hosting of feasts.

Gran Quivira and Pueblo Colorado are located approximately 20 kilometers apart within the southernmost cluster of sites in the Salinas district, the Jumanos pueblo cluster (Graves 1996; Hayes 1982). The two sites share a similar layout of numerous large room blocks arranged to form several plaza areas. The sites are also roughly comparable in size. Gran Quivira is composed of approximately twenty-two room blocks, and Pueblo Colorado consists of approximately eighteen room blocks (Spielmann and Eshbaugh 1988:1). Villages in the Salinas district were all occupied beginning in the late A.D. 1200s or early A.D. 1300s. Occupation of the Salinas pueblos continued into the historic period, circa A.D. 1670 (Hayes 1981:8, 1982:15; Spielmann and Eshbaugh 1988:1), with the exception of Pueblo Colorado, which was abandoned by the early 1500s, prior to Spanish contact.

Residents of the Salinas pueblos participated in two kinds of long-distance exchange: exchange with Plains hunter-gatherers for bison prod-

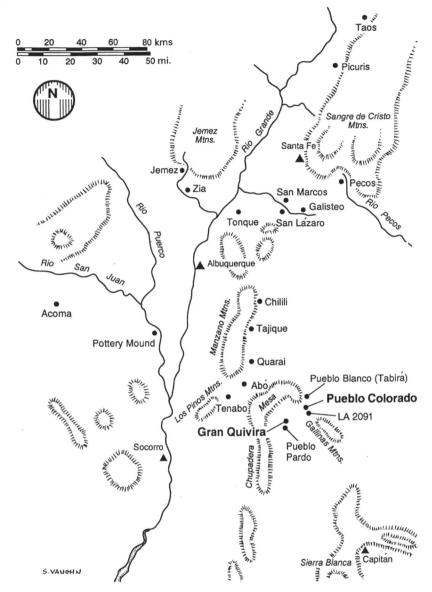

FIGURE 3.1. Protohistoric pueblos in the Rio Grande Valley.

ucts and exchange with pueblos from other clusters primarily to acquire glaze-decorated ceramics. Evidence from the Salinas pueblos indicates that there was differential participation in these long-distance exchanges but that residents of both pueblos were actively involved in such prestige-enhancing activities.

With regard to Plains-Pueblo exchange, Potter (1995) has recently ex-

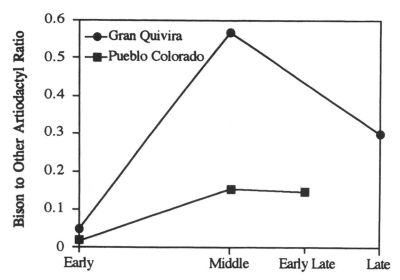

FIGURE 3.2. Trends over time in the ratio of bison to other artiodactyls at Gran Quivira and Pueblo Colorado (Potter 1995:423, reprinted by permission of *Kiva*).

amined faunal remains from the excavations at both Gran Quivira and Pueblo Colorado. His data, summarized in Figure 3.2, reveal that bison bone occurs in much greater quantities relative to other large game in the Gran Quivira assemblage (Potter 1995:423–25). Demand for bison was apparently fueled by depletion of large-game resources in the local area during the protohistoric period (Potter 1995; Spielmann 1988) and by a demand for bison hides, which were an important long-distance exchange item within the protohistoric Pueblo world (Spielmann 1994). Although Pueblo Colorado lies some 20 kilometers closer to the Plains (see Figure 3.1), it is clear that the inhabitants of Gran Quivira enjoyed much greater access to highly valued bison products through their closer exchange relations with Plains groups. Something other than geographic proximity must have determined the availability of bison at these two sites, and Potter (1995:425) argues that Gran Quivira was able to "dominate the local social and economic spheres of exchange," emerging as the preeminent pueblo in the cluster.

The data concerning long-distance exchange of glaze-decorated ceramics are also compelling concerning interpueblo differences in the manipulation of long-distance exchange ties (Table 3.1). Petrographic sourcing of glaze-decorated ceramics recovered from Gran Quivira and Pueblo Colorado (Graves 1996; Herhahn 1998; Warren 1981a, 1981b) indicates that both pueblos imported the majority of their glaze wares. A significant

Table 3.1 SOURCES OF PROTOHISTORIC GLAZE WARE BOWL RIM SHERDS FROM GRAN QUIVIRA AND PUEBLO COLORADO (FROM HERHAHN 1998).

Site	n	Percent Local Salinas Sources			Percent Nonlocal Regional Sources				
		Abo/ Tenabo	Other Salinas	Gran Quivira	Central Rio Grande	Lower Middle Rio Grande	Tonque	San Marcos	Unknown
Gran Quivira	77	55	3	8	9	4	17	3	3
Pueblo Colorado	47	26	0	4	2	4	32	26	6

Chi^2=27.19, p< 0.0001, df=7

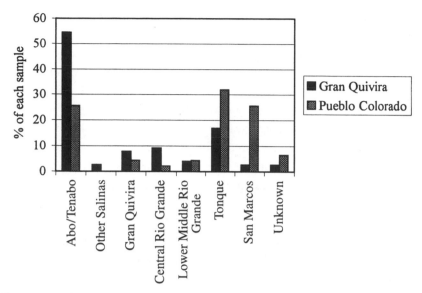

FIGURE 3.3. Glaze ware sources for Gran Quivira and Pueblo Colorado samples.

proportion of these imports came from Abo and Tenabo Pueblos, within the Salinas cluster of sites. Tonque and San Marcos Pueblos, however, which lie roughly 100 kilometers north of the cluster, were also important sources of glaze bowls for Gran Quivira and Pueblo Colorado. The petrographic data reveal that both pueblos were heavily involved in long-distance exchange relations with these two villages but that there were significant differences in their participation in this exchange.

The data we consider here are taken from Herhahn's (1998) petrographic analysis of Glaze C and D ceramics from protohistoric deposits excavated at the two sites (Spielmann 1991a, 1992, 1998a). Table 3.1 and Figure 3.3 show the percentage of local and nonlocal imports in a sample of protohistoric glaze ware bowl rim sherds from Gran Quivira (n = 77) and Pueblo Colorado (n = 47). The percentages of local, Salinas district imports at the two sites differ substantially. Roughly 58 percent of the Gran Quivira assemblage consists of vessels obtained from Abo and Tenabo Pueblos and the eastern Manzanos. Only 30 percent of the Pueblo Colorado assemblage represents local importation, mostly from the Abo/Tenabo area. The nonlocal assemblages at each site also differ substantially. The Pueblo Colorado assemblage is dominated by imports from Tonque and San Marcos Pueblos, 32 and 26 percent, respectively. Imports from these two sites make up only 20 percent of the Gran Quivira sample.

Warren's (1981a, 1981b:182–83) petrographic data, however, present a different picture of long-distance exchange relationships at Gran Quivira during the protohistoric period (see also Graves 1996). The Glaze C and D bowl sherds (n = 154) in her analysis were taken from extensive National Park Service excavations at the site (Hayes 1981) and reveal a much greater reliance on nonlocal glaze ware sources, both in terms of relative proportions of nonlocal sources and the diversity of sources represented. Nearly one-third of her sample was sourced to Tonque Pueblo. In addition, she identified five different sources within the Galisteo basin, constituting roughly 10 percent of her sample. Given that Warren's (1981a, 1981b) data come from a much larger area of the site, it is perhaps not surprising that the variety of nonlocal sources represented in her sample is greater than Herhahn's (1998).

These petrographic data present a relatively complex picture of long-distance exchange relationships in the Jumanos cluster. The inhabitants of both pueblos were apparently active in networking and pursuing strategies of multiple exchange partnerships with a number of different areas. Although Herhahn's (1998) data suggest Gran Quivira may have been less active in long-distance exchange, Warren's (1981a, 1981b) analysis suggests that Gran Quivirans may have acquired vessels from a greater diversity of sources than Pueblo Colorado. However, in terms of sample proportions, Pueblo Coloradans apparently relied much more heavily on acquiring vessels from nonlocal, or long-distance, sources, especially Tonque and San Marcos Pueblos. Evidence for large-scale feasting at Gran Quivira may help explain this marked difference in patterns of importation.

What fueled the sizable demand for these glaze-decorated vessels at Pueblo Colorado and Gran Quivira? We do not argue that glaze bowls were wealth items per se. However, the effort expended in acquiring visually distinctive glaze bowls from such long distances suggests that they were a valuable commodity in the protohistoric Rio Grande. Spielmann (1998b) has argued that the adoption and rapid dissemination of glaze ware bowls in the Rio Grande valley is linked to the importance of public ceremonial feasting in the context of the Southwestern Cult as defined by Crown (1994). Glaze bowls became *the* serving bowls for households throughout the Rio Grande, and household contributions to ceremonial feasts would publicly display an individual household's glaze bowl repertoire. The public use of glaze bowls obtained through long-distance exchange could have been a prestige-enhancing activity on the part of individual households within a pueblo.

Recent research (Graves 1996) examined feasting behaviors at both Gran

Table 3.2 CONCENTRATIONS OF SERVING, STORAGE, AND COOKING VESSEL REMAINS
IN THE PROTOHISTORIC MIDDEN DEPOSITS AT GRAN QUIVIRA AND PUEBLO COLORADO
(IN KILOGRAMS OF CERAMICS/KILOGRAMS OF LITHICS) (FROM GRAVES 1996).

Site	Glaze Ware Serving Bowls	Utility Storage Jars	Utility Cooking Jars
Gran Quivira	5.3	5.4	8.5
Pueblo Colorado	1.0	2.2	0.8

Quivira and Pueblo Colorado. The analysis focused primarily on the discard of ceramics from excavated trash midden deposits at the two sites. Ceramic discard rates, or densities, were calculated in grams of ceramics per grams of lithics rather than grams per unit volume of dirt to mitigate against potential differences in midden depositional processes (Graves 1996:58–60). Table 3.2 and Figure 3.4 show that the excavated protohistoric midden deposits at Gran Quivira contain five times the amount of serving bowl remains and eleven times the amount of cooking jar remains than the midden deposits at Pueblo Colorado.

How can two villages of similar size, layout, and likely similar populations have such drastically different discard rates of ceramic vessels? The sheer volume of ceramics in the midden deposits of Gran Quivira, especially the high density of cooking jar remains, strongly suggests the frequent occurrence of large-scale food preparation and consumption at this village. These data indicate that feasts were probably being hosted at a much higher frequency or at a greater scale at Gran Quivira than at Pueblo Colorado.

Given the far greater magnitude of food serving documented at Gran Quivira, it is perhaps not surprising that proportionately more glaze ware bowls were imported locally at Gran Quivira than at Pueblo Colorado. The prestige associated with the ownership and use of Tonque and Galisteo bowls may have been accrued to individuals or households, while communal feasting reflected the abilities of larger units such as ceremonial societies.

If feasting events were being hosted more often at Gran Quivira, how, then, were they structured, and at what scale did they occur? Unfortunately, the available data do not allow the distinction between different types of feasting behaviors (such as competitive feasting, ritual feasting, etc.). However, several factors allow us to begin assessing the scale and structure of feasting at Gran Quivira.

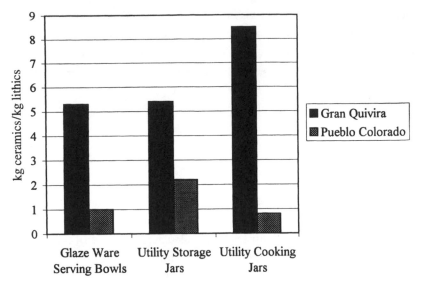

FIGURE 3.4. Concentrations of serving, storage, and cooking vessel remains in proto-historic midden deposits at Gran Quivira and Pueblo Colorado (in kilograms of ceramics/kilograms of lithics).

Feasting in middle-range societies may often take the form of competition, whereby ambitious groups or individuals within a community compete with each other for prestige and social power. Feasts provide a context in which, through public displays, a feast organizer appears successful and powerful to other ambitious community members and may be able to attract a faction of supporters (Clark and Blake 1994; Hayden 1995; Johnson and Earle 1987; Sahlins 1972). It does not appear that the feasting activities identified at Gran Quivira represent such within-community, competitive feasting sponsored by rival groups or individuals within the village. The sustained intensity of feasting we see in the data occurred throughout most or all of the protohistoric period, perhaps 150 to 200 years. It is unlikely that a pattern of competitive feast hosting would be sustained in a single community for such a long period of time (Hayden 1995:24–25). It is more likely that the evidence of feasting at Gran Quivira represents the hosting of large, intercommunity events through time. The sheer magnitude of difference between the ceramic discard rates of the two sites suggests that people from neighboring villages, including Pueblo Colorado, participated in these large gatherings and that this evidence of feasting at Gran Quivira represents the hosting of intercommunity events throughout the protohistoric period (Graves 1996:65–67).

Feasts in middle-range societies are often held in the context of religious events (Aldenderfer 1993; Blitz 1993a; Hayden 1995; Rappaport 1979a). Ritual knowledge has been shown to be a source of power in many middle-range societies (Aldenderfer 1993; Brandt 1980; Burns and Laughlin 1979; Chowning 1979), and there appears to be a strong relationship between the control and restriction of sacred knowledge, as evidenced through the hosting of ritually sanctioned feasts and ceremonies, and the acquisition of power and leadership (Aldenderfer 1993; Feinman and Neitzel 1984; Johnson and Earle 1987; Sahlins 1972). If access to sacred knowledge becomes restricted, then only those who control such knowledge possess the authority and sanction to conduct ritual or ceremonial activities, allowing some members of a society to gain considerable power.

Data from prehistoric and historic Puebloan contexts suggest that feasts hosted at Gran Quivira may have been ritually sanctioned events. Blinman (1989) and Toll (1984) have identified feasting activities in the archaeological record that are clearly associated with ritual contexts. Moreover, feasts in modern pueblos are organized and hosted by the religious leaders of communities (Brandt 1985). If the gatherings at Gran Quivira did take place in ritual contexts, then some aspects of ritual control may have been present as well. A system of ritual dependency may have existed that integrated the pueblos of the Jumanos cluster. Certain critical religious institutions and knowledge may have been controlled and maintained by groups or individuals at Gran Quivira.

Discussion

In his discussion of the dual-processual model, Feinman (1995) highlights a key concept that is critical in understanding the development of leadership in human societies, the "dialectic of control" (Giddens 1984; Spencer 1993). According to this concept, the growth of strong leadership and inequality "follows from the successful coordination and articulation of two sets of potentially opposing relations. The first is defined by the ties between a leader and his local faction [of supporters], while the second represents that individual's links to the extra-factional [or regional] arena" (Feinman 1995:262). It is the interplay and combination of these two sets of relations that fuels the emergence of institutionalized inequality and leadership in middle-range societies. We see such a combination in our case study from the Rio Grande, in the pattern of prestige enhancement through within-cluster relations among particular pueblos, and through the acquisition of prestige-enhancing goods derived through long-distance exchange.

Similarly, we see a role for the establishment and manipulation of inter-community relations, especially long-distance exchange, in both network and corporate strategies. Whether long-distance relations develop within a corporate system, such as the protohistoric Rio Grande, or a network system determines the *form* of such interaction but not its existence. For example, according to the dual-processual model, the establishment of long-distance relations in a network system will take the form of competi-tive exchanges in wealth items, often within the structure of a prestige goods economy (Blanton et al. 1996a:4–5). In our case study, although long-distance exchange appears to have been a significant prestige-enhancing activity in the protohistoric period, a prestige goods economy did not develop. Nonetheless, if glaze-decorated bowls were important in commu-nal feasting, long-distance exchange appears to have been a fully integrated component of an overall corporate-based system.

A heterarchical approach is also quite informative to our understanding of prestige-enhancing behaviors in the Jumanos cluster. Although our data indicate that Gran Quivira residents were more active than those at Pueblo Colorado in exchange with Plains hunters and in the hosting of feasts, the glaze bowl data document that some Pueblo Colorado residents were at least as active as, if not more than, Gran Quivirans in long-distance ex-change. What emerges, then, is a dynamic picture of prestige-enhancing activities within the Jumanos cluster, one in which economic activities (exchange) were at least somewhat independent of the hosting of the feasts in which these bowls were used. Although Gran Quivira was apparently the more prominent pueblo in the cluster, the inhabitants of this pueblo did not hold a monopoly of control over the local social and economic spheres. The inhabitants of each pueblo were able to utilize various strat-egies, with varying degrees of success, in the acquisition of prestige, power, and leadership.

Conclusion

The data from the Jumanos pueblo cluster suggest that both participation in long-distance exchange and the hosting of feasts, and by extension control over ritual knowledge, were activities that could have been used by aspiring leaders to enhance their prestige and power. These activities were an out-come, in large part, of the increasing intensity of intercommunity relations during the protohistoric period. As we have noted, settlement clustering in the Rio Grande marks a fundamental transformation in the scale and scope of interactions among individual pueblos. It is within the context of this increasing scale of social interactions that these particular prestige-enhancing activities became the potential sources of differential power and the bases of leadership in protohistoric Puebloan society.

ACKNOWLEDGMENTS

Funding for excavations at Gran Quivira and Pueblo Colorado and analysis of the materials recovered was provided through grants to Spielmann from the National Science Foundation (SBR-9423194 and BNS-8418586) and the Wenner-Gren Foundation for Anthropological Research (Grant-in-Aid #5202 and #4655). We would like to thank Barbara Mills for organizing such a stimulating session and for seeing the papers through to publication.

4

Ritual as a Power Resource in the American Southwest

JAMES M. POTTER AND ELIZABETH M. PERRY

RECENT ARCHAEOLOGICAL AND ethnological discussions of Puebloan political organization have emphasized ritual as the basis for leadership in Puebloan society and have made the argument that ritual-based social hierarchy
indeed exists (or existed) in these societies (Adams 1989; Brandt 1994;
Potter 2000; Spielmann 1998b; Upham 1989; Whiteley 1988). Each of
these analyses has noted that the control of rituals and ritual knowledge
is the fundamental basis for social ranking in Pueblo societies. While this
conclusion is not in dispute, there has been little discussion of how groups
or individuals come to control rituals, the conditions under which ritual becomes a potent power resource, and the ways in which ritual may
distribute power as well as consolidate it. Moreover, how the actual *performance* of rituals may amplify social differences has not been addressed.
Indeed, the performative aspect of ritual as a power resource in Puebloan
society has either been conflated with the control of ritual or ignored
entirely.

In this chapter we suggest that the control and performance of ritual may
be potent power resources because they have the unique capacity to dis-
perse power and establish social hierarchy simultaneously. For example,
while the control of various rituals and ritual responsibilities may be widely
distributed within a community, as in the case of Hopi society, ranking and
highly structured social differentiation do occur among the controllers of
ritual, as well as between those in control of ritual and those not in control,
precisely because of the inherent hierarchical nature of many ritual structures. Thus, even if control of ritual is not highly centralized, decision-
making units may be firmly ranked according to the importance of the
ritual(s) they control. Moreover, this seemingly contradictory aspect of

ritual power may be reinforced during ritual performance, which has the capacity to simultaneously integrate and rank social units though mediating the processes of inclusion and exclusion.

The overarching goal of this essay is to deconstruct ritual practice as a resource of social power in middle-range societies, particularly Puebloan society. We begin with a detailed discussion of how the control and performance of ritual may operate both to distribute power and to establish hierarchy. We note that hierarchy is inherent to ritual-based structures due to the subtle ability of ritual to simultaneously integrate and rank social units, the intrinsic authority that ritual confers upon those who control it, the capacity of ritual to create a context for the production and internalization of ideology, and the fact that ritual and the knowledge necessary for its successful performance may be controlled and monopolized. Moreover, we suggest that a system of leadership based on ritual control and performance, *especially if distributive of power,* may provide a highly stable hierarchical power structure, since competition is reduced and overt resistance to the dominant power structure and subversive action are often provided a real but innocuous outlet during ritual performance. We conclude the essay with a brief case study that exemplifies the dual nature of ritual as a power resource, and we explore some of the unique aspects of early Pueblo IV period ritual in the Zuni area that may have been particularly effective in structuring power relations.

Although historic and modern Zuni accounts of ritual are provided throughout the paper, we stress that our use of the Zuni ethnographic record should be viewed as an illustrative example of how ritual operates, rather than an attempt at direct historic analogy. Moreover, our focus on Zuni and Melanesian ethnography is a product of the specific limitations of our knowledge of the cross-cultural record, the richness of the literature for these two culture areas, and the limitations of space.

We view social power as the ability of people to motivate actions and to secure access to material, social, and ideological resources. While not denying coercion as a viable means to these ends, this definition recognizes the importance that other, often more subtle, resources of power can have in achieving them, particularly in small-scale societies. As Foucault (1980) and Giddens (1984) suggest, power is the ability to structure the possible field of action of others. We argue that this can be accomplished effectively through controlling access to ritual and ritual knowledge and through the use and manipulation of symbols during ritual performance.

The Control of Ritual

Several aspects of ritual make it a controllable and thus monopolizable power resource, including the facts that access to the knowledge, ceremonial objects, and places necessary to perform important rituals may be restricted and that control of certain rituals may be limited to specific clan or society affiliations. Each of these aspects may operate to either disseminate or consolidate control. Regardless, the control of ritual may translate into puissant religious and/or secular authority. As Brandt (1994:15) notes, "Ceremonial knowledge and ceremonial property, including objects, songs, and chants, must be considered as resources because they enable the control of other resources."

An effective strategy for controlling access to ritual knowledge, and thereby monopolizing ritual, is the practice of secrecy (Barth 1975; Brandt 1977, 1994; Harrison 1985). Ritual secrecy preserves the "scarcity value" of ritual knowledge (Harrison 1985). Brandt (1977, 1985, 1994) has convincingly argued that Pueblos as a society type in the Southwest represent nonegalitarian, hierarchical communities, "with inequalities created and maintained by a well-developed system of information control managed through secrecy, surveillance, and privacy" (Brandt 1994:14).

Initiation rituals are another means through which knowledge may be highly controlled. Among the Baktaman on New Guinea, for example, access to ritual knowledge is contingent upon successful participation in a series of seven initiation rituals (Barth 1975). As individuals successfully participate in these rite-of-passage rituals over their lifetime, they gain access to more (and more powerful) ritual knowledge, ultimately allowing them to become leaders of the community. The particular individuals who become initiated, and the rate at which they participate in the seven rite-of-passage rituals, is highly variable and is dependent upon decisions of the existing ritual leaders.

Sacred objects that are necessary for the conduct of ritual also are often tightly controlled and monopolized. Status and leadership in the Baruya society of New Guinea, for example, is contingent upon the possession of sacred objects for male initiation. These objects signify who has the right to become a leader, and access is restricted to specific lineages (Godelier 1982, 1991).

In addition to knowledge and ceremonial objects, the distribution of ceremonial responsibilities is also greatly structured and controlled in many middle-range societies, including Puebloan society. Although the distribution of control and responsibility may be widely dispersed and crosscutting within communities (e.g., Ladd 1979:484), at some level *social hierarchy is always a result of ritual control*. For example, the importance of particular ceremonies often varies within societies and can thus result in the ranking of controlling groups. As Brandt (1994:14) notes of Puebloan society, "The hierarchically ranked groups include religious societies, clan groups, lineages, and households . . . which are ranked by ideological justifications based on such factors as order of emergence in this world, order of arrival, and *the importance of the ceremony they control*" (emphasis ours). The differential importance of ritual may relate to the importance of knowledge and ceremonial property associated with the ritual, variations in the number of participants in a ritual, or the importance of the season and amount of time of which a group is in control (Brandt 1994:15).

Ranking may also relate to the order of importance of the cardinal direction and/or color symbolically represented by groups controlling specific ceremonies. Cushing (1979:190–91), for instance, notes that at Zuni, "the tribal division made up of clans of the north takes precedence ceremonially, occupying the position of elder brother or the oldest ancestor, as the case may be. The west is the younger of this, and in turn, the south of the west, and east of the south, the upper of the east, the under of them all."

Finally, the actual structures within which rituals occur may be ranked in importance, resulting in a ranking of the groups in control of the rituals associated with specific structures. Zuni kivas, for example, are hierarchically arranged according to a counterclockwise circuit of the village, and this ordering system "determines the sequence in which kivas perform dances during a given season" (Tedlock 1979:502). Here it is apparent that even in one of the most distributive of ritual systems, ranking and hierarchy occur.

It is important to emphasize that even in middle-range societies in which membership in ceremonial organizations crosscuts kinship and clan boundaries, there are usually some ceremonial groups or societies in which membership is restricted to specific kinship groups or clan affiliations.

For example, among the Zuni, the rain priesthood, which historically wielded great authority and decision-making power, was restricted to members of certain clans (Bunzel 1992:478; Ladd 1979:485). In this way, while some elements of ritual responsibility and authority are often distributed widely within the community, others may be quite restricted and centralized.

The Performance of Ritual

Four aspects of communal ritual performance may enhance and reinforce the hierarchy inherent in the control of ritual and ritual knowledge. Ritual performance is often a context in which 1) messages about hierarchy are communicated, 2) authority is instilled in messages communicated and in those who communicate them, 3) ideology may be manipulated and presented for "internalization," and 4) resistance to the dominant structure may be expressed and dispelled.

As Rappaport (1979b) has made clear, ritual performance communicates both canonical and indexical messages about the significance of the ritual performance and its performers. Canonical messages are encoded in the liturgical order and are more or less invariant from ritual performance to ritual performance. Symbolically, they express the enduring aspects of nature, the immutability of structure, the sanctity of tradition, and the timelessness of the social and cosmic order. Canonical messages evoke *authority* through the repetitive and redundant use of sanctity-invoked symbols, actions, and words. By contrast, indexical messages communicate the ritual performer's immediate physical, social, and spiritual state of being (or the image of these that the performer wants to project) and rely upon whatever opportunities a more or less invariant liturgy offers for variation. Indexical messages communicate social distinction and status. They emphasize the strength and power of the performer and the wisdom of those who control the power and knowledge to successfully perform rituals.

The interplay of canonical and indexical messages tends to produce social distinctions that are not easily challenged. Indexical messages establish social distinctions, while canonical messages simultaneously imbue these distinctions with a sense of sanctity and authority. As James Turner (1992:298) suggests, "Ritual typically both expresses category distinctions and refutes their arbitrariness." At the same time that these distinctions are being expressed, however, communal ritual promotes social integration by encouraging participation of the whole group. Ritual "demonstrates a relatively unified corporate body, often leading participants to assume that there is more consensus than there actually is" (Bell 1992:210). Moreover, because ritually communicated information is sanctified, ritual can serve to sanctify and hence promote the communal acceptance of important social decisions. It is the dualistic nature of ritual that makes it a powerful force that both ranks and integrates social units.

A second aspect of ritual performance that makes it a particularly effective power resource is the inherent authority that the structure of ritual confers on ritual performers. For example, canonical messages evoke authority through their recurrent reference to eternal phenomena, such as the immutability of the cosmos and the social order. Moreover, Rappaport (1979b:175–76) notes that formality is an obvious aspect of all rituals: "Rituals tend to be stylized, repetitive, stereotyped, often but not always decorous, and they also tend to occur at special places and at times fixed by the clock, calendar, or specified circumstances." Bloch (1974) submits that the inherent formality of ritual produces and maintains "tradition" while simultaneously creating a form of authority, "traditional authority," that is rooted in the appeal to the past. Furthermore, the efficacy of formality as an authoritative power resource is due in part to the fact that formality is an intangible aspect of social control. Formality puts people in a situation that discourages challenge and compels acceptance (Bloch 1975:3–4, 9); it is difficult to argue with a ritual. Furthermore, much of the strength of ritual-based authority lies in the fact that rituals depersonalize authority by placing it in an office or a formal status rather than in a person (Bloch 1974).

Another aspect of ritual performance that may enhance and solidify social differentiation is its capacity for generating belief among participants. Geertz (1966), for instance, views ritual as a symbolic modeling of the social order that actively defines social norms and presents them for internalization. Ritual performance is a mechanism for transforming norms into sentiments and sentiments into significance. As such, ritual performance creates a context in which people experience the effectiveness of symbolic meanings and strong emotional responses are incited (Turner 1969). "Meaning" is derived from the way in which the symbolic material emerges in the interaction, and, depending on how these are manipulated, new "realities" may be evoked and *internalized* through performance (Bloch 1992:129; Schieffelin 1985).[1]

For example, James Turner (1992:294) suggests that the sheer repetitiveness of some rituals allows the power relations created in these rituals to become "embodied" and then reproduced in nonritual behavior: "While behavioral routines are grounded in a conceptual framework (e.g., opposed categories such as 'male' and 'female'), through repetition they become embodied and can be activated without conscious reference to cognitive categories. But if embodied habit is crucial to the reproduction of power relations, it needs to be recognized that ritual can be a potent force in the structuring of habit." Thus, Turner notes that the social hierarchy established and enacted in the Fijian *yaqona* drinking ritual persists in non-ritual contexts. Schieffelin (1985:711) maintains that "the reality of symbolic meanings" is evoked in ritual performances such as the Kaluli seance rituals of New Guinea and that once the "seance reality" is created, it may spill over into everyday life. This concept of the embodiment of ideology through routinized bodily experience parallels Bourdieu's (1977, 1990) notion of *habitus* and Foucault's (1980) concept of the ritualized body. However, these scholars refer not to the efficacy of religious rituals per se but to the rituals of daily practice. Giddens (1984:60) also stresses that routinized behavior such as ritual plays an important role in the production and reproduction of power relations, which are "often most profoundly embedded in modes of conduct taken for granted by those who follow them."

Finally, ritual performance provides opportunities for individual expression and avenues for resistance and dissension while reinforcing authoritarian structures. Indexical messages create the opportunity for participants in ritual performance to communicate individualistic and even subversive information within the context of a canonical, authoritarian ritual structure. The structure of the ritual itself and thus the authority of the leader in control of the ritual is not damaged by such acts of individual expression. On the contrary, it contains subversive action within an authoritarian structure and provides community members with an outlet for dissent that is ultimately innocuous. In Abu-Lughod's (1986) ethnography of Bedouin women's poetry, the spontaneous composition and delivery of poems that communicated potentially subversive attitudes constituted a culturally acceptable ritual genre. Such poetry could be viewed as an outlet for resistance that pacified a dominated group while leaving authoritarian structures in place. Individuals who feel as though outlets for resistance exist are less likely to comprehensively challenge leaders. Leaders who are able to ritually construct avenues for resistance are bound to be more successful (see also Gluckman 1954).

In summary, hierarchical social relations are created and maintained through the control of various aspects of ritual and through ritual performance. While control may or may not be dispersed within a community, hierarchy does emerge in all ritual structures, and ritual performance enhances and reinforces this hierarchical structure. A short case study illustrates the effectiveness of ritual as a power resource in the late prehistoric period of the American Southwest.

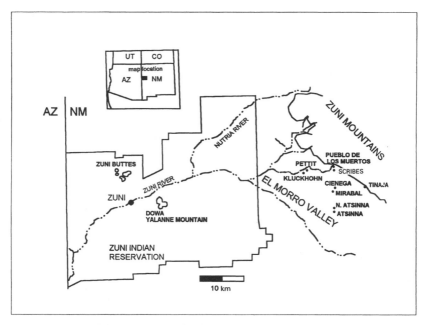

FIGURE 4.1. Map of the Zuni area with relevant sites plotted.

Ritual Power in the Southwest: A Case Study

The Pueblo IV period (circa A.D. 1275–1300) was marked by extraordinary changes in community structure, social organization, and ritual practices across the Southwest (Adams 1989; Crown 1994; Kintigh 1985; Lipe 1989; Ortman 1998; Potter 1997b). Communities in the El Morro Valley in the Zuni area, for example, underwent a major reorganization of population at about A.D. 1275 as aggregated settlements comprising unplanned, dispersed room blocks were abandoned and large, highly planned, plaza-oriented communities were established (Figure 4.1). The Scribe S to Pueblo de los Muertos transition in A.D. 1275 is an example of this community reorganization (Figures 4.2 and 4.3).

The reorganization of population into nucleated, plaza-oriented settlements at this time marks a major shift in ritual practice. Prior to A.D. 1275 unroofed and roofed Great Kivas were the focus of much communal ritual activity (Kintigh 1994). After A.D. 1275, large, enclosed plazas replaced Great Kivas as the dominant locus of communal ritual. While there are exceptions to this (e.g., some later sites, such as the Kluckhohn site and Atsinna, had Great Kivas in addition to large, central, enclosed plazas), it is nonetheless a fairly strong trend in the Cibola region. The Pueblo IV period plazas of the Zuni area were unique in comparison to the formally

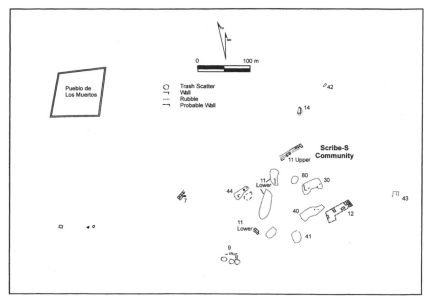

FIGURE 4.2. Map of the Pueblo III community Scribe S (foreground) and of the Pueblo IV community Pueblo de los Muertos (background) (from Watson, LeBlanc, and Redman 1980).

defined spaces of earlier Chacoan and Mimbres sites and the large central spaces of Pueblo IV period sites such as Grasshopper Pueblo in that they were completely defined and enclosed by the entire community, and they were planned and enclosed during their initial construction. When they did grow, these communities expanded inward as tiers of rooms were added along the already-defined plaza space (Watson, LeBlanc, and Redman 1980).

Adams (1989) contends that the shift to plazas as the dominant communal ritual space was associated with the adoption of new religious rituals that functioned to help integrate diverse social units within large communities. Furthermore, Adams (1991) has suggested that the Kachina Cult got its start in the Western Pueblo region at this time, and Crown (1994) has argued that a Southwestern Cult spread across the Southwest. Crown argues that the sudden appearance throughout the Southwest of polychrome vessels that depict animals, birds, feathers, and masked figures is related to the spread of this new ritual system.

In addition to the adoption of formal plazas as the focus of public rituals and the advent of new ceramic styles that may have been related to new ritual forms, control of certain aspects of ritual appears to have become more highly centralized during the Pueblo IV period as access to at least

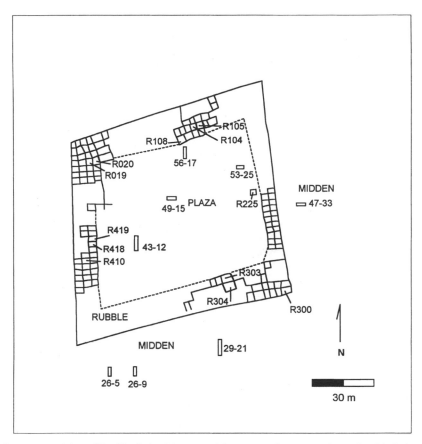

FIGURE 4.3. Map of Pueblo de los Muertos with excavated rooms and trenches labeled.

some elements of ritual became more restricted. This shift is evidenced in the dramatic increase in the ratio of habitation rooms to ceremonial rooms (or rooms to kivas) (Steward 1937; Lipe 1989), as well as the more highly restricted distribution of ritually important fauna such as wild birds and carnivores within the Pueblo IV period community (Potter 1997b). This access constriction suggests that the control of certain aspects of ritual was a source of differentiation within communities, those with access to particular elements of rituals versus those without such access. At the same time, other aspects of ritual became more inclusive and "communal" than before as the large, open, central plaza became the primary locus of ritual participation. This new communal ritual system, once adopted, potentially created and maintained political-economic strategies that were reliant upon the simultaneous interplay of communal and exclusionary practices.

This restriction of access to ritual knowledge associated with kiva cere-

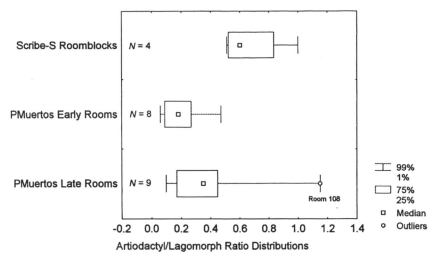

FIGURE 4.4. Box plots of artiodactyl-to-lagomorph ratio distributions at Scribe S and the early and late phase occupations of Pueblo de los Muertos. Note the highly skewed (right) distribution from the later PM rooms, indicating the unequal proportions of artiodactyl remains among rooms during this phase.

monies was coterminous with the increasingly unequal distribution of certain economic resources during the Pueblo IV period. For example, numbers of hunted deer and antelope became markedly uneven among residential units at Pueblo de los Muertos, an eight-hundred-room plaza-oriented pueblo in the El Morro Valley (Figures 4.3 and 4.4).[2] This differentiation can be attributed in part to the strong ritual component of the organization of communal large game hunts in Puebloan society. Animal species such as pronghorn antelope and jackrabbits that are traditionally hunted communally became more prevalent at these communities after about A.D. 1300.

A communal hunting strategy is commonly employed to compensate for the uncertainty of success of individual hunters, especially in areas impacted by sedentary communities (Driver 1990; Speth and Scott 1989). The organization of successful communal large game hunts, while bringing more large-bodied game into the community, would have simultaneously legitimized and empowered those in control of the ritual related to hunting. Communal large game hunting is a practice that, historically, requires specific ritual knowledge that only certain individuals within the community can operationalize. The hunting of deer and antelope communally, for example, is a task that may be organized and enacted only by the leading men or specific societies within a Puebloan community (Anell 1969:61;

Gnabasik 1981:45, 48, 103; White 1974:302). Moreover, social agents organizing successful communal hunts would, by analogy, have had primary
access to the resources procured in such hunts prior to the distribution of
these resources within the community. The spoils of such hunts are often
differentially apportioned according to the level of an individual's involve-
ment in the hunt, and often the primary ritual specialist in the community,
or the head of the society organizing the hunt, or both, receive a sizable
portion of the game killed in the hunt. For example, at Zia, "a deer is
divided into two parts, one for the *cacique,* the other for the hunter who
killed it. The hunter gets the head, the skin and part of the backbone and
the chest from the neck down to and including the fourth rib, and a part of
the belly. The rest goes to the *cacique*" (White 1974:303). Similarly, at Taos,
when deer drives were held, "the slayer got a hind leg, the hide and antlers;
the man who was next to come up on the slain animal got a shoulder; all
the hunters had a share. The first two deer to be killed went to the Hunt
Chief who had 'made the talk,' i.e. prayed before the hunt began, asking the
deer not to be afraid to give themselves to the hunters" (Gnabasik 1981:48,
quoting Parsons 1920, footnote 37 on page 19). Here it is evident that it is
by virtue of the ritual knowledge that the hunt chief possesses that he is
entitled to a portion of the deer.

Communally hunted antelope are also distributed by and among the
most powerful ritual specialists within many Puebloan groups. At Zia, for
example, after a successful hunt, the antelope meat is brought to the cacique's office, where the war chief decides when it is to be divided among
the heads of the curing and weather control societies, be it one, two, or
even three days after the hunter's return (Stevenson 1894:119–21).

From these examples it is apparent that individuals in control of important ritual knowledge often have primary access to the most desirable
portions of large game, especially those from communally hunted deer and
antelope. Ritual specialists and society heads also control the distribution of
these resources to a much greater extent than even those individuals involved in the hunt. Historic accounts of the Eastern Pueblos have also
mentioned that in communal hunts, larger shares of the animals killed were
given to leaders (Benavides 1630:39, 128–29). Brandt (1994:19) has made
similar observations in her work.

This reinforcing relationship among ritual-based status, the organization
of communal activities (e.g., hunts), and access to resources may ultimately
have translated into more enduring expressions of social differentiation
within the Pueblo IV community and may account for the increasingly

uneven distributions of highly valued faunal resources within the community. In particular, this tendency would be the case in natural environments that are susceptible to the impact of large sedentary populations as these environments become overhunted and therefore more risky and unpredictable over time. Those who were successful in operationalizing their ritual and organizational abilities to cope with this increased uncertainty were undoubtedly accorded great prestige and power within the community.

In addition to differentiation within the community, ritual-symbolic differentiation reveals itself in patterning across several large Pueblo IV communities within the El Morro Valley. Pueblo IV period communities were often planned at their inception, and thus their morphology could be controlled by the builders of these settlements. Data on wall bonding and abutting from several early Pueblo IV period sites such as Pueblo de los Muertos and Atsinna in the Zuni region, Homol'ovi II in the Hopi region, and Gran Quivira in the Salinas region indicate that whole sites or large portions of sites were laid out and constructed in a single communal effort (E. Charles Adams, personal communication 1995; Hayes 1981; Watson, LeBlanc, and Redman 1980). Plaza-oriented sites in the El Morro Valley most often conformed to either a circular or a rectilinear shape.

The earliest Pueblo IV sites in the area, however, such as the Kluckhohn site and Archeotekopa II, consisted of a conjoined square and a circle (Kintigh 1985). Each of these settlements is estimated to have over one thousand rooms. The fact that the symbolic duality of the square and circle began as a single community structure suggests that *intercommunity* relations were also influenced by this duality once communities began to be built as either circles or squares. In other words, the presence of distinctly square and distinctly circular settlements that were contemporaneously occupied in the El Morro Valley suggests a symbolic duality occurring above the level of the single community. Moreover, this morphological duality may have been a reflection of the complementary roles of square and circular settlements within a system of ritual interdependence. Some of the strongest distinctions among these communities are in the spatial distributions of remains from fauna that, ethnographically, are extremely important for religious ritual, specifically, wild birds (Potter 1997a). On the whole, rectilinear sites, such as Pueblo de los Muertos and Atsinna, exhibit a preponderance of raptors and perching birds, while circular sites, such as Cienega and Mirabal, are dominated by waterfowl (Figure 4.5). Although it is indeed possible that the residents of the circular sites had differential access to migratory waterfowl for the simple reason that one (Cienega) was associ-

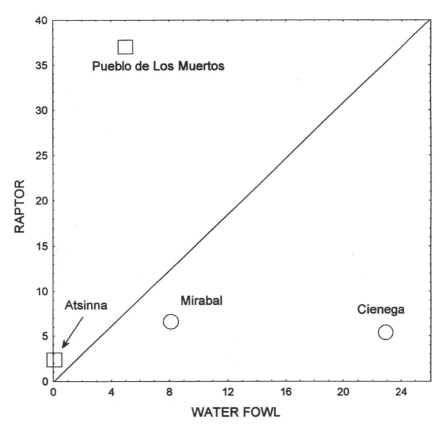

FIGURE 4.5. Counts of raptors versus waterfowl elements at "square" and "circular" Pueblo IV sites in the study area.

ated with a standing-water spring, the likelihood of migratory birds consistently opting to land in the midst of an occupied town seems remote. There were less heavily utilized areas for water birds to exploit throughout the region, including many other springs and the marshy areas around the Zuni Salt Lake. This reasoning also does not account for the high waterfowl proportion at the Mirabal Site.

We suggest instead that various types of birds were acquired for their ritual/symbolic significance. Although specific interpretations of the symbolic meanings of these patterns are at present premature, we can suggest that the differential proportions of various types of birds among Pueblo IV period communities were the product of each community or community type (e.g., circular vs. square) having a different suite of roles and responsibilities within a regional ritual system. That is, circular communities procured waterfowl, including various ducks, cranes, and geese, as

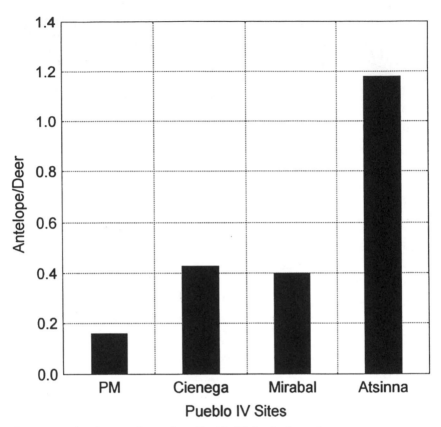

FIGURE 4.6. Antelope-to-deer ratios at Pueblo IV sites in the study area.

part of their role within a valley-wide system of ritual integration, while square-site occupants sought raptors such as falcons, hawks, and eagles as well as perching birds such as woodpeckers and ravens for their role in the system.

Pueblo IV communities are differentiated not only by their morphology and ritual fauna but also by their ratios of local to nonlocal large game remains. The El Morro Valley is in prime deer-hunting territory, while antelope range in lower grassland areas. This being the case, sites in the El Morro Valley should have had fairly equal access to local deer populations. When antelope-to-deer ratios are compared among sites, however, the uniquely low ratio at Pueblo de los Muertos is comparable to other Pueblo IV sites, especially Atsinna, which actually exhibits more antelope than deer in its assemblage (Figure 4.6). Since geographic proximity to resources cannot fully account for these differences, social proscriptions to access may have played a role. Specifically, occupants of some sites might have had better access to certain hunted resources because of their community's position within this proposed regional ritual system.

Thus, such a system, while not highly centralized, appears to have structured power relations and facilitated differential access to resources. Ignoring momentarily the dangers of ethnographic analogy, it is interesting to note that at Zuni, where the six directions are ranked in terms of their importance (Cushing 1979:190–91), the game animals have directional assignments: mule deer (north), mountain sheep (west), antelope (south), whitetail deer (east), jackrabbit (zenith), and cottontail (nadir) (Stevenson 1904:441; Tedlock 1979:500–501). Furthermore, dual organization (as potentially expressed by the morphological duality of settlements in the El Morro Valley) is common in modern and historic Pueblo society, and ranking and power differentiation are created and maintained by this non-centralized structure. For example, while leadership responsibilities alternate between Winter and Summer moieties in Tanoan communities, one group controls for a far greater portion of the year than the other (Ortiz 1969).

In sum, religious ritual emerged as a potent social power resource that structured interactions both within and among early Pueblo IV communities in the Zuni area and was simultaneously distributive of power and hierarchically organized. In addition, within a new communal structure, ritual was used by those in control as a strategy to secure access to certain economic resources, specifically highly valued food resources.

Conclusion

Drawing upon the above case study, we conclude by addressing two questions that have wider anthropological relevance. First, what are the conditions that eventuate the manipulation of ritual as a source of social power in middle-range societies? Potter (2000) has argued that under certain conditions ritual knowledge may be more effectively monopolized and controlled than economic resources and thus may tend to emerge as a potent source of social power. In particular, he argues, ritual tends to emerge as a power resource under conditions of social and economic uncertainty. Bender (1985) notes that a system in which status is established through the manipulation of ritual power *naturalizes* that power by associating it with the general well-being of the group. Potter (2000) suggests that if the general well-being of the group is perceived to be threatened, then those in control of the ritual knowledge necessary to cope with that threat may be accorded great prestige and authority, potentially to the point of allowing the development of considerable degrees of social inequality (cf. Aldenderfer 1993). In other words, ritual-based social hierarchies appear to develop in contexts where the control of ritual translates into the control over people's *perception* of risk and survival.

New ritual forms that appeared in the Southwest at about A.D. 1275, for example, were used as an authoritative resource (as defined by Giddens 1984) in the face of social and environmental uncertainty. The beginning of the Pueblo IV period in the Southwest was marked by high levels of social conflict (Adams 1988; Haas and Creamer 1993; Lightfoot and Kuckelman 1994; Wilcox and Haas 1994), unpredictable rainfall and drought (Dean 1993; Dean and Robinson 1977, 1978; Watson, LeBlanc, and Redman 1980), massive population migrations (Duff 1998; Haury 1958), and, as discussed above, extraordinary changes in community structure, social organization, and ritual practices across the Southwest (Adams 1989; Crown 1994; Kintigh 1985; Lipe 1989; Ortman 1998; Potter 1997b).

Indeed, it was a time of extreme environmental, social, and ideological uncertainty. Consequently, the potential existed for the development of social differentiation through controlling the rituals that dealt with this uncertainty. Ritual in particular and knowledge in general operated as monopolizable resources available to leaders.

The second question we address relates to how and why ritual is a particularly potent resource of social power. As suggested above, ritual power is specifically effective as the foundation of leadership because of the way in which ritual mediates the processes of inclusion and exclusion. The communal, integrative aspects of ritual solidify inter- and intracommunity ties (Hegmon 1989; Rappaport 1979b). Materially, the communal aspects of ritual are expressed in architectural changes that occurred across the Pueblo III to Pueblo IV transition, as nucleated, plaza-oriented communities replaced communities of more dispersed room blocks. Plazas often function as ritual gathering places and tend to facilitate social interaction and the creation of a sense of community (Adams 1989; Potter 1998). Additionally, with the emergence of plaza architecture, economic activities such as corn grinding, once performed inside domestic rooms, shifted to communal areas such as plazas (Ortman 1998). Both ceremonial and daily household activities thus occurred regularly in open, visible spaces. While such activities inevitably facilitate social interaction and consequently social integration (Potter 1998), they also promote visibility and potentiate observation among community members. The spatial relocation of domestic activities from relatively nonobservable to observable areas would have allowed leaders and other community members opportunities for surveillance of individuals. Moreover, it would have facilitated the visibility of ritual performance, enhancing the potency of ritual messages such as community cooperation and consensus and the authority of ritual leadership as well as reinforcing the hierarchical structure inherent in the ritual system. Visible public performances are public displays of power and ideology and demonstrate and objectify the "capacity to be an organizer of society in general, including all the complex organism of services, [an] activity of organizing the general system of relationships" (Gramsci 1971:5).

This architectural shift coincided with the increasingly restricted access to use of kiva space by particular individuals. Whereas small kivas in the Pueblo II and Pueblo III periods were probably used on occasion for domestic as well as household ceremonial activities, Pueblo IV period and historic kivas were more specialized both in terms of who had access to them and the range of activities that occurred in association with them (Ciolek-Torrello 1985; Lipe 1989; Ortman 1998; Parsons 1939).

Architectural trends across the Pueblo III to Pueblo IV transition thus appear to signify a movement of community members into communal, visible, and observable space and a movement of leaders into restricted, unobservable space (Adams 1989). Thus, the processes of inclusion and exclusion are highlighted through the plaza/kiva dichotomy. Community members were spatially integrated by an architectural apparatus that increased the visibility of their activities and promoted their powers of observation, while at the same time individuals with the appropriate ritual knowledge and position were not observable during "secret" activities performed in the enclosed and restricted space of kivas. It is important to emphasize here that the *performance* of ritual in this case would have been as important as the differential *control* of ritual in the promotion and sanctification of social differences.

The increased importance of communal game hunting in Pueblo IV society also reflects the increased importance of integrative activities. Yet, if historic analogues are any guide, only certain individuals controlled the knowledge required to organize and lead such hunts. Hunting activity became increasingly both inclusive and exclusive as it ranked certain individuals with respect to the rest of the social body while simultaneously bringing much of the community together. Understanding the dialectic between inclusion and exclusion is key to understanding the operation of leadership, the distribution of power, and the existence of hierarchy in early Pueblo IV society.

ACKNOWLEDGMENTS

This essay benefited tremendously from the editorial help of Jean Ballagh at SWCA. Jean is not only a terrific editor but an insightful archaeologist, and her comments on the content of the essay improved it as well. In addition, we would like to thank one anonymous reviewer for his or her critical but ultimately helpful comments on an earlier draft. Thanks also to Barbara Mills for supporting this research and including us in this volume. This research was supported by National Science Foundation Dissertation Improvement Grant SBR 96-28617 awarded to the senior author.

NOTES

1. The fact that symbols are polysemous and can have vastly different meanings to people within a single community does not negate the fact that meaning in general can be created and manipulated during ritual performance. Indeed, it is this flexibility of meaning that allows symbols to be effectively manipulated.

2. These patterns are not due to variable lagomorph frequencies. Similar patterns are produced when the artiodactyl frequencies are divided by the assemblage totals, as well as when a Correspondence Analysis (CA) is performed on the data. Moreover, since CA uses straight counts rather than assemblage percentages, the closed-sum problem is circumvented (Baxter 1994).

5

Ceramic Decoration as Power

Late Prehistoric Design Change in East-Central Arizona

SCOTT VAN KEUREN

ARTIFACT STYLE IS fundamental to inferring social interaction and status in archaeological settings. In complex societies, painted pots, murals, textiles, and other decorated media directly legitimize sociopolitical hierarchies or advertise the rank and life history of elite individuals or lineages (e.g., Earle 1990; Freidel and Schele 1988; Morris 1995). In cultural systems that lack formal hierarchies, decorated artifacts mediate interaction and status across gender, kinship, and other social categories (e.g., Welbourn 1984). Although decorated artifacts are a salient feature of politically complex societies, the link between decorated media and elite status in complex societies does not provide an inferential model for linking artifact decoration to prehistoric leadership strategies in middle-range societies. Archaeological research has narrowly focused on the unequal distribution of or access to the material "carriers" of decoration, but these strategies can be predicated on a range of both material and nonmaterial sources of social power.

Flanagan (1989:246) reminds us that a range of inequities exists on the basis of gender, age, craft production skills, and diverse categories of knowledge in so-called egalitarian or middle-range societies. Because social knowledge is occasionally recorded by the decoration of material culture, the analysis of stylistic variability can be used to infer nonmaterial sources of social power in archaeological contexts (Blanton et al. 1996a:2–3; Feinman 1995:268). This model can be used to investigate the role of leadership strategies in systems that lack a rigid social hierarchy, elites, and other evolutionary traits used to define complex societies. Artifact decoration is thus an important signal of episodic and occasionally sustained reorganization of social relations, regardless of whether leadership strategies lead to permanent, institutionalized hierarchies.

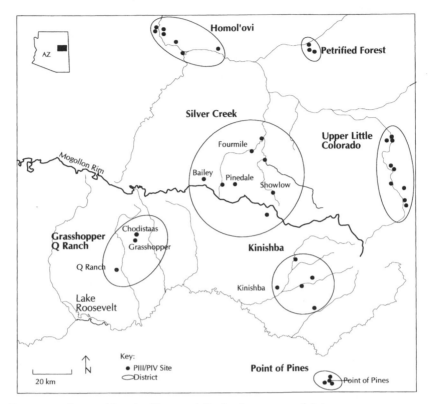

FIGURE 5.1. Late prehistoric villages and districts in east-central Arizona.

Leadership strategies can draw upon both material and nonmaterial sources of power. Recent models call attention to the latter category, citing the role of ritual knowledge and other social information as an important source of social power in ethnographic settings (Barth 1975; Brandt 1980; Burns and Laughlin 1979; Chowning 1979; Keen 1994; Strathern 1988). Because decorated artifacts transmit a diverse range of implicit and overt social knowledge (Wobst 1977:326–28), the content, regional expanse, and contextual use of artifact decoration are the most pervasive evidence of information exchange and manipulation in archaeological settings (Blanton et al. 1996a).

In the American Southwest, painted pots record a diverse range of information, including but not limited to mythical events, religious beliefs, and esoteric knowledge. Recent studies reiterate the importance of painted ceramics as an archaeological residue of prehistoric belief systems (e.g., Adams 1991; Brody 1977; Crown 1994; Hays 1994). Leadership strategies in this region were predicated on, in part, the control or restriction of certain socially valued categories of knowledge that potentially influenced the decorative content, function, and discard of decorated pots.

In this chapter I outline basic expectations for the influence of both wealth-based (or material) versus knowledge-based (or nonmaterial) foundations of social power on community or regional styles. This model is then used to assess the social correlates of ceramic change across the Pueblo III to IV periods and evaluate the role of painted pottery in knowledge-based leadership strategies at fourteenth-century pueblos in east-central Arizona (Figure 5.1).

Artifact Decoration as a Leadership Strategy

Artifact style is a possible correlate of two or more possible leadership strategies in changing social systems. Renfrew (1974), A. Strathern (1969), Lindstrom (1984), and more recently Blanton et al. (1996a) outline a model that differentiates two basic leadership trajectories (see Mills this volume; Feinman this volume). In the first, power is centralized by individuals on the basis of the exchange and control of economic resources, including trade goods and agricultural surplus. In the second, social power is more diffuse across social groups and is based on the control of or unequal access to a diverse array of social information, including ritual knowledge, land tenure histories, craft-producing skills, or mythological expertise. Because decorated material culture plays a role in the exercise of social power in these two basic leadership strategies, community-level or regional style variability can be used to model these changing social relationships. Although the archaeological record does not preserve dialogue and other channels in which social power was manifest in prehistory, the production and use of decorated pottery and other visual media are potential sources of both material (the pots themselves) and nonmaterial (the information conveyed by pottery decoration) leadership strategies.

The relationship of artifact decoration to material-based leadership strategies is a conventional theorem in archaeological essays on power, complexity, social structure, and community reorganization in the archaeological record (e.g., Earle 1990; Kroeber 1957; Morris 1995; Pauketat and Emerson 1991; Pollock 1983; Wobst 1977; Wonderley 1986). These leadership strategies are often centered on the production and exchange of limited-circulation or "exotic" commodities. Decoration on these objects can depict standardized icons or images that are sanctioned by specific social groups or individuals. The emulation of these regional styles may occur at the periphery or boundaries of communities as social segments compete for status recognition, but the underlying behavioral message is resistant to alteration by all but a handful of individuals. Decorative styles emphasize the social or political preeminence of individual actors who in turn directly control the content and presentation of imagery. In addition to other social markers, including the differential distribution of prestige goods in mortuary or residential spaces, the referents of styles are associated with the ancestry, importance, and achievements of living individuals. Because these styles operate to enhance the social power of a limited part of a community, visibility and prominence are key factors. Archaeological examples include regional developments along the Peruvian coast, the American Bottom, and lowland Mesoamerica, where cross-media styles were used to validate social inequalities by limiting presentational art to elite themes or portraiture. In these examples, decorated artifacts and their semantic referents functioned with architecture and other forms of expressive material culture to sanction the status or social positioning of emerging or established elites.

Although style adds a nonmaterial (or symbolic) dimension to leadership trajectories that are essentially wealth-based, the link between style, information, and social power is of central importance to the analysis of social change in archaeological communities that lack the social and economic resources to sustain wealth-based leadership strategies. In these societies, decorated objects, body ornamentation, clothing, and architecture (including murals) communicate a diverse array of trivial or esoteric, personal or group knowledge. I am specifically concerned with social information that is shared, pertinent to community integration and well-being, or plays a functional role in ceremonial events but is unequally known or accessed by members of the community. When these knowledge categories are expressed through collective styles, they often emphasize community-wide value systems in place of themes associated with elite prominence or ancestry. The semantic content of these media may be understandable to a wide audience, but social restrictions limit their accessibility in ceremonial events or other opportunities in which individuals apply or reinterpret design imagery. Decorated objects can include limited-use items or widely circulated utilitarian objects, but the production and exchange of these items are not formally restricted or controlled, and the context of presentation can fluctuate between low-visibility items such as interior murals and ceramic bowls to high visibility clothing and body ornamentation.

A key social behavior that prevents unabated diffusion of knowledge is secrecy (Barth 1975:217–18; Brandt 1980:125–29; Burns and Laughlin 1979:251; Herdt 1990:360–61; Keen 1994:251; Keesing 1982:245). For instance, Brandt argues that the "fundamental basis for social ranking in Pueblo societies is possession and ownership of ceremonial property, knowledge, and ceremonial participation" (1994:15; see also Brandt 1980:127–28; Levy 1992:25–26). Secrecy serves to maintain the partitioning of knowledge and, inevitably, to sustain imbalances in the allotment of ceremonial roles or prominence of groups in loosely or nonstratified middle-range social systems. Although there is little evidence of formal political stratification at late prehistoric pueblos in the western upland Southwest (Reid 1985:170–72; cf. Saitta 1994), ceremonial prestige, social group membership, and uneven access to ritual knowledge and paraphernalia were potential sources of social power. In societies that lack formal political institutions, social power is rarely exerted as direct control of one group over another. Instead, as M. Strathern (1988:119) has sensibly noted, power is often construed through the "status of proposition," as in a claim to land, ritual property, or ancestral prominence.

The daunting challenge to archaeologists is the measure of secrecy, knowledge control, and other ephemeral behaviors in the prehistoric record. Access to both ritual and domestic spaces within pueblos can be used to infer modes of secrecy and architectural privacy (e.g., Ferguson 1996). The distribution, variability through time, and context of presentation of regional ceramic styles in the Southwest are also crucial denominators used to investigate prehistoric leadership strategies (S. Plog 1989, 1990; Upham, Lightfoot, and Feinman 1981; Upham 1982). Earlier research used regional patterns to infer the presence of sociopolitical entities (e.g., Upham 1982), but I narrow the focus of this essay to social change at the scale of individual villages.

The identification of communication barriers is key to inferring knowledge-based leadership strategies with artifact style. According to Hardin, stylistic behavior is dependent, in part, on the "opportunity to see, the ability to decode, and the disinclination to replicate" designs (1984:600). Style boundaries result in part from social barriers that interrupt the transmission of decorative (or technological) knowledge. Although these differences are often viewed by archaeologists at a regional scale (e.g., Braun and Plog 1982), the availability of provenance data from chemical compositional analyses of late prehistoric whole vessels assemblages now provides a basis for measuring intraregional style boundaries (Van Keuren 1999).

In the remainder of this chapter, I refer to two important ceramic style events in the upland Southwest that are the foundation of recent efforts to infer prehistoric belief systems (Adams 1991, 1994; Crown 1994) and socio-political complexity (Upham 1982; Upham, Lightfoot, and Feinman 1981). Although the role of ceramics in private and public ritual was at times peripheral, painted pottery is one of the strongest signals of information categories in the prehistoric American Southwest. A brief and dramatic episode of ceramic design change occurred at the Pueblo III to IV period transition in eastern Arizona (A.D. 1275–1325). I argue that this event is possible evidence of leadership strategies predicated on access to or control over two possible categories of social information.

Community Reorganization in Fourteenth-Century East-Central Arizona

Regional styles appear throughout the prehistoric sequence of the upland Southwest, but style events during this period are unprecedented. Beginning in the late thirteenth century, intermittent periods of population migration, aggregation, and abandonment resulted in transformed Southwestern communities. These social processes impacted the cultural landscape of the Mogollon Rim region in eastern Arizona, as evidenced architecturally by site aggregation and increased focus on public space, and stylistically in the expanse, content, and perhaps even function of painted ceramics. Change in public architecture, site layout, and the decorative imagery of ceramics are the most parsimonious archaeological evidence of community reorganization at the Pueblo III to IV period transition in east-central Arizona (Adams 1989, 1991, 1994; Crown 1994, 1996; Mills 1998; Reid 1989; Reid et al. 1996).

By the early Pueblo IV period (ca. A.D. 1325), the majority of pueblo populations in the Little Colorado River drainage and surrounding archaeological regions were living in aggregated villages. Populations in the Silver Creek drainage resided at a handful of large, plaza-oriented sites, including Fourmile Ruin and Pinedale Ruin (Figure 5.1; Kintigh 1996; Mills 1998). Contemporary and similarly sized villages were occupied south of the Mogollon Rim, including Grasshopper Pueblo, Q-Ranch Pueblo, Kinishba, and Point of Pines Pueblo (Reid 1989; Reid et al. 1996). These sites represent the zenith of late prehistoric pueblo settlement patterns in this area prior to pueblo residential abandonment at the end of the fourteenth century. At these large pueblos, as well as contemporaneous sites

FIGURE 5.2. Pinedale-style vessels (above) and Fourmile-style bowls (below). (Courtesy of the Arizona State Museum. Museum numbers [left to right]: top: A43,550; A35,299; and A39,096; bottom: 75-11-579; A41,973; and A29,590.)

in surrounding archaeological districts (see Adams 1989; Kintigh 1996), a formal hierarchy of both private and public ritual architecture included large enclosed plazas, kivas within plazas and room blocks, and ceremonial rooms (Adams 1991:125–26; Reid and Whittlesey 1982:697). The efficacy of public ceremonial events for integrating households or other social groups is evidenced by the focus of these sites around large, often enclosed central plazas (Adams 1994:42–44).

The widespread abandonment of the Colorado Plateau and subsequent migration and resettlement of northern groups at pueblo settlements in the Little Colorado River drainage, the Mogollon Rim region, and the Tonto Basin are responsible for a suite of technological and design changes in painted ceramics (Crown 1996:247). I narrow the focus of this presentation to two important stylistic events that occur in the decorated assemblages of Mogollon Rim region pueblos (Figure 5.2). The first is the appearance and widespread adoption of the Pinedale style by about A.D. 1300. The second is the emergence of the Fourmile style, which replaces Pinedale style on White Mountain Red Ware bowls at about 1325 in east-central Arizona. Building on recent work by Adams (1991) and Crown (1994) and my analyses of White Mountain Red Ware whole vessels from sites in east-central Arizona (Van Keuren 1998a), I argue that these two episodes of design change involved the application of ritual knowledge or other information to painted ceramics. This information was a potential nonmaterial source of social power used by households or other social groups to enhance their status, perhaps contributing to important changes in the organization of or relations between social groups at late aggregated pueblos in the Silver Creek drainage and surrounding areas.

By the late 1200s, the Pinedale style was applied to three decorated wares in eastern and central Arizona and western New Mexico (Cibola White Ware, Roosevelt Red Ware, and White Mountain Red Ware). Pinedale-style designs appear first in the Mogollon Rim region in the 1270s to 1280s on Roosevelt Red Ware and Cibola White Ware (Crown 1994; Montgomery and Reid 1990). Within a few decades, the design style is ubiquitously applied to early Pueblo IV period painted ceramics produced throughout eastern Arizona and western New Mexico (Crown 1996:241). The ceramic assemblages of sites in the Silver Creek drainage, including Bailey Ruin, recently tested by the University of Arizona Archaeological Field School (Mills, Herr, and Van Keuren 1999), consist almost exclusively of Pinedale-style Roosevelt Red Ware (Pinto Polychrome), White Mountain Red Ware (Pinedale Black-on-red and Polychrome and Cedar Creek Polychrome), and Cibola White Ware (Pinedale Black-on-white). Pinedale-style Cibola White Ware and White Mountain Red Ware were produced almost exclusively at Upper Little Colorado River drainage villages and less frequently at sites south of the Mogollon Rim (see Triadan 1997; Zedeño 1994, 1995).

In an early statement on the development of White Mountain Red Ware production, Carlson (1970) argued that the origin of this omnipresent design style in early Pueblo IV period decorated assemblages was a product of the southward movement and resettlement of Kayenta groups into east-central Arizona beginning in the late 1200s. According to him, Pinedale style was the product of direct "cultural interchange between somewhat diverse peoples" (1970:109; see also Crown 1994:204–5). By the Pueblo IV period, the style appears almost exclusively on polychrome bowls probably used for food serving and other domestic activities. The geographic extent of the style equals or exceeds all earlier regional styles in the Southwest, but it does not appear to coincide with prestige goods trade or exchange. In fact, Crown's (1994) analysis of Pinedale-style Salado Polychromes demonstrates that these pots were widely produced and easily obtainable through exchange or manufacture with local materials.

Haury's (1934) excavations at Canyon Creek Pueblo in the Mogollon Rim region, as well as early excavations in the Silver Creek drainage (see

FIGURE 5.3. Pinedale Polychrome, Fourmile Polychrome, and Grasshopper Polychrome bowls. (Courtesy of the Arizona State Museum. Museum numbers [left to right]: A35,299; A35,297; and A34,999.)

Haury and Hargrave 1931), show that Pinedale style was replaced by about 1325 with Fourmile-style designs on White Mountain Red Ware. By this time, the production of white ware had waned in eastern Arizona (Zedeño 1994:104), and shortly thereafter, classic Pinedale-style designs on Roosevelt Red Ware were replaced by bolder Gila-style (or "late" Pinedale-style) designs on Pinto/Gila and Gila Polychrome (Reid and Whittlesey 1982). Fourmile style is distinguished by the use of asymmetrical design layouts on bowls, the use of representational forms on the interior of bowls (as well as geometric designs), and the standardization of exterior designs on bowls (Figures 5.2 and 5.3). I have argued elsewhere that the movement of iconic designs from the exterior of Pinedale-style bowls to the interior of Fourmile Polychrome and the use of standardized geometrics on the exterior of this late type are important consequences of the changing social role of painted ceramics in east-central Arizona pueblos (Van Keuren and Reid 1996). The appearance of Fourmile style on White Mountain Red Ware foreshadows later Pueblo IV period changes in Hopi Yellow Ware and Zuni Glaze Ware (Adams 1991; Woodbury and Woodbury 1966).

Fourmile Polychrome occurs as bowls typically placed in mortuary contexts with little or no use-wear compared to earlier White Mountain Red Ware types (Pinedale Black-on-red and Polychrome). Although Fourmile Polychrome was produced at Silver Creek drainage pueblos, it was widely emulated at late Mogollon Rim region pueblos (Triadan 1997; Triadan, Mills, and Duff 1997). At Grasshopper Pueblo and Point of Pines Pueblo, it appears that both local and migrant potters produced polychrome bowls in Fourmile style using locally available resources. Local production of this type may have continued in other regions, but the abandonment of Silver Creek drainage pueblos at the end of the fourteenth century marks the cessation of Fourmile-style White Mountain Red Ware production in eastern Arizona.

Ceramic Design Approaches to Social Complexity in the Upland Southwest

Pinedale- and Fourmile-style ceramics are cited as a central point of evidence for inferring the emergence of sociopolitical complexity (see Lightfoot and Most 1989; Upham 1982, 1989; Upham, Lightfoot, and Feinman 1981). According to Upham, Lightfoot, and Feinman (1981:133), the distribution and use of polychrome bowls were controlled by elites at fourteenth-century villages in east-central Arizona. Evidence of decision-making processes also includes site hierarchies, surplus accumulation, agricultural intensification, and elite exchange of rare items (F. Plog 1989:124; Upham 1982:200–202). Although hotly debated a decade ago, these parameters of complexity have not materialized in the archaeological record of Pueblo villages in eastern Arizona. The debate resulted in a schism between those who focused on material-based power and the placement of Southwest villages into a complex category of traditional evolutionary schemes (e.g., Upham 1982) and other archaeologists who questioned the methodological basis for these inferences (e.g., Reid 1985). The exchange has now been erroneously recast as a debate between a complex versus egalitarian perspective on late Pueblo prehistory.

The migration, abandonment, and aggregation of groups with diverse cultural backgrounds in large villages during the brief period from 1275 to 1325 likely followed diverse social trajectories. Differences in access to land, natural resources, or ceremonial knowledge and participation between both well-established and recently arrived households at early Pueblo IV period villages were conceivable preconditions for social change. The organization of village groups did not result in formal discrepancies in material wealth. Instead, as I argue here, leadership strategies were predicated on the restricted utilization of social information or ideas (including ritual knowledge) in the realm of public ceremony. By the close of the Pueblo III period, it appears that painted ceramics in eastern Arizona began to articulate these nonmaterial sources of social power.

Ceramic Design, Belief Systems, and Alternative Leadership Strategies in the Early Pueblo IV Period

Pottery design change at the close of the Pueblo III period is at the core of recent analyses of regional belief systems and community reorganization in east-central Arizona (Adams 1991, 1994; Crown 1994; Hays 1989, 1994). Crown argues that the spatial expanse of the Pinedale style and its appearance on multiple wares are evidence of a regional belief system beginning in the late 1200s. That late Pueblo III and IV period ceramic designs begin to codify shared belief systems seems evident, and there is general consensus among archaeologists that pottery decoration played either an indirect or a direct role in signaling information about community beliefs or ceremony. There is little substantive evidence to suggest, however, that Pinedale-style pottery played a role in exchange networks manipulated by emerging elites or that the style legitimized social inequality as part of a prestige goods economy (Crown 1994:195–98). Moreover, ceramics are rarely used as prestige items on a cross-cultural basis (Peregrine 1991). The exact interpretation of ceramic decoration is impractical, but I concur with the inference that Pinedale-style pots served as visual markers of a shared belief system that potentially facilitated economic exchange or social interaction at late prehistoric communities. The wide-ranging appearance of Pinedale style by 1300 indicates that the accompanying belief system, whatever its referent or function, was potentially decipherable to a wide, culturally diverse audience (Crown 1994:212).

The expanse of the Pinedale style was short-lived, and by the second or third decade of the fourteenth century, diversification in artifact styles occurred throughout eastern Arizona. In the upper and middle Little Colorado region and Mogollon highlands to the south, Fourmile style appears on a specific ceramic type and perhaps other media. Based on the occasional appearance of masked figure imagery, Adams argues that Fourmile Polychrome is one marker of a widespread belief system that helped integrate (along with public architecture) culturally diverse populations at large aggregated villages (Adams 1989, 1991, 1994; see also Hays 1989, 1994).

Several points of research hint that the organization of production and consumption of this late type differs from that of earlier types. First, chemical sourcing analyses confirm that the production zone of classic Fourmile Polychrome was restricted to the Silver Creek drainage by the mid-1300s (Triadan 1997; Triadan, Mills, and Duff 1997). Triadan's (1997) sourcing study of White Mountain Red Ware from Pueblo IV period sites in the

Mogollon Rim region shows, however, that Fourmile Polychrome was widely imitated using local resources at villages south of the Mogollon Rim. For instance, imported Fourmile Polychrome and a local copy in Fourmile style (Grasshopper Polychrome) predominate in the decorated household and mortuary assemblages at Grasshopper Pueblo (Triadan 1997:106). Second, De Atley's comparison of Pinedale- versus Fourmile-style White Mountain Red Ware indicates more diversity in Fourmile Polychrome glaze paint recipes, which is possible evidence of more restricted access to specific paint recipes or resources for this later type (1985:328). Third, on the basis of a comparative study of mending holes on White Mountain Red Ware and other early Pueblo IV period decorated types in eastern Arizona, Senior (1995) argues that cracks in Fourmile Polychrome bowls were repaired more frequently than other contemporaneous decorated and undecorated types. According to her, these patterns indicate that the social value of this type was greater than that of earlier decorated pots. And finally, use-wear comparisons of Pinedale-style White Mountain Red Ware and Roosevelt Red Ware with Fourmile Polychrome bowls and the fact that Fourmile Polychrome rarely appears in nonmortuary contexts at Pueblo IV period sites both hint that the function of this pottery type varies from earlier and contemporaneous polychrome bowls. These diverse data suggest that a shift took place in the production, geographic extent, social value, and even function of Fourmile Polychrome versus earlier Pinedale-style pottery.

If Pinedale-style pots mark the appearance of a regional belief system, as Crown (1994) argues, then the knowledge associated with these designs may have been an integral part of public ceremonies or other events in which information control enhanced the social prominence of certain groups (see Upham 1989). If the style was indeed part of an information-based leadership strategy, how and for whom was social power augmented? A handful of rich burials at large pueblos suggests that at least a few individuals were able to achieve extraordinary social prominence (e.g., Griffen 1967). However, social inequality was more likely to arise horizontally among households, clans, or other corporately based social groups. These strategies may have evolved from differential access to *operational* knowledge, which can include information about land tenure, histories of group interaction, or ritual calendars (Keesing 1982:208; Lindstrom 1984:293). Plaza architecture was the primary locus of public ritual events that indirectly sanctioned, by way of ownership of ceremonial knowledge and paraphernalia, access to land and other economic resources. Thus, Pinedale-style pots are one possible manifestation of early-fourteenth-century operational knowledge that was widely understood by members of pueblo communities but unevenly put to use in community events by specific individuals or groups. At postmigration communities in the upland Southwest, uneven access to operational knowledge was a conceivable source of social inequalities between migrants and locals.

The knowledge necessary to produce Pinedale-style pots and, more specifically, to apply the grammatically correct structure of the designs was widely accessible (Crown 1996:246). Thus, the standardized production of Pinedale-style pots throughout the upland Southwest suggests that style barriers were either minimal or penetrable at the start of the Pueblo IV period. Because it was widely shared and understood, the ritual knowledge, belief system(s), and other referents of Pinedale-style designs were not the direct source of social power. Instead, behaviors associated with public ceremony (of which Pinedale style played a part) were the conceivable context in which social inequalities were articulated.

The Pinedale to Fourmile style transition may have involved a basic alteration in the type of knowledge associated with community ritual. Although Pinedale style can be seen to correspond with operational knowledge, intricate Fourmile-style designs signal the greater importance of *interpretive* knowledge. This category of information focuses on the management or creation of meaning in social systems (Lindstrom 1984:294; also see Brandt 1980:127). In addition to asymmetrical images of macaws and other birds, Fourmile Polychrome bowl interiors depict a diverse range of visual subjects. The complexity of these bowl designs marks an important transition in the application of painted designs on Southwestern pottery. Fourmile Polychrome was not the focus of a prestige goods economy but perhaps relayed information that was unequally accessible to some members of pueblo communities in east-central Arizona. Compared to Pinedale style, the extent of Fourmile style is restricted in space to sites in the Mogollon Rim region of east-central Arizona (Carlson 1970), and classic Fourmile Polychrome was possibly produced at only a handful of villages within the region (especially those in the Silver Creek drainage).

The appearance of Grasshopper Polychrome, a Fourmile copy produced with local resources in the Grasshopper region, suggests that either immigrant potters arrived in this region and continued to produce polychrome bowls or that local potters emulated a nonlocal technology. That Plateau migrants arrived and resettled at Grasshopper Pueblo during the fourteenth century is clearly evident in the archaeological record (Reid 1998). The local emulation of Cibola White Ware and White Mountain Red Ware can be attributed to a direct transfer of technological knowledge (Van Keuren 1999; Zedeño 1995:119–120). My analyses of design structure in both nonlocally and locally produced White Mountain Red Ware indicate that the majority of local Grasshopper Polychrome bowls exhibit important differences in the application of Fourmile-style designs. Classic Fourmile Polychrome exteriors are present on ninety-four of ninety-eight Grasshopper Polychrome bowls in the Grasshopper Pueblo assemblage. Of these vessels, only twenty-four have Fourmile-style interior designs, and the remainder exhibit either earlier Pinedale-style designs, a mixture of Pinedale and Fourmile styles, or designs that defy classification (Van Keuren 1998a; Figure 5.3). These examples stand in contrast to the nonlocally produced Fourmile Polychrome assemblage that depicts asymmetrical geometric or representational imagery on bowl interiors. Design differences between Fourmile and Grasshopper polychrome bowls suggest that the local vessels were produced by potters in the Grasshopper region with limited experience in the decoration of polychrome ceramics. These potters were able to produce the local type by copying a reference collection of Plateau-produced Fourmile Polychrome but did so with hypothetical or old-fashioned designs on bowl interiors.

Two important clues suggest, however, that local potters also acquired stylistic knowledge directly from northern potters recently settled in the Grasshopper region. First, a small number of "local" Fourmile Polychrome pots with thick slips, local tempering materials and crushed sherds, and well-executed interior and exterior designs are present in the Grasshopper Pueblo assemblage. These pots were probably produced by Plateau migrants residing in the Grasshopper region. Second, the overall execution sequence of white and black paint on Grasshopper Polychrome mirrors that of Fourmile Polychrome and earlier White Mountain Red Ware. Interior and exterior designs on imported Fourmile Polychrome in the Grasshopper Pueblo assemblage are always outlined by thin white brushstrokes prior to the application of black paint. This subtle step in the application of painted designs was a fundamental behavior learned at a young age through direct observation of experienced potters. White paint was applied prior to black paint in all Grasshopper Polychrome vessels where paint was still preserved, indicating that at least one inherent design rule was learned by Grasshopper Pueblo potters through direct observation of migrant potters. Despite interaction between these groups, a formal style barrier prevented the complete transfer of decorative know-how between migrants and locals at Grasshopper Pueblo. These decorative patterns are also evident in the whole vessel assemblages at Point of Pines Pueblo and at sites north of the Mogollon Rim (e.g., Fourmile Ruin).

The style barrier may reflect information boundaries between social groups at this village. Although I have little insight as to the precise reading of prehistoric pottery designs, Fourmile-style designs may refer to the allegories or origin myths of different corporate groups at large pueblos and are thus one material item that authenticated the ceremonial legitimacy (and right to land) of migrant groups at this site and other fourteenth-century villages. Thus, leadership strategies may have arisen in the context of access to or control over public thought and ceremony, perhaps even influencing who was allowed to produce, paint, or even use polychrome bowls in specific contexts.

Conclusion

I have argued that ceramic design change in the early Pueblo IV period is a material residue of knowledge-based leadership strategies that potentially reorganized the social composition of villages in the uplands of eastern Arizona. These social processes are manifest in two style shifts in poly-chrome pottery decoration, the first beginning in the late 1200s with the appearance of the Pinedale style on multiple wares, and the next at 1325 with the shift to Fourmile style on White Mountain Red Ware. Although it is impossible to interpret the exact meaning of pottery decoration, both of these style events hint that the semantic content of polychrome ceramics was elevated at the beginning of the fourteenth century. I suggest that these styles may have articulated two different but overlapping types of knowl-edge that served as a potential basis for social power. According to Crown (1994), Pinedale-style pots articulated basic, widely shared, and perhaps even mundane concepts that could have easily played a role in facilitating social cohesion in public ritual and other community events. These widely produced vessels were standard parts of household assemblages throughout the upland Southwest during the late 1200s and early 1300s.

By contrast, Fourmile style marks the application of new categories of social knowledge in public and ritual life to ceramics, perhaps emphasizing the social value or prominence of certain groups within pueblo commu-nities. The latter knowledge was articulated, at least in part, through the manufacture and decoration of high fired, red-slipped bowls during the early to mid-1300s in east-central Arizona. These pots were restricted to a tighter geographic range when compared to earlier Pinedale-style ceramics, but their distribution *within* villages does not indicate that they were restricted in access or served as objects of elite status (cf. Upham, Lightfoot, and Feinman 1981). Instead, they appear to be active carriers of information that enhanced the ceremonial prominence of the households that either produced them or were directly familiar with the semantic (and allegorical) content of the designs. Because barriers determine the accuracy of copying behavior, these social processes are recorded by decorative variability or heterogeneity. Evidence that local potters at villages in the Mogollon region copied Fourmile-style designs with hypothetical and ultimately inaccurate design execution schemes is material evidence of an important design barrier. This barrier hints at unequal access to information about manufacturing skills or resource procurement, ceremonial participation, or perhaps even esoteric knowledge. The presence of both "classic" Fourmile Polychrome and Fourmile-style imitations at Fourmile Ruin and other pueblos at the northern edge of the Silver Creek drainage hints that these social barriers also shaped community relations north of the Mogollon Rim. Change in the elaboration of design, value, and consumption of polychrome bowls thus reflects the possible role of painted ceramics in the articulation of knowledge-based social power at early Pueblo IV period villages in eastern Arizona.

ACKNOWLEDGMENTS

Barbara Mills, Jeff Reid, Susan Stinson, Sarah Herr, William Graves, and Carol Kramer offered helpful comments during the preparation of this essay. Barbara Mills drafted Figure 5.1. The Arizona State Museum, the Museum of Northern Arizona, the Smithsonian Institution, the Field Museum of Chicago, the Museum of New Mexico, and the Museum of Northern Arizona provided access to whole vessel collections. This work was supported by grants from the National Science Foundation (SBR-9802381) and the Wenner-Gren Foundation for Anthropological Research.

6

Leadership Strategies in Protohistoric Zuni Towns

KEITH W. KINTIGH

UNTIL RELATIVELY RECENTLY, neo-evolutionary typologies and the Direct Historical Approach have dominated interpretations of the protohistoric western Pueblos. Protohistoric pueblos were widely assumed to have been organized like the nineteenth-century pueblos and to be adequately characterized as egalitarian "tribes," a concept long established in Elman Service's (1962) typology of social organization. This position is no longer tenable in light of withering attacks on the archaeological use of neo-evolutionary typologies in general (see, for example, references cited by Yoffee [1993:63–65] and Blanton and his colleagues [1996a:1–2]), arguments about the appropriate use of ethnographic analogy (e.g., Levy 1994; Upham 1987), and reinterpretations of Pueblo ethnography (Brandt 1977, 1980, 1994; Ortiz 1969; Whiteley 1988).

In the Southwest, archaeological critiques of this "traditional" position were first articulated by David Wilcox (1981) and most forcefully conveyed by Steadman Upham (1982; Upham and Reed 1989; Lightfoot and Upham 1989). I will highlight two of the central critiques. The first critique was that the historic Pueblo people were not (and still are not) as egalitarian as they have been depicted and that there are notable concentrations of power in religious officials (Brandt 1994). Much of this critique derived from Elizabeth Brandt's (1977, 1980) and Alfonso Ortiz's (1969) important ethnographic work and reinterpretations of ethnohistoric evidence.

The second critique posits that there is no reason to believe that Pueblo organization in the nineteenth century bore any strong resemblance to the situation in the fifteenth century; that is, the analogy to the protohistoric/ethnographic present is inappropriate. Spanish accounts are used to suggest quite different organizational forms (Wilcox 1981; Upham 1982). Further, epidemics associated with the Spanish *entrada* would have decimated Pueblo populations, and this depopulation would have substantially disrupted extant organizational forms (Brandt 1994; Reff 1990; Upham 1987).

These critiques laid the groundwork for Upham's (1982) radical reinterpretation of late prehistoric and protohistoric period Pueblo society. His model placed Western Pueblo society at a different stage in the neo-evolutionary framework, arguing that it was hierarchically organized, with elites controlling access to items associated with elite status, including polychrome ceramics. Upham's publication unleashed a torrent of substantive and theoretical criticism of his argument for a strongly hierarchical model of Pueblo society. Many if not most scholars have rejected his hierarchical interpretation of protohistoric Western Pueblo social organization.

At the same time, the underlying critiques have gained considerable acceptance. Although scholars today may, with some caution, map ethnographic descriptions on the protohistoric pueblos, the nature of our *understanding* of the ethnographic case has shifted markedly. There seems to be an emerging consensus favoring rejection of neo-evolutionary models; we now tend to see Pueblo society as neither a chiefdom nor an egalitarian tribe but as a form with considerable "complexity" that does not neatly fit into the standard social organizational pigeonholes.

In the Southwest, increasing attention is being paid to the strategies of leaders (Potter 1997a, 1997b; Varien 1997) and to the basis of power in control over ritual knowledge. Such power often has both ascriptive and achieved components but is typically *not* marked by inordinate differences in material wealth. To this end, scholars such as Crown (1994), Adams (1991), and Spielmann (1998a; Graves and Spielmann this volume) have recently offered innovative and nuanced interpretations of the late prehistoric archaeological record. Although there remain vocal holdouts (Reid and Whittlesey 1990), advocacy of a straightforward egalitarian view of late prehistoric Pueblo organization has waned dramatically.

This intellectual shift, which has been under way for some years in Southwestern archaeology is, of course, quite compatible with theoretical developments in the general anthropological and archaeological literature (Blanton et al. 1996a; Crumley 1995; Hayden 1995; Wills et al. 1994). This essay represents an attempt to understand the nature of the political organization of protohistoric Zuni towns and the leadership strategies employed in creating and maintaining that organizational form. Because we have a rich ethnographic record, in evaluating alternative models I explicitly attend to archaeological, ethnographic, and ethnohistoric data and to the similarities and differences between the ethnographic and protohistoric situations as we now understand them.

The Zuni Case

The Zuni case is particularly interesting in this regard because we have rich, abundant, and early ethnographic accounts, starting with those of Frank Cushing in the 1870s (Green 1979). It is interesting because there is one obvious and important difference between the protohistoric and ethnographic cases (aside from the usual consequences of European contact). Prior to the Pueblo Revolt of 1680, the Zuni lived in from six to nine distinct towns (the fabled cities of Cíbola), whereas after the reconquest in 1692, only one village, Zuni, was reestablished.

Zuni is also interesting because there have been large-scale excavations at two protohistoric towns. The Museum of the American Indian, Heye Foundation, sponsored the Hendricks–Hodge Expedition, which, from 1917 to 1923, excavated extensively at Hawikuh (Smith, Woodbury, and Woodbury 1966) and did more limited excavations at Kechipawan (Hodge 1920). One of the largest Zuni towns, Hawikuh (Figure 6.1), was occupied from sometime in the mid- to late 1300s until the Pueblo Revolt in 1680 and was the location of Coronado's first encounter with the Pueblos. Co-operating with the Hendricks–Hodge Expedition, in 1923 the Cambridge University Museum of Archaeology and Anthropology excavated Kechipawan (Figure 6.2), a large, contemporaneous town about 3 kilometers east of Hawikuh (Bushnell 1955).

Todd Howell's dissertation examined the mortuary data from the excavation of nearly a thousand graves at Hawikuh (1994; see also Howell 1995; Howell and Kintigh 1996) and yielded some strong conclusions about the internal organization of this important protohistoric Zuni town. Howell developed expectations for the mortuary record based on a number of organizational models: a complex chiefdom, a simple chiefdom, a sequential hierarchy (Johnson 1982), a big man system, and what might be called a revisionist historic Zuni model.

Howell showed that the Hawikuh data best fit the revisionist historic Zuni model. In this model, power is concentrated in religious offices that are maintained within only a few of the many lineages at Zuni. Notably, he identified a small number of graves with a great diversity of offerings, which he interpreted as the graves of leaders. Spatial and dental trait data indicated that these leaders came from a small number of kin groups.

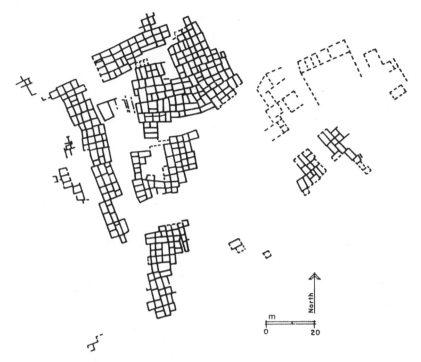

FIGURE 6.1. Plan of Hawikuh.

In the language of dual-processual theory (Blanton et al. 1996a), this would seem to indicate "exclusionary" power, because power was apparently concentrated in a very few kin groups and not shared (insofar as we can see it) across different sectors of Hawikuh society. However, the architectural and mortuary evidence do not indicate the degree of differentiation of individual wealth that one might expect to accompany monopoly control over power. Thus, the exclusionary power was probably balanced by strong "corporate" aspects of the political organization. Ethnographically, there is a strong corporate ideology that seems to preclude extraordinary accumulation of power and wealth.

Even if we accept Howell's reconstruction for Hawikuh, it remains for us to understand how this single town fits into the protohistoric Zuni polity consisting of six to nine distinct towns with about 25 kilometers separating the most distant towns.[1] Six or seven towns were occupied when Coronado arrived in 1540, and another two precontact protohistoric towns are known (Figure 6.3). Early Spanish accounts emphasize the size and importance of Hawikuh and Matsaki (Hodge 1937), but little else is known of the nature of the political relationships among the protohistoric towns.

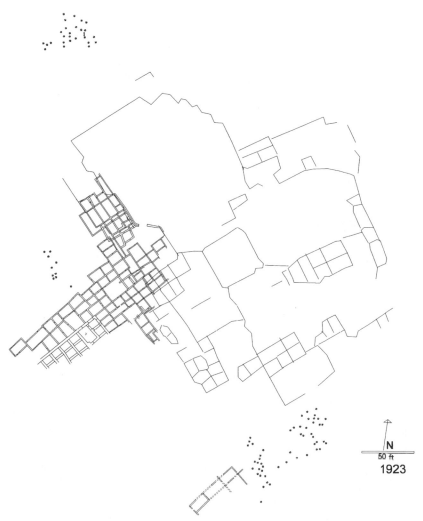

FIGURE 6.2. Plan of Kechipawan.

This essay describes the available evidence on the organization of the multitown, protohistoric Zuni polity, emphasizing a comparison of Kechipawan's previously unreported mortuary data with Hawikuh's. This evidence is evaluated in terms of current theoretical arguments that have been offered to replace the neo-evolutionary schemes. Again in the language of dual-processual theory, I will argue that at both the level of the polity and the level of the town, network strategies, while present, were largely subordinated by corporate strategies of leadership. It appears that the Zuni polity had no single centralized authority but consisted of a number of towns that not only possessed unequal political and ritual power but also

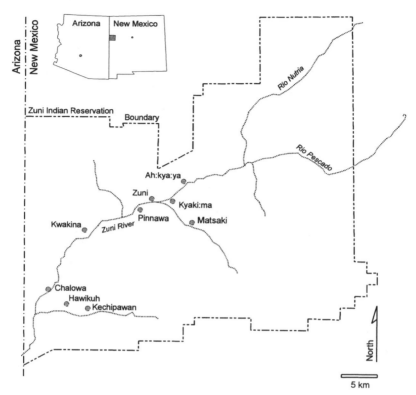

FIGURE 6.3. Location of the nine protohistoric Zuni towns.

maintained distinctive group identities throughout the protohistoric period. This situation appears inconsistent with Upham's (1982) argument for hierarchical organization and may incorporate important elements of heterarchy (Crumley 1995).

Leadership Strategies and Organizational Models

In developing this argument, we must first establish that there existed something that can reasonably be identified as a "Zuni polity." The early Spanish accounts (including those based on native informants) make clear that there was an entity they called Cíbola and another known as Totonteac. In the late nineteenth century Bandelier (1892, 1981) clearly associated Cíbola with Zuni and Totonteac with Hopi. It seems clear that by 1539 these separate cultural identities were firmly established in relatively distant locations (about 160 kilometers apart). Ethnographic (that is, nineteenth-century) Zuni, while sharing important similarities with Hopi, markedly contrasts not only in language but in having only a single large village (Zuni), while Hopi villages of different sizes and ritual importance are spread across three mesas.

Given Howell's reconstruction of village-level social and political organization at Hawikuh, we can still envision a number of organizational forms for the protohistoric Zuni polity that were driven by different leadership strategies.

CENTRALIZED MODEL

One model is that the protohistoric Zuni had a relatively centralized or hierarchical organization. Although there are undoubtedly other ways in which such a system could be organized, it seems likely that in such a case there would be a major town that housed the key leaders and central religious institutions. This would make the post–Pueblo Revolt coalescence into a single town easily understandable, especially in light of likely population decline. (It may be noted that Levy [1994] argues that such a model would be highly implausible ethnographically.)

CONFEDERACY–OF–EQUALS MODEL

Another model would have the Zuni towns more or less equal and quasi-autonomous, perhaps forming a loose confederacy (Levy 1994; Spielmann 1994) when cooperation was needed. In this case, we would see political/ religious leadership positions replicated in each town. The post-Revolt coalescence into a single system would likely have required a substantial reorganization, though such a reorganization might, in any event, have been required by the disease-induced depopulation.

HOPI MODEL

Another model would be similar to the ethnographic Hopi case best described by Whiteley (1988). Here, we would expect core towns that are likely large and quasi-independent of the other large towns and also smaller "daughter" villages that are ritually dependent on one of the mother towns. In this case, the religious hierarchy would be more or less replicated in the major towns but have diminished expression in daughter villages.

Of course, these are not all of the possibilities, but they serve for heuristic purposes. In this essay I examine two major forms of evidence that affect this question. First, I look at the data on site size and location. Second, I compare the mortuary practices and assemblages.

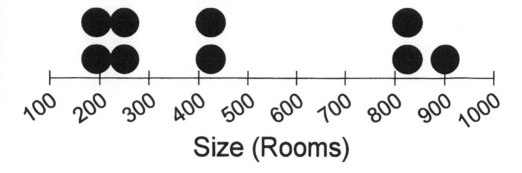

FIGURE 6.4. Dot plot of protohistoric Zuni site sizes.

Settlement Pattern Data

Although there are substantial problems in estimating the size of the proto-historic Zuni towns, these estimates were developed using archaeological data that conform reasonably well with accounts derived from Coronado's 1540 expedition (Kintigh 1985:74–75). It can be seen from the dot plot (Figure 6.4) that there are three major size modes, with three sites between 800 and about 900 rooms, two sites with about 400 rooms, and four sites between 150 and 250 rooms (Anyon 1992; Kintigh 1985). Two or three of these were abandoned prior to 1540. Candidates for precontact abandonment are the two medium-size sites, Chalowa and Ah:kya:ya (Anyon 1992), and a smaller site, Pinnawa (Kintigh 1990).

Perhaps the major conclusion we can draw from these data is that they are not compatible with the centralized model, in which one would expect a single dominant site and a hierarchy of site sizes below that. A rank-size plot (Hodder and Orton 1976:69–73) of such a distribution would tend to show sites plotted on a straight line. By contrast, a rank-size plot of the Zuni settlements (Figure 6.5) shows a remarkably convex distribution, more consonant with either the Hopi or confederacy-of-equals model.

One might also wonder if an upstream (eastern) polity was centered at Matsaki and a downstream (western) one was centered at Hawikuh. However, in this case, there would be two equally large towns, Hawikuh and Kechipawan, in the downstream polity. Mills notes this spatial pattern and

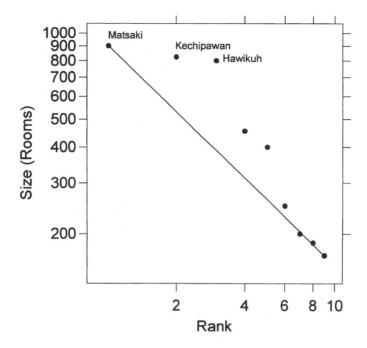

FIGURE 6.5. Rank-size plot of protohistoric Zuni sites.

shows that clays used for glazed Zuni ceramics (Heshotauthla types, Kwa-kina Polychrome, the Pinnawa types, Kechipawan Polychrome, and the historic Hawikuh types) were not readily available to sites in the western cluster (1995:201–2, 213–14). Because, as is discussed later, these glazed types are found in substantial frequencies at the western sites, including Hawikuh and Kechipawan, either long-distance procurement of clays or, more likely, significant movement of ceramics from towns in the eastern cluster to those in the western cluster is indicated.

Mortuary Analysis

Following the approach pioneered by Howell, I have analyzed the mortu-ary data from Kechipawan. I made a concerted effort, after consultation with Howell, to record the data in a comparable manner. Furthermore, the excavations at the two sites were going on at the same time and the excavators were cooperating closely, so the recovery techniques were probably comparable. In contrast to the 955 graves Howell analyzed at Hawikuh, I had information on 255 graves from Kechipawan. In neither case do we have anything like the complete population of graves; the sample size differences are due to differing amounts of archaeological excavation at the two sites, not any difference in their populations.

GRAVE RICHNESS

If a diverse assemblage of funerary objects is indicative of the multiple roles that leaders have within a community, as Howell argues, then graves with a high richness can be interpreted as those of leaders. Figure 6.6 shows a histogram of grave richness, by which I mean the number of *different classes* of items present in the grave. The proportions of graves with seven or fewer classes out of about ninety different classes of items recorded are roughly equal at the two sites, and the mean number of classes is also close, 2.1 for Hawikuh versus 1.9 for Kechipawan.

However, Hawikuh has a much greater *range* of richness values, up to twenty-four, compared with a maximum of thirteen at Kechipawan. At Hawikuh a comparatively large percentage, 4.5 percent (forty-three), of the graves have a richness greater than seven compared to only a third of that percentage (1.6 percent, four) at Kechipawan. Using a binomial distribution, it can be calculated that if a sample of 255 (Kechipawan's sample size) is drawn from a population with 4.5 percent rich graves (the proportion found at Hawikuh), then the probability of finding four or fewer rich graves (the observed number at Kechipawan) is a little less than 1 percent. That is, a sample as depleted in rich graves as Kechipawan is quite unlikely if drawn from a population with Hawikuh's proportion of rich graves.[2] It may also be noted that there are six very rich graves (richness greater than thirteen) at Hawikuh and none at all at Kechipawan, although this result is not statistically unlikely using the same logic ($p = .19$).

Despite the fact that the sites are about the same size (using either historical accounts or archaeological evidence) and are strictly contemporary (based on ceramic and historical data), Kechipawan appears lacking in rich graves when compared to Hawikuh, suggesting that Kechipawan may lack the full range of leadership positions found at Hawikuh. This corresponds with the early Spanish documents that stress the importance of Hawikuh and Matsaki but make little mention of Kechipawan, despite its proximity and large size.

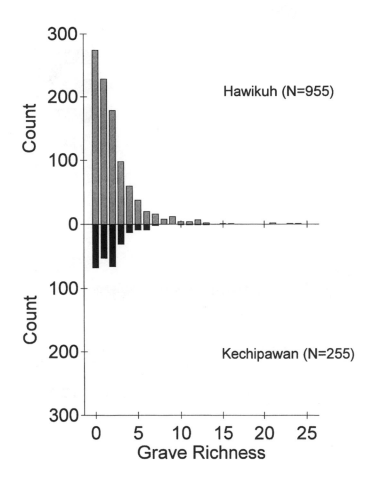

FIGURE 6.6. Side-by-side histograms of grave richness at Hawikuh and Kechipawan.

GRAVE ACCOMPANIMENTS

We can follow this line of reasoning a bit farther. If the grave accompaniments are grouped for comparison, some interesting patterns appear (Figure 6.7). Hawikuh, in the right-skewed bars, shows greater percentages of graves with one or more types of chipped stone, ritual items, weapons, and weaving tools. In the left-skewed bars, Kechipawan shows mainly a greater percentage of graves with one or more categories of ceramics. (These percentages are based on the number of graves at each site with at least one burial accompaniment; 187 at Kechipawan and 681 at Hawikuh.) Weapons

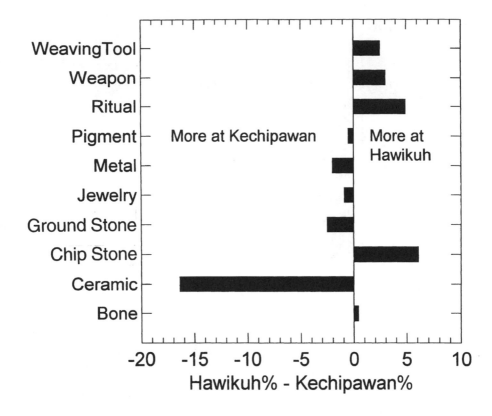

FIGURE 6.7. Side-by-side bar graphs comparing percentage differences in categories of materials from mortuary contexts at Hawikuh and Kechipawan.

and ritual items, found more commonly at Hawikuh, were identified by Howell as associated with graves of important leaders.

In the absence of any additional data, the patterns of grave richness and the differential distribution of the categories of grave goods seem contrary to a confederacy-of-equals model and might suggest a mother-daughter relationship between Hawikuh and Kechipawan, especially given their proximity. The convex rank-size relationship is also consistent with this interpretation. However, further analysis indicates that although important elements of this Hopi model may hold, the situation is likely to be more complicated.

If such a mother-daughter relationship obtained, the ceramic assemblages from Hawikuh and Kechipawan should be similar, or if certain types had restricted usage, the ceramics found at Kechipawan should be a subset of those at Hawikuh. However, while the major types are shared, the distributions are remarkably different. The most comparable data sets available are the whole or reconstructible vessels found in graves. While provenience was unfortunately lost on many Hawikuh vessels and recovery procedures may have differed slightly, there is no reason to expect any particular bias in the representation of the types, except perhaps for the utility pottery, which is excluded from the following analysis.

CERAMIC ASSOCIATIONS

Figure 6.8 illustrates large differences in the percentages of major ceramic types, based on 120 identified vessels at Kechipawan and 333 at Hawikuh. Types that are notably more common at Kechipawan than Hawikuh are the Salado types (Gila and Tonto Polychrome), with three times the percentage at Kechipawan when compared with Hawikuh (21 versus 7 percent); Unnamed Red-on-buff, with eight times more (12 versus 2 percent) at Kechipawan; and Matsaki Brown-on-buff, with three times more (11 versus 4 percent). Types more common at Hawikuh are Matsaki Polychrome, with twice the percentage (37 versus 62 percent) and the historic Hawikuh types with three times more (3 versus 8 percent).

The quite different representations of ceramic types do not seem to be due to differing interregional exchange relations of groups populating the two towns. The only contemporary Pueblo settlements are at Hopi (170 kilometers or more northwest), at Acoma (about 115 kilometers east), and along the Rio Grande (at least 200 kilometers east). Pottery from Hopi is easily recognizable and accounts for less than 1 percent at each site. Only one Rio Grande vessel has been identified at either Kechipawan or Hawikuh (Mills, personal communication, 1999). Although no Acoma ceramics have been identified from either site, Zuni and Acoma have similar ceramic traditions, so Acoma ceramics may not always be easily distinguished based on their surface characteristics.

The Matsaki types and the Hawikuh types are certainly made at Zuni and are rare outside these protohistoric towns. Unnamed Red-on-buff appears to be part of the local Zuni buff ware sequence, probably a variant of Matsaki Brown-on-buff in which red paint is substituted for brown (similarly, Woodbury and Woodbury [1966:324–25] see this as a buff-slipped variant of Pinnawa Red-on-white). Interestingly, despite the quite

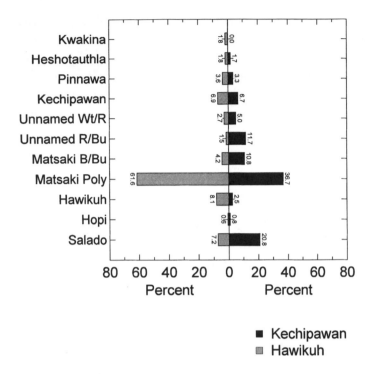

FIGURE 6.8. Side-by-side bar graphs comparing percentages of different ceramic types from mortuary contexts at Hawikuh and Kechipawan.

different representation of Matsaki Polychrome, Matsaki Brown-on-buff, and Unnamed Brown-on-buff at the two sites, their combined percentages are fairly similar (69 percent at Hawikuh versus 59 percent at Kechipawan).

The other major difference is in the Salado types (Roosevelt Red Ware), Gila and Tonto Polychrome. Gila Polychrome production started about A.D. 1300, and Tonto Polychrome production started somewhat later, in the mid-1300s. While both types were made until A.D. 1400, the terminal dates are unclear, but probably no later than 1450 (Crown 1994:19–20). In any case, these types probably ceased production relatively early in the occupations of these sites. Based on INAA analysis, Crown and Bishop argue that there exists a northeastern source for the Salado types. (Their figure and text [1994:27] suggest that their hypothesized HNorth source, which includes both Hawikuh and Homolovi samples, may be further divisible.)

Andrew Duff (personal communication, 1998) now has strong evidence that Salado types were produced in the Upper Little Colorado. However, the Upper Little Colorado sites were abandoned near the time the protohistoric Zuni towns were established. Barbara Mills's INAA analysis of Zuni sources (personal communication, 1998) indicates that Crown's Salado Polychrome samples from Hawikuh did *not* use the local clays from which Zuni buff ware and glazed types were produced. If they were not made at Zuni, they must have been either traded early in Hawikuh's occupation or brought as heirlooms from places such as the Upper Little Colorado. All of the Hawikuh sherds whose source was identified by Crown and Bishop were from this northeastern source (i.e., they were not from central Arizona or elsewhere). However, Salado Polychrome ceramics from Kechipawan were not chemically sourced and could conceivably have a different origin.

Most of the types showing the largest differences were locally made. If there are differences in exchange, they are largely if not entirely intraregional, not interregional. The differences between the sites also do not appear to be chronological; in particular, the diagnostic Zuni glaze wares have very similar proportions, suggesting similar beginning dates, and both sites are known to have been abandoned at the time of the Pueblo Revolt in 1680.

GRAVE ORIENTATION

Burial practices also vary substantially between Hawikuh and Kechipawan. The most dramatic difference is in grave orientation, which according to ethnographically recorded tradition at Zuni follows the "old custom," with heads to the east (Stevenson 1904:306). At both sites eastern orientations are the most common. However, Figure 6.9 shows that fully 35 percent of 533 graves at Hawikuh have north and south orientations, while at Kechipawan, less than a third of that percentage (10 percent of 158 graves) have north or south orientations. In this radial bar chart, the percentage of graves with a given orientation is indicated by the length of the wedge-shaped bar, with each dotted ring indicating 10 percent.

It has been known since Hodge's excavations early in this century that cremation, which is unknown in earlier Zuni area sites and unknown ethnographically, was widely practiced at Hawikuh.[3] Indeed, about a third of the graves at both sites were cremations: 33 percent at Hawikuh and

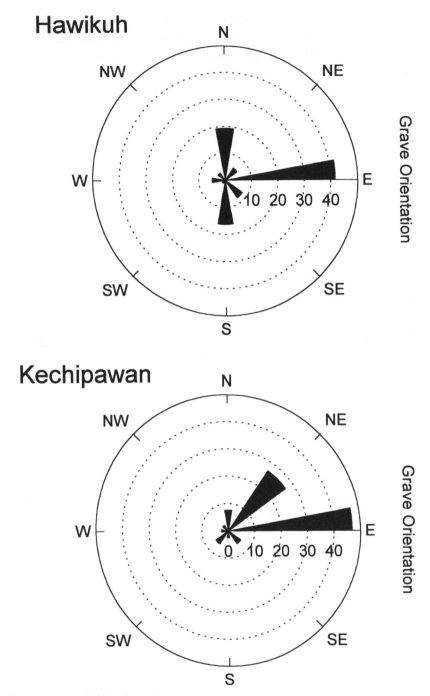

FIGURE 6.9. Radial bar chart of grave orientations at Hawikuh and Kechipawan.

28 percent at Kechipawan. It may be added that ceramic types associated with cremations are quite strongly differentiated from those with inhumations, although all major ceramic types do appear with both types of graves.

Conclusion

Without comparable data from other Zuni sites, particularly Matsaki, we cannot fully reconstruct the organization of the Zuni polity. Nonetheless, ethnohistoric references indicate that there was a cultural identity encompassing the Zuni towns, an inference that is consistent with the spatial separation of the Zuni towns from the nearest other groups (the most distant protohistoric Zuni towns were 25 kilometers apart, while Acoma and Hopi were about 115 and 170 kilometers away, respectively). Further, the historic sources suggest there were two central towns, Hawikuh and Matsaki. The strongly convex rank-size relationship and the location of what were apparently the most important settlements near the extremes, rather than near the center of the settlement distribution, suggest that the polity was not highly centralized and may, in some senses, have been split.

Despite the large sizes and spatial proximity of the two towns investigated, Hawikuh apparently possessed important leaders, while Kechipawan seems to have lacked them, presumably indicating greater ritual and political centrality for Hawikuh. This seems inconsistent with a polity that was organized as a confederacy of equals.

The strong differences between the sites in burial practices, as illustrated by orientation, the differences in representation of the categories of grave goods, the dramatically different assemblages of ceramic types found in mortuary contexts, and the practice of cremation at both towns suggest that disparate group identities that may reflect ethnic differences were maintained at Hawikuh and Kechipawan. This is *not* what one would expect of daughter communities budding off from a mother town.

Overall, this suggests a more complex organization for the Zuni polity than is implied by any of the three models. While it seems reasonable that all these towns would have cooperated if and when the need arose, it appears that the Zuni polity was composed of a mixture of politically and ritually *unequal* towns. Distinctive group identities were maintained between and probably within these towns throughout the protohistoric period.

These differing group identities could have and probably did result from the many migrations characterized in traditional histories from Zuni and other Pueblos (Cushing 1988; Ferguson and Hart 1985; Parsons 1996). It may be that long-standing group differences were maintained, or perhaps migrant groups entering Zuni late in the protohistoric period were establishing new towns or quite unevenly distributing themselves among existing towns and maintaining separate identities.

Of course, this possibility should not surprise us, because we know from the archaeological evidence that there was apparently quite a lot of settlement instability through the Pueblo IV period (Kintigh 1985) and that there was great population movement at about the time of establishment of the protohistoric towns at Zuni (between 1350 and 1400). There was a massive movement of people from villages upstream (east) in the Zuni River valley, such as Atsinna, Pueblo de los Muertos, Cienega, the Pescado ruins, and Heshotauthla (Kintigh 1985). Also, full-time occupation of the Upper Little Colorado River valley and the Mogollon Rim region ended at about this time (Kintigh 1990, 1996). We need to look more closely at the Pueblo IV period to see whether the source of the protohistoric diversity is from the earlier Zuni towns (in which case, ethnic differences were *maintained* through the Pueblo IV period, rather than integrated or suppressed) or whether they derive from immigrants from farther away or both.[4] In particular, we need to understand how migrations by different groups of people and the local reactions to the migrants shaped protohistoric Pueblo political structures.

For too long we have projected back into the past the strong and distinct cultural identities that characterize modern pueblos such as Hopi or Zuni. A growing body of archaeological evidence, as well as Pueblo traditional histories, seems to indicate that considerable cultural diversity was common, even within what we identify as local prehistoric "cultures." Indeed, this study has presented evidence that such diversity persisted through the protohistoric period at Zuni. Additional insight may come from the traditional histories of the Zuni people.

Where does this leave us with respect to our discussion of leadership strategies and their origins? To put it in Crumley's (1995) terms, the Zuni polity would appear to be heterarchical, indicating a lack of unidimensional hierarchy and a presence of multiple and noncongruent sources of power that come into play in different situations. This characterization would also be consistent with ethnographic descriptions of Zuni (e.g., Kroeber 1917) that emphasize, for example, the crosscutting roles of kinship, the priesthoods, and Kachina groups and that decouple ritual and economic status.[5] Howell (1994:137–39), relying on analyses by Stodder (1990), argues that leaders "generally did not lead longer, healthier lives than their fellow villagers," although his analysis did show that kin groups supplying leaders were mildly advantaged. Nonetheless, models of hierarchy and heterarchy are perhaps more helpful in describing what protohistoric Zuni is *not* (hierarchical) than in illuminating the interplay of groups or factions (Brumfiel 1992) within the social, political, and economic systems.

As Blanton and his colleagues (1996a) suggest in their dual-processual theory, both corporate and network strategies can coexist in different mixes. The fact that important leadership positions are concentrated at Hawikuh and are rare or absent at Kechipawan and the concentration of these leadership positions in a very few kin groups indicate that power was not widely shared and that a network strategy was employed to a degree by leaders within the Zuni polity. The apparent lack of political centrality of a single town and the absence of great differentiation in grave wealth indicate that a corporate strategy coexisted with and seriously limited the effectiveness of the network strategy.

This interpretation of a dominant corporate strategy fits well with Blanton and his colleagues' (1996a:3) association of a strong network strategy with a large spatial scale and wealth-based political economy based on extragroup exchange of prestige goods. In fact, there is little material evidence of extragroup exchange in protohistoric Zuni (though there was somewhat more than there had been preceding the Pueblo IV period). While some marine shell and turquoise have been found, mainly in funerary assemblages, the scale of exchange does not appear great, nor it is clear what prestige goods might have been exchanged in return.[6] We are, unfortunately, generally unable to assess exchange in feathers (which undoubtedly existed). Webster (1997) concludes that it is unlikely that there was much, if any, cotton production at Kechipawan or Hawikuh (most textiles were yucca fiber).

This interpretation also fits with the posited association of a corporate strategy with a knowledge-based system where political action takes place primarily within the local group. A knowledge-based local system, of course, fits well with our current understanding of Pueblo ethnography.

In recognition of the argument that explanations of cultural developments be understandable in terms of individual decision making, dual-processual theory is concerned with the leadership strategies utilized by emergent leaders, strategies that over a period of time result in the societal types described as corporate and network.

Brian Hayden's (1995) discussion of "pathways to power" presents a refined series of actor-oriented models of the acquisition and maintenance of power in middle-range societies. His models seem largely oriented toward understanding the acquisition and maintenance of individual power. Periodic feasting, warfare, and creation of debt obligations (all of which rely to a degree on surplus production) play major roles.[7] In the examples he describes (on the Northwest Coast and in New Guinea), there seem to be relatively stable organizational structures, even if the individuals or groups holding power frequently change.

However, we must also recognize that most of the organizational forms that we observe archaeologically or ethnographically are the outcomes of multigenerational sequences of decision making by leaders who are influenced by the concurrent responses of those affected. Thus, corporate and network seem better described as long-term outcomes of such a multigenerational process than as "strategies" in the everyday sense of the term, that is, explicitly formulated plans to achieve specific results.

In some cases, perhaps including those described by Hayden, there are individual or elite strategies that result in relatively stable organizational forms in which the nature of the strategies for the maintenance of power remains somewhat transparent or at least subject to inference. In other cases, I suspect that these multigenerational interactions of self-interested individuals result in organizational forms with associated ideational and ritual legitimations that are not readily decomposed into strategic antecedents or constituents, at least in part because of the unintended consequences of the actions of leaders. Additional insight on this process may be provided by Santa Fe Institute–style complexity theory (Lewin 1992; Wills et al. 1994; Yoffee 1994). In this conception, some of the organizational structure we observe may have "emergent" properties that come from the interaction of many actors pursuing their self-interested individual strategies. However, to disentangle that process will be difficult indeed.

Protohistoric Zuni organization was undoubtedly shaped by many interested individuals, yet we must understand that the overall configuration was a result of the consequences, intended and unintended, over four centuries that exhibit dramatic social and organizational change (Kintigh 1985, 1994, 1996; Kintigh, Howell, and Duff 1996). While many of us will agree that the result does not neatly fit the standard neo-evolutionary niches, it may also not be readily classifiable into these more recent organizational typologies.

ACKNOWLEDGMENTS

An earlier version of this paper was presented in the symposium "Corporate or Network? Alternative Leadership Strategies in the Greater Southwest," at the 63rd Annual Meeting of the Society for American Archaeology in Seattle, March 25–29, 1998. I am most grateful to Barbara Mills, Andrew Duff, Brenda Shears, Katherine Spielmann, and David Wilcox for insightful comments on an earlier draft of this paper. Todd Howell graciously provided access to his Hawikuh data and provided assistance in making the Kechipawan data set comparable to it. I am also grateful to Eulalie Bonar, who facilitated access to the National Museum of the American Indian collections, and to David Phillipson, Christopher Chippindale, and Robin Boast, who made possible the analysis of the Kechipawan materials at the Cambridge University Museum of Archaeology and Anthropology. Compilation and analysis of the Kechipawan data presented here were funded by grants from the National Endowment for the Humanities (RK-20034-93) and the National Science Foundation (SBR-9318701), whose support is gratefully acknowledged.

NOTES

1. By "polity" I imply an identity and some degree of cultural integration but no specific organizational form.

2. Despite this statistic, an unresolvable sampling problem remains. At Hawikuh, the rich graves were quite unevenly distributed across the eleven different cemetery areas that were excavated. It is probably the case that fewer cemeteries (but at least five) were excavated at Kechipawan. If a particularly rich cemetery existed but was missed at Kechipawan, the true richness distribution might be quite similar.

3. Stevenson (1904:305) reports, "The Zuni always buried their dead. They insist that should they incincrate the bodies, there would be no rain, for their dead are the u'wannami (rain-makers)." The appearance of cremation at Zuni has widely been interpreted as resulting from a direct or indirect diffusion or migration from central Arizona populations along the Gila and Salt rivers (see Crown 1994:110–11). In the late fourteenth and early fifteenth centuries, cremation was practiced in the Point of Pines area, in Cliff phase sites in southern New Mexico, and along the Verde River in central Arizona. Indeed, cremation is often thought to have become relatively rare in central Arizona by the time these Zuni towns were founded. At the major Classic (A.D. 1200–1450) Hohokam site of Pueblo Grande, less than a third (29 percent) of the 854 individuals were cremated, with similar proportions in both Early and Late Classic (Mitchell 1994:74, 134). By contrast, at the Late Classic site of Los Muertos, more than two-thirds of the individuals (370 of 522) were cremated (Brunson 1989:339, 386).

4. In contrast to the protohistoric case, contemporaneous Pueblo IV Zuni towns seem to have relatively uniform (nonmortuary) ceramic assemblages.

5. Kroeber (1917:183) says: "The clans, the fraternities, the priesthoods, the kivas, in a measure the gaming parties, are all dividing agencies. If they coincided, the rifts in the social structure would be deep; by countering each other they cause segmentations which produce an almost marvelous complexity, but can never break the national entity apart."

6. There are about 8,400 catalog records of the National Museum of the American Indian and Cambridge University Museum of Archaeology and Anthropology associated with the excavation of about 1,200 burials and 450 rooms at Hawikuh and Kechipawan. Of these, 7 refer to copper bells (not all of which may be prehistoric), 54 refer to turquoise, and about 265 refer to marine shell.

7. LeBlanc (1989a, 1999) would argue for warfare in Pueblo III and Pueblo IV contexts at Zuni, though that viewpoint is controversial. We now do have some evidence for feasting in Pueblo IV Zuni towns (Potter 1997b).

7

Organizational Variability in Platform Mound–Building Groups of the American Southwest

MARK D. ELSON AND DAVID R. ABBOTT

Approximately 120 platform mounds from 96 archaeological sites have been recorded in the American Southwest. Even though twenty-four platform mound sites have now been tested or excavated in some manner, most within the past twenty years (Doelle 1995), the function of the mounds and the leadership structure and social organization of the groups that built them remain the subject of heated debate. This controversy has been ongoing since the earliest days of the century, and archaeologists are still debating the same basic functions originally proposed by Frank Hamilton Cushing, Adolph Bandelier, and J. Walter Fewkes (Elson 1998; Howard 1992).

Simply defined, platform mounds are cultural features that were deliberately raised or filled to construct an elevated platform. Some mounds had associated structures on top of their elevated platforms, whereas others did not. In the Southwest, platform mounds were largely confined to southern and central Arizona in the region traditionally defined as the Hohokam culture area. They were most numerous during the Classic period between A.D. 1150 and 1375, when the great majority of mounds were constructed, although a few earlier mounds are also known.

In the 1500s, Spanish explorers in the southeastern United States such as Hernando de Soto and Juan Pardo visited villages where platform mounds were still in use, providing a link with mound-building peoples of the prehistoric past (Hudson 1990; Swanton 1946). These accounts have greatly aided the archaeological interpretation of mounds in that area (Anderson 1994; Blitz 1993b; Neitzel 1965). Unfortunately, in the Southwest direct ethnographic parallels are absent.

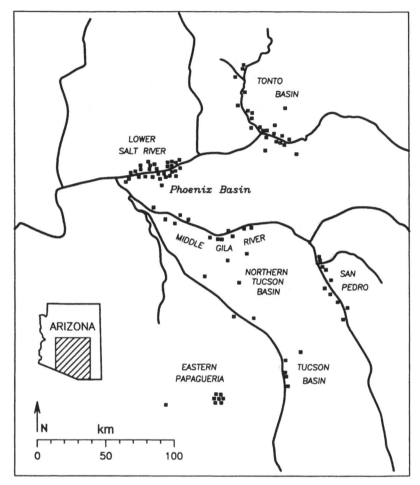

FIGURE 7.1. The regional distribution of platform mound sites in central and southern Arizona (from Elson 1998:fig. 1.1, reprinted by permission).

Although there is variability in these features, Southwestern platform mounds can be generally characterized as follows (Doelle, Gregory, and Wallace 1995; Elson 1998; Gregory 1987). The mounds are distributed over an area of approximately 45,000 square kilometers largely confined to the Sonoran Desert, from the eastern Papaguería, Tucson Basin, and San Pedro River Valley in the south to the Phoenix and Tonto basins in the north (Figure 7.1). They have a raised surface area averaging around 500 square meters with an average volume of fill of 1,500 cubic meters. Their height above the surrounding ground surface averages approximately 2 meters. Most, although not all, Southwestern platform mounds are enclosed within a masonry or adobe compound wall usually containing room spaces and

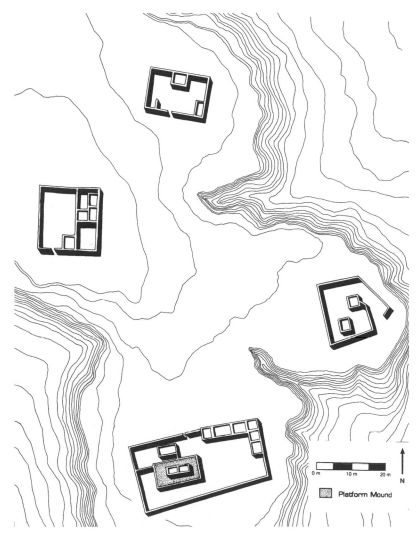

FIGURE 7.2. An idealized example of a platform mound site containing three compounds and a platform mound compound with two rooms on top of the mound (bottom center) (from Elson 1998:fig. 1.2, reprinted by permission).

open plaza areas, and they are often associated with other compounds without mounds that were primarily for residential purposes (Figure 7.2).

Relatively speaking, the platform mounds in the Southwest are not exceptionally large monuments whose construction necessitated a huge investment in labor and resources. The smallest mounds were constructed with less than 500 cubic meters of artificial fill, and the two largest mounds, at Pueblo Grande and Mesa Grande in the Phoenix Basin, are both estimated to contain around 14,000 cubic meters of rock, dirt, and debris (Doelle, Gregory, and Wallace 1995). Even these large Hohokam mounds are relatively small in comparison to many mounds found in the New World and elsewhere. Nonetheless, Southwestern mounds can be considered as monumental architecture because, as Trigger (1990:19) notes, their "scale and elaboration exceed the requirements of any practical functions . . . [they were] intended to perform."

The significance of platform mounds lies in the fact that mound construction, even of the relatively small mounds like those found in the Southwest, was almost certainly a group effort, one oriented toward a non-subsistence-related task that necessitated some form of cooperation above the family level. However, the nature of this social organization—that is, whether mound-building groups were organized by leaders filling formal and ascribed offices of authority or whether they were organized through less formal nonhierarchical mechanisms—has been the subject of significant debate and controversy.

Archaeological Models of Southwestern Platform Mounds

Platform mounds in the prehistoric Southwest have been most commonly investigated through the use of archaeological data on architecture, room and feature function, and patterns of artifact distribution (Bayman 1994; Bostwick and Downum 1994; Ciolek-Torrello, Callahan, and Greenwald 1988; Craig and Clark 1994; Doyel 1974; Elson 1994; Fish, Fish, and Madsen 1992; Gregory 1987, 1988; Howard 1992; Jacobs 1994; Lindauer 1995, 1996; Wilcox 1987a). These studies have produced a general consensus among archaeologists that platform mounds served to integrate portions of their surrounding settlements, probably through ritual means, and functioned in resource redistribution and the management of irrigation and other subsistence activities (Crown 1991; Doelle, Gregory, and Wallace 1995; Doyel 1981; Elson, Stark, and Gregory 1996; Fish and Fish 1992; Gregory 1987). Yet within this general framework, two sets of competing models have been proposed, each with a number of permutations.

One set of models suggests that the mounds were, for the most part, not residential. Instead, they were ceremonial and used by relatively undifferentiated groups for ritual, feasting, and other socially integrative activities (Bostwick and Downum 1994; Ciolek-Torrello 1988; Ciolek-Torrello, Whittlesey, and Welch 1994; Craig and Clark 1994; Whittlesey and Ciolek-Torrello 1992). These models dispute the notion that mound-building groups were ranked and hierarchically organized. In these scenarios, leadership was achieved and derived through religion and the kinship system; rule was by consensus rather than birthright or force.

In direct contrast, a second set of models suggests residence on top of the mounds by managerial elites, although there are several variations on this theme. Some propose that elite power was legitimized through ritual activities and based on the redistribution of subsistence resources and the control of trade goods (Bayman 1994; Fish and Fish 1992; Wood 1989, 1995). Others stress that the mounds were associated with irrigation management (Doyel 1981; Gregory 1988; Gregory and Nials 1985; Howard 1987, 1990), while still others emphasize political alliances among high-status personages from across a broad swath of the desert Southwest (Wilcox 1987a). Finally, some models posit that elite power had different bases depending on specific environmental and economic contexts of the community (Doelle, Gregory, and Wallace 1995; Henderson 1993; Rice 1987a, 1990).

The elite, or managerial, models are particularly well developed for the lower Salt River Valley in the Phoenix Basin, where large-scale irrigation agriculture was practiced and the connection between platform mounds and irrigation is believed to be strong. This is due to the fact that a set of canals with a common headgate location, called a "canal system," served several mound villages equally spaced along the canal routes (Gregory and Nials 1985). A number of different models have been proposed to explain the functioning of these systems, distinguished by how communities are delimited and the manner in which they were integrated for agricultural purposes. For example, some researchers argue that the mound sites along the same canals were aligned as a single, integrated political and social unit with the greatest political power at the end, assuring equitable water deliveries to all parts of the canal system (Gregory 1987; Gregory and Nials 1985). Others believe that each mound was the central focus for an individual community (Fish 1996; Fish, Fish, and Madsen 1992), implying that the communities located in the same canal system were joined through alliances among their leaders to form a beneficial cooperative. Still others suggest that platform mounds were the integrative foci for individual communities that formed alliances only through the threat of force and warfare. Residents of settlements at the end of the canal system coerced those living near the headgates to supply them with sufficient water (Rice 1998).

Finally, changes in mound function over time have also been noted. In the Phoenix and Tonto Basins, the earlier (Soho and Roosevelt phase) platform mounds are suggested to be primarily nonresidential, ceremonial features, as compared to the later (Civano and Gila phase) mounds, which many believe to have had a residential component (Doyel 1974, 1981; Gregory 1987, 1988; Wood 1989). This change implies a shift in socio-political organization: earlier mounds are believed to have been used by groups of more limited social differentiation than later mounds, where occupation by elite groups with strong leaders is implied.

The above studies have obvious implications for the leadership structure of mound-using groups. In the following sections we suggest that the Hohokam mound-building social units were organized differently than previously believed. We concentrate our analysis on the irrigation-dependent communities along the lower Salt River of the Phoenix area but then expand our discussion to encompass the platform mounds and surrounding settlements in other parts of the Southwest. We argue that while aspects of hierarchical structure were most likely present, crosscutting horizontal ties were also pervasive, ordering communities through kinship. The mounds functioned in the regulation and territorial marking of irrigation systems and were perhaps ritually focused on the glorification of the descent group and associated ancestors.

We present two lines of evidence for our assessment. The first is based on a recent study of historic platform mound–building groups using ethnographic or ethnohistoric information (Elson 1996, 1998). The other derives from a detailed analysis of utilitarian ceramic production and distribution networks among platform mound sites in a single canal system in the Phoenix area (Abbott 1994a, 1994b, 2000).

Analysis of Historic Mound-Building Groups

The analysis of ethnographic or ethnohistoric mound-building groups suggests the following common attributes: (1) platform mounds were constructed by well-defined, ranked descent groups with institutionalized leadership positions; (2) the mounds themselves probably served to demarcate descent group territory and glorify the descent group in general, often through the practice of ancestor worship; and (3) perhaps most important in terms of the reconstruction of prehistoric leadership, there is a correlation between the size and diversity of the platform mounds and the leaders' rights and responsibilities to lead. That is, the more energy invested in mound construction and the greater the number of functionally different mounds present in a group, the greater the social differentiation and the authority of leaders (Elson 1996, 1998:51–52).

Seven groups were chosen for analysis: the Ifaluk and Yap islanders of Micronesia, the Samoan and Marquesan islanders of Polynesia, the Choctaw and Natchez of the southeastern United States, and the Mapuche of central Chile. These groups were selected based on the quality of available information and on the need to investigate a range of types and levels of social organization. They included only those that fell into the "middle-range" category, which essentially subsumes the previous and now largely discarded neo-evolutionary stages of "tribe" and "chiefdom" (Feinman and Neitzel 1984; Upham 1982). The use of only middle-range societies was to avoid analyzing groups that were either far less complex (such as "bands") or far more complex (such as "states") than the types of social organization present among the mound builders of the prehistoric Southwest. Although many other middle-range mound-building groups are known ethnographically, there is no evidence that these other groups have attributes significantly different from those discussed here.

The ethnographic data indicate a high degree of variability in both the social organization of middle-range mound-using groups and the manner in which the platform mounds were used. Mound-building groups encompass many different kinds of subsistence systems, descent systems, residence rules, and religious practices. The number of individuals and the ethnic composition of these groups are also highly variable, as are the function, form, and size of the mounds themselves, which differ greatly both within and between social units. Even with this variability a number of common attributes are present among middle-range mound-building societies, several of which have important implications for the social organization and leadership structure in the prehistoric Southwest.

First, most of the analyzed ethnographic groups have several different types of mounds that are used contemporaneously. In fact, only one of the seven analyzed societies had only a single mound type. Mounds were used as general domestic residences (Ifaluk, Yap, Samoa, and Marquesa), chiefly residences (Yap, Samoa, Marquesa, and Natchez), community meeting areas (Ifaluk, Yap, Samoa, Marquesa, and Mapuche), temples (Yap, Samoa, Marquesa, and Natchez), burial features (Yap, Marquesa, Mapuche, and Choctaw), charnel houses (Natchez and possibly Choctaw), areas for staging and/or viewing public ceremony (Marquesa and Mapuche), places for redistributing food (Yap, Marquesa, and possibly Natchez), and hunting platforms for chiefly sport (Samoa). The four most common uses are as residential mounds, community mounds, temple mounds, and burial mounds. Perhaps most significantly, the data strongly indicate that mound architecture and morphology are not necessarily directly indicative of mound function and that most platform mounds are multifunctional. Function and use may also change over the lifetime of a mound.

Second, all of the mound-using peoples examined, including groups not directly used in the analysis, are either ranked or stratified with well-defined, inherited leadership positions. Platform mounds were not found among band-level groups or middle-range groups with very limited social differentiation. This indicates that some form of institutionalized, hierarchical leadership is typically associated with mound construction.

The data further suggest that architecture may be one of the best measures of social differentiation and the nature of the leadership (Abrams 1994; Trigger 1990). That is, outside of architecture, the ethnographic data indicate that clear material signatures of status are not necessarily to be expected in the archaeological record, particularly for middle-range groups (see also Feinman and Neitzel 1984). This point is important, because controversy over what are true status markers in the Southwestern archaeological record forms the basis for much of the disagreement between the two opposing sets of models for Hohokam platform mound use and the organization of the associated social units. For the seven ethnographic groups where data were available, status was primarily distinguished through the carrying of wooden artifacts (Samoa), the wearing of elaborate clothing (Marquesa, Yap, and Natchez), tattoo patterns (Marquesa and Natchez), and deferential behavior to chiefs and nobles by those in lower positions (Samoa, Yap, Marquesa, and Natchez). In fact, in Samoa, Yap, Marquesa, and Natchez, which are the most socially differentiated groups in the analysis, the above traits are the primary nonarchitectural indicators of status. In societies that include inherited leadership roles but with relatively less power and authority, like the Choctaw and Ifaluk, there are very few, if any, artifacts indicative of social differentiation. Yet in all of these groups, mound architecture can be directly correlated with individual and group status.

Furthermore, the accumulation of personal wealth was not considered to be a positive attribute in any analyzed group. Chiefs and nobles may at times accumulate more goods than others, primarily through control of trade, gift exchange, tribute collection, or cultivation of larger plots of productive land. However, the ceremonial and social obligations of chiefs, including giving feasts and staging rituals, periodically involve the redistribution of accumulated goods, thereby minimizing (but not eliminating) material differences. Although redistribution of resources in this manner is often used as a means to raise status (Hayden 1995), it also acts as an equalizing

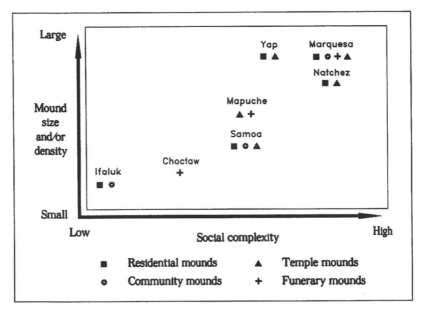

FIGURE 7.3. Schematic relationship between social differentiation and platform mound size and diversity for the seven analyzed groups (from Elson 1998:fig. 3.1, reprinted by permission).

factor in the individual possession of material goods. These data suggest that the absence of archaeologically visible material indicators of status, such as in the prehistoric Southwest, does not necessarily correspond with an absence of status differentiation (see also Feinman 1995; Plog 1995).

The third common attribute among mound-building groups is that the greater the elaboration in the types of mounds used by a group and the greater the size of the mound (as measured by volume), the greater the social differentiation and the power of group leaders. This relationship is demonstrated by the historic analysis: Yap, Natchez, and Marquesa are clearly stratified societies where leaders have coercive force and the power of life and death over those in the lower ranks. These groups also have the largest mounds, the greatest degree of functional diversity in mound type, or both (Figure 7.3). This association can be translated into labor energy measures (see Abrams 1989, 1994) by stating that the greater the degree of energy expended in mound construction, the greater the social differentiation of the group. Mound construction can occur in stages and even over several generations, but the ethnographic information indicates that it is the accumulated energy expenditure that is related to the degree of social differentiation. Only those societies that have the strongest and most effective leaders construct large (or numerous) monuments to reflect their own and their group's status. Status is achieved regardless of whether the mounds are constructed all at once or whether they are constructed by the same group over an extended period of time.

Fourth, platform mounds in middle-range societies are generally used by an entire descent group, particularly those constructed by communal, rather than household, labor. Descent group use may be related to a general pattern of ancestor worship or at least a concern with lineage ancestors. This association was noted in most of the analyzed mound-building groups, although further research is needed. Mounds tend to be used for the glorification of the entire descent group, which can take the form of lineages, sublineages, clans, or some bilateral form. All of the group members share, although not necessarily on an equal basis, in the attributes and status associated with the mound. This is true regardless of whether the mound is inhabited by a particular individual. In fact, mound-top occupation is variable and cannot be directly equated with the degree of group social differentiation or the nature of leadership.

Fifth, platform mounds are never truly abandoned as long as the descent group that constructed the mound still inhabits the general territory, although as noted, mound function may change. Platforms that are no longer actively used are often considered to be the home of descent group ancestors and are important in group history and for promoting group solidarity: they are the scene of ceremonies and the location of shrines, and they are often associated with ritual proscriptions. Furthermore, as Anderson (1994) has documented in the ethnohistoric record of the southeastern United States, mounds and mound centers undergo their own cyclical historical processes, involving both the rise and fall of leaders and groups. Ethnographic data collected for the historic study also suggest that mounds can be and often are used sequentially over generations: not all mounds in a single settlement or local system may be in use at the same time. One archaeological implication is that the site with the highest frequency of mounds was not necessarily the largest or most powerful site in the local settlement system at any one point in time.

Sixth, ceremonial activities are associated with all platform mound types and functions. Mound construction, including that of even the smallest residential mounds built by household or extended household labor, is always accompanied by some sort of religious sanctification that usually involves feasting and food redistribution.

And finally, mounds are commonly used as territorial markers. They are ostentatious features generally built to be seen from a distance, and one of their functions, as indicated by the ethnographic data, is to demarcate descent group territory. Among the Mapuche, platform mounds are used to legitimize lineage land claims by marking long-term occupation of a particular area (Dillehay 1990). Although a territorial function is not present among all mound types and all cultural groups, it appears to be generally true for the larger classes of mounds built with communal labor.

Ceramic Distribution in Canal System 2

Recent research involving platform mound sites in Canal System 2 of the Phoenix area provides new information on the social networks of prehistoric mound-building groups (Abbott 1994a, 1994b, 2000). Canal System 2 is one of four major Phoenix-area canal systems with headgates on the Salt River. In the Soho (ca. A.D. 1150–1275) and Civano (ca. A.D. 1275–1375) phases of the Hohokam Classic period, the time of most platform mound construction, Canal System 2 contained ten platform mounds spread over eight large main canals (Figure 7.4). The canals emanated from headgates near Pueblo Grande, and most ended near the site of Las Colinas, some 10 kilometers to the west (Howard and Huckleberry 1991). As first noted by Gregory and Nials (1985) and Gregory (1987), mounds in the Phoenix Basin are regularly spaced every 5–8 kilometers along irrigation canals, strongly suggesting that they functioned in the management of the hydraulic infrastructure.

Through patterns of ceramic exchange from a large sample of plain ware ceramics, Canal System 2 was likely coterminous with a cohesive social grouping during the Early Classic period. At that time, plain ware pots were commonly exchanged among the residents in Canal System 2 from one end of the system to the other, crosscutting both mound and non-mound sites. However, few plain ware containers were transported across canal-system boundaries, even between villages that were proximally situated on opposite sides of the Salt River.

This pattern of ceramic exchange can be interpreted in social terms, suggesting that the residents in Canal System 2 shared numerous social and, presumably, kinship connections with one another (Abbott 2000). The movement of vessels within the canal system was so intensive that instead of the system being composed of a number of allied but otherwise unrelated groups, it was more likely to have contained a single, socially bounded community. This is supported by ethnographic data that suggest that utili-

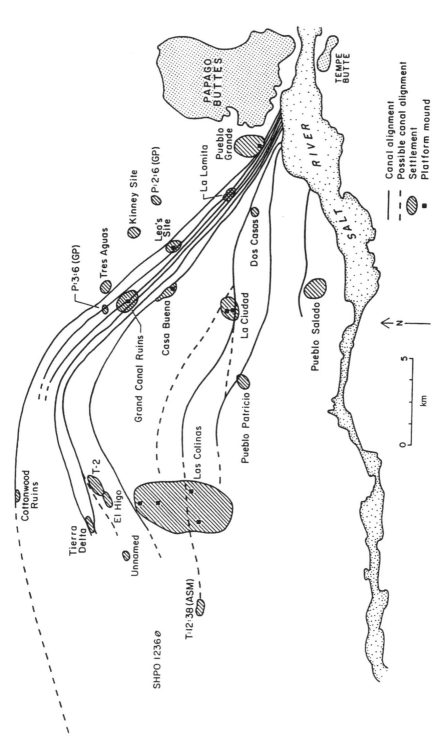

FIGURE 7.4. Canal System 2 during the Classic period (after Howard and Huckleberry 1991).

tarian pottery primarily moves within limited and closely connected social networks (Stark 1993, 1995, 1998). The presence of these horizontal and crosscutting relationships, then, implies that the managerial structure did not depend on powerful elites or some other form of coercion at the end of the canal system to assure agricultural success throughout the cooperative.

The Soho phase social pattern broke down during the following Civano phase. Utilitarian ceramics from other Phoenix Basin canal systems entered Canal System 2 in appreciable numbers, suggesting the formation of new exchange networks and social connections with people on the opposite side of the river. In addition, the social networks participated in by different domestic units within villages were reconfigured so that some residence groups were pulled closer together, while other residence groups in the same settlement were largely excluded. For example, at Pueblo Grande, a set of residence groups were more closely tied to one another and with people across the river than they were to other domestic units in their own village. Other residence groups at Pueblo Grande were more provincial in their social networks, engaging in exchange relationships primarily within their own community (see Abbott 2000).

The Organization of Southwestern Mound-Building Groups

Recent research by Doelle and colleagues (1995) has indicated that the platform mounds can be divided into six spatially discrete clusters: the lower Salt River, middle Gila River, Tonto Basin, Tucson Basin, lower San Pedro River, and Papaguería, with a more-or-less diffuse cluster in the northern Tucson Basin/Picacho Peak area (see Figure 7.1). There are significant differences between clusters in the size, diversity, and number of platform mounds (Table 7.1). The Salt River cluster is by far the largest, containing more platform mound sites with more mounds than any other. Size data show that the mounds along the Salt River are also significantly larger by a factor of almost two than the mounds in the other clusters, and at least three distinct types of mounds have been recognized—true platform mounds, tower mounds, and great houses (Doelle, Gregory, and Wallace 1995; Elson 1998). Although the total number of measured mounds for all clusters is somewhat small, encompassing around a third of the known mounds (and some systems, like the Salt River, are skewed by a few relatively large mounds, hence the large standard deviations in Table 7.1), these data are thought to be generally representative. It is likely, given the ethnographic data and the wide range in the Phoenix Basin mound sizes, that

Table 7.1 VOLUME OF PLATFORM MOUNDS (IN CUBIC METERS) IN MOUND CLUSTERS IN CENTRAL AND SOUTHERN ARIZONA (DATA FROM ELSON 1998:TABLE 6.1).

System	No. of Mounds	No. of Mounds Measured	Range (m³)	Average (m³)	Standard Deviation
Lower Salt	43	4	1,584–14,000	8,063	5,949.4
Middle Gila	13	4	1,056–4,050	2,119	1,145.0
Tonto Basin	26	7	300–2,142	864	578.0
Tucson Basin	7	3	257–892	512	335.3
Lower San Pedro	14	10	111–538	316	165.7
Papaguería	8	7	130–476	230	116.9
Northern Tucson Basin	6	4	788–2,360	1,617	709.2

Note: Platform mounds of less than 100 m³, which may have been tower mounds, are excluded. Based on data from Doelle (1995) and Doelle, Gregory, and Wallace (1995).

more than the three currently recognized types of mounds were present and that the mounds had varying functions.

The Salt River cluster can be contrasted with the other mound groups, which have fewer and smaller mounds with more limited diversity. In the Tonto and northern Tucson Basins, the two best-researched outlying areas, each mound cluster and associated irrigation system appears to contain one or, at most, two platform mounds (Elson, Stark, and Gregory 1996; Fish and Fish 1992). Although irrigation agriculture was practiced in these areas, its scale and importance were far less than in the Phoenix Basin. Furthermore, unlike Phoenix Basin mounds, which were used and remodeled over relatively long periods of time, the great majority of mound sites investigated in the outlying areas appeared suddenly and were relatively short-lived, with little evidence for extensive remodeling. Temporal information suggests a thirty- to fifty-year span for the few mounds with available data. The mounds were also initially constructed at a date significantly later than the Phoenix Basin mounds. In the Tonto Basin, which is the best dated group, mounds first appeared around A.D. 1275, some seventy-five to a hundred years later than similar mound forms in the Phoenix Basin (Elson 1995, 1998). The temporal lag in mound development in the outlying areas strongly suggests that some form of emulation of Phoenix Basin mounds was occurring. However, as we discuss below, this circumstance does not necessarily mean that the mound clusters were equivalent or that they had identical leadership and forms of social organization.

What can the analysis of historic mound builders combined with the results of the study of ceramic exchange in Canal System 2 tell us about the leadership structure of these groups? First of all, perhaps the most important point is that both the historic analysis and the ceramic data strongly suggest that during the Soho phase, Canal System 2 was a bounded community with social organization most likely based on kinship. The plain ware exchange pattern indicates that the social networks crosscut the platform mounds and individual settlements within the canal system. This idea is supported by the historic analysis that showed that among middle-range groups, platform mounds were primarily constructed and used by descent groups. Although mounds for individual use were built by the Natchez, Marquesans, Samoans, Yap, and Mapuche, all of these leaders were part of a larger set of codescendants who traced their common heritage to an apical ancestor, and the mounds reflected overall group membership and status.

We suspect that the Soho phase congruency between Canal System 2 and a socially bounded community was repeated in other canal systems and may have been stimulated by the partial collapse of the Hohokam regional system. At the beginning of the Classic period, large upland tracts north of the Salt River Valley were abandoned, and numerous platform mounds sprang up along the Salt and Gila Rivers. We suggest that platform mound construction and immigration were connected. As immigrants streamed into the riverine zones, a need to formalize and mark territories ensued. The irrigation-based communities built platform mounds, and on their tops were usually placed one or two pit structures of an anachronistic style. These constructions may be related to ancestor worship and possibly marked possession of the irrigable land and hydraulic infrastructure by affiliating the mounds with particular ancestor spirits and their living descendants (see also Abbott 2000).

By the Civano phase, the web of social networks in the Phoenix area was reconfigured at a time when some mound tops became crowded with what many (but not all; see Bostwick and Downum 1994) analysts believe was residential architecture. Some small, side-by-side platform mounds (such as at Pueblo Grande) were encased in a single massive construction, others were substantially enlarged, and a new diversity of mound types and sizes was created. As the utilitarian wares indicate, the social order was one in which communities were no longer aligned with individual canal systems, suggesting that the relationship between irrigation management and the sociopolitical organization had been altered. And, based on the ethnographic and ethnohistoric data, the larger size and diversity of the mound complexes suggest that at this time social differentiation and ranking among subgroups and individuals became more pronounced, although there is admittedly little artifact evidence to support this. It is possible that changes seen at this time are also partly related to immigration, although the exact relationship between migrant groups and Civano phase changes is currently unclear. However, the start of the Civano phase corresponds to a time of environmental stress when large areas of the northern Southwest were being depopulated (Cameron 1995; Clark 1997; Dean, Doelle, and Orcutt 1994), and, although difficult to discern archaeologically, it is likely that some migrants were relocating into the well-watered Phoenix Basin.

We speculate that by the Civano phase the subgroups of highest rank may have become directly associated with the mounds themselves, regardless of whether the mound top was inhabited or not. The Civano phase platform mounds within Canal System 2 were of varying sizes, with Pueblo Grande, at the head of the canal system, being by far the largest (Table 7.1). The construction of the Pueblo Grande platform necessitated a much greater outlay of labor and resources than did the construction of the other mounds. Although the relationship between the large and small mounds within each canal system and their degree of contemporaneity are not clear, it is possible that the smaller mound sites represent the home of related but lower ranked leaders of the same subgroup.

The non-elite members of the descent group, who constituted the majority of the population and were most likely spread over a number of different kin-based subgroups, lived in the habitation areas of the mound villages and in the small hamlets and farmsteads. As the ceramic data demonstrate, group membership was not localized by village; instead, the various social networks crosscut the settlements to a considerable degree.

The dual-processual leadership framework recently proposed by Feinman (1995) and Blanton and his colleagues (1996a) may fit well with the prehistoric Hohokam data. This model of corporate- or network-based leadership strategies represents alternative paths toward inequality. The corporate strategy is group oriented and knowledge based and emphasizes kinship affiliation and minimal economic differentiation, whereas the network strategy is individual oriented and wealth based and is focused on personal long-distance exchange and alliance, often with nonkin, and the gaining of prestige (Blanton et al. 1996a:6; Feinman 1995:268). As Feinman (1995:264) notes, while the two may be seen as parts of a continuum, they are structurally antagonistic, and therefore one mode may dominate at any point in time.

The ethnographic and ethnohistoric analysis found that a combination of both network and corporate political-economic strategies was present among all mound-building groups; no group used one strategy to the complete exclusion of the other. Among the Yap, Marquesans, and Natchez, for example, tribute and trade were the domains of the group leader, who amassed personal wealth for redistribution at feasts and other social events, thereby gaining individual status. Corporate structure, however, was the predominant mode in all analyzed historic groups. This emphasis is indicated by the overall orientation of the mounds as belonging to the entire descent group. Even if the mound itself was inhabited, it was generally used to glorify the group rather than a specific individual. Many, although not all, of the mounds were also used as locales for learning and distributing ritual knowledge, supporting the statements by Feinman (1995:268) and Blanton and his colleagues (1996a:6) that public architecture is commonly associated with a corporate strategy.

There is an interesting relationship between the presence of network or exclusionary strategies in the historic groups and platform mound characteristics. That is, as network behavior increases, so do the size and diversity of the platform mounds, the energy invested in mound construction, and, therefore, the authority and power of group leaders. This relationship is clearly illustrated in the historic analysis, where the collection of goods by leaders through tribute or formalized trading expeditions played a much larger role in groups such as the Yap, Marquesans, and Natchez, who had either a great diversity in mound types, or very large mounds, or both. Leaders of these groups were the most powerful and individually wealthy in the analysis. By contrast, accumulation of goods played little role in the social systems of groups with small mounds of limited diversity.

These data suggest several points. For one, a corporate strategy was most likely the dominant mode of leadership at prehistoric Southwestern platform mound communities. This is true for both the Early and Late Classic periods and is based on the association of ritual goods and features with some mounds and the generally accepted function of the mounds as group-oriented integrative locales for the collection and dispensing of ritual knowledge and power (Bostwick and Downum 1994; Craig and Clark 1994; Doyel 1981; Elson 1994; Fish, Fish, and Madsen 1992; Jacobs and Rice 1997). However, it is also possible that groups with larger and more diverse mounds, such as those in the Phoenix Basin during the Late Clas-

sic period Civano phase, had leaders who used a more mixed network/
corporate strategy.

During the Civano phase, elite households may have taken possession of
the mounds at a time when the association between canal system and
community was significantly altered. Along with it, the corporate basis for
leadership may have been remodeled to include a greater emphasis on
network behavior. This new foundation for inequality included alliances
with people outside the canal system and, perhaps, depended on the factionalism that became pronounced at Pueblo Grande (and presumably
elsewhere) during the Late Classic period. The ceramic data clearly indicate changes in the social system, which possibly involved leaders pursuing
new strategies for consolidating authority and power.

The platform mounds outside of the Phoenix Basin appear to have been
used by leaders with a more corporate leadership strategy. In these systems,
although the ethnographic and ethnohistoric data indicate that ranked
leaders were present, the smaller size and limited diversity of the mounds
suggests that social differentiation was not as extreme as in the Phoenix
Basin during the Late Classic and that the mounds may have been primarily
the property of the entire descent group instead of a single highly ranked
subgroup. These leaders had higher status, may have been deferred to,
accumulated greater resources than others, were the repositories of ritual
knowledge, and probably controlled the redistribution of selected goods
but in general were probably not that much different from the rest of the
group. Although in the Tonto Basin, for example, there is differential
distribution of some artifact types, there is little evidence that the mound
sites contained significantly higher quantities of any type of manufactured
goods (Jacobs and Rice 1994; Stark 1995). Differential distribution of certain high value or exotic goods, however, has been claimed for the Marana
mound village in the northern Tucson Basin (Bayman 1994; Fish and Fish
1992; Harry 1997), and it is possible, if not likely, that each mound system
contained varying combinations of network and corporate behavior.

Given the temporal priority of Phoenix Basin mounds, the mounds in
the outlying systems likely stemmed from some form of emulation and
were perhaps associated with a larger ideological system, the nature of
which is at present unclear. As noted above, however, this does not necessarily mean that the form of social organization was also emulated (see also
Doelle, Gregory, and Wallace 1995:438–39). Mounds in the outlying areas
may have also been initially constructed to consolidate and mark descent
group territory; there is a direct correlation between the appearance of

mounds in some outlying systems and the onset of environmental and social stress, including immigration of culturally distinct populations, that affected large areas of the Southwest after A.D. 1250. Prior to this time, the physical marking of territories with imposing architecture may not have been as critically important.

Conclusion

Our discussion indicates that traditional neo-evolutionary models for social organization fail to adequately explain the variability found among both historic mound-using groups and those of the prehistoric past. Although the ethnographic data strongly indicate that hierarchically ranked leaders were present in all platform mound–building groups, and we suggest that these leaders, both religious and secular, were directly associated with the mounds themselves, we also suggest that crosscutting social relationships were equally critical in the functioning of the various platform mounds and canal systems. Data from the ethnographic and ethnohistoric analysis of mound-building groups show that these relationships were based along kinship lines and that the platform mounds themselves were associated with specific descent groups. On the other hand, we recognize the possibility that other, non-kinship-based forms of crosscutting social organization, such as sodalities or work groups, may have also been present. These other facets of Hohokam social organization remain to be examined with the increasing wealth of archaeological data and judicious use of the ethnographic record.

ACKNOWLEDGMENTS

The authors would like to thank Barbara Mills for inviting us to participate in this volume and for her comments on this paper. Comments from two anonymous reviewers were also helpful. Research into historic platform mound–building groups was facilitated by comments and general support from Charles Adams, Jeffrey Dean, Barbara Mills, Alice Schlegel, Thomas Sheridan, Deborah Swartz, and Desert Archaeology, Inc. Institutional support for the ceramic analysis came from the Arizona Department of Transportation and Soil Systems, Inc. The ceramic analysis was aided by loans from the Pueblo Grande Museum, Arizona State Museum, Arizona State University, Mesa Southwest Museum, and Museum of Northern Arizona. Additional funding for the ceramic analysis was provided by a Robert H. Lister Fellowship in Southwest Archaeology from Crow Canyon Archaeological Center, National Science Foundation (Grant: DBC9201161), and Sigma Xi Grants-in-Aide-of-Research.

8

Leadership Strategies among the Classic Period Hohokam

A Case Study

KAREN G. HARRY AND JAMES M. BAYMAN

ARCHAEOLOGISTS HAVE STRUGGLED to identify appropriate models to describe the social, political, and economic organization of prehistoric societies within the Greater Southwest. In the 1970s and 1980s, Southwestern literature was dominated by debates that derived from the explicit or implicit use of neo-evolutionary models. These debates focused on the level of complexity present in prehistoric societies and what place they should be assigned on the evolutionary scale (for a partial review of these debates, see McGuire and Saitta 1996). In recent years, however, it has become increasingly apparent that neo-evolutionary models are inadequate for explaining the range of variation present in prehistoric Southwestern societies (Fish and Yoffee 1996). As a result, new models, based on such concepts as simultaneous versus sequential hierarchies (Johnson 1982), heterarchy (Rautman 1998), dialectics (McGuire and Saitta 1996), and corporate versus network leadership strategies (Blanton et al. 1996a; Feinman 1995), are being examined.

The most public of these discussions has focused on the puebloan Southwest. Similar theoretical trends, however, have characterized the Hohokam culture area. Whereas studies in the 1980s focused on whether the Hohokam had achieved a chiefdom-level society (Ciolek-Torrello and Wilcox 1988; Rice 1987c, 1990), more recent researchers (Bayman 1995; Fish and Yoffee 1996; Yoffee, Fish, and Milner 1999) have questioned the adequacy of models based on evolutionary theory to describe Hohokam society. Accumulating evidence further suggests that substantial organizational variation existed between Hohokam communities, even among those that were contemporaneous. As a result, we contend that any discussion of Hohokam social organization must be presented on a case-by-case basis,

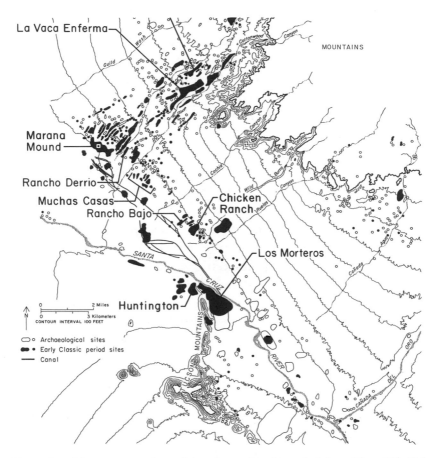

FIGURE 8.1. Marana community and sites discussed in this study (adapted from Fish, Fish, and Madsen 1992:fig. 3.2).

using available archaeological data. This essay presents just such a study. Here we examine the strategies used by the leaders of one Hohokam political entity—the Marana community of southern Arizona—to solidify and strengthen their power within the community.

Research Setting

The Marana community is a vast multisite community located just north of the Tucson Basin (Figure 8.1). It is defined by an Early Classic (ca. A.D. 1100–1300) period cluster of habitation, agricultural, and miscellaneous activity sites, around which lies an uninhabited buffer zone (Fish, Fish, and Madsen 1992). The community spans an area of 146 square kilometers and contains more than two dozen habitation sites. Based on site size, visible architectural remains, and ceramic assemblages, Fish, Fish, and Madsen (1989) have demonstrated that a three-tiered settlement hierarchy was present. The largest habitation site contains the platform mound. Centrally located within the community, the Marana platform mound site spans a 1.5-by-1.0-kilometer area and contains the remains of between twenty-two and twenty-five residential compounds (Fish, Fish, Brennan, Gann, and Bayman 1992).

The area encompassed by the Marana community contains Preclassic as well as Early Classic period sites, although the densest occupations occurred during the Classic period. During the Preclassic period the area contained two dispersed site clusters, one centered on the floodplain and lower bajada and a second on the upper bajada (Fish, Fish, and Madsen 1992). Each of these communities contained a single site with a ball court that undoubtedly served as the focal point for its respective community. Despite these similarities, there is evidence that the two communities maintained slightly different cultural affiliations. Whereas the lowland community is characterized by high percentages of decorated ceramics associated with the Tucson Basin, sites in the upland settlement cluster exhibit low proportions of these wares. These data suggest that the lowland community maintained closer ties with sites in the Tucson Basin than did sites in the upland community. By the end of the early twelfth century, the two ball courts were abandoned, and a new habitation site—the Marana platform mound village—was founded in the previously unoccupied middle bajada. Coincident with these changes, additional villages were also settled in the middle bajada, resulting in the coalescence of the two communities into one larger community focused on the centrally located platform mound village.

The Early Classic community incorporated both newly established and previously occupied settlements. Of the habitation sites discussed in this essay, the middle bajada sites (the sites of Marana Mound, Rancho Derrio, Muchas Casas, Rancho Bajo, and Chicken Ranch) were established at the terminal Preclassic/Early Classic transition. The remaining sites all have Preclassic components. Three of the sites (Casa de Piedras, La Vaca Enferma, and Sueño de Saguaro) are located in the upland zone and were affiliated with the upland community during the Preclassic period. The remaining two sites (Los Morteros and Huntington) are located in the lowland zone and were affiliated with the Preclassic lowland community (Table 8.1; see Figure 8.1). Several lines of evidence suggest that by the start of the Classic period, the residents of these and the newly founded hamlets had integrated into a single functioning community. This evidence

Table 8.1 INTERSITE COMPARISONS.

Site	Preclassic Affiliation	Classic Period Occupation				
		Percent Tanque Verde Red-on-brown Ceramics	Standardized Exotic Pottery Count	Standardized Shell Count	Standardized Obsidian Count	No. of Sherds in Sample
Middle Bajada Sites						
Marana Mound[1]	Unoccupied	18.7	2.8	34.2	7.6	14,387
Rancho Derrio/ Muchas Casas/ Rancho Bajo[1]	Unoccupied	3.4	0.0	12.1	0.4	2,314
Chicken Ranch[2]	Unoccupied	8.5	N/A	N/A	N/A	744
Lowland Sites						
Los Morteros[3]	Lowland Community	20.8	2.0	26.5	12.4	3,960
Huntington	Lowland Community	high	N/A	N/A	N/A	N/A
Upland Sites						
Casa de Piedras/La Vaca Enferma[1]	Upland Community	<4	0.0	8.8	0.8	1,251
Sueño de Saguaro[2]	Upland Community	<4	N/A	N/A	N/A	264

[1] Data derive from excavated midden contexts.

[2] Data derive from surface collections.

[3] Data derive from excavated midden contexts. Includes all sherds from single-component, Classic period trash deposits. Information for Los Morteros derives from Wallace (1995).

N/A = data not available.

includes the presence of a settlement hierarchy surrounded by an unoccupied buffer zone, the existence of a single, centrally located platform mound, and the occurrence of an irrigation canal that connected the sites of Los Morteros and Marana Mound (Fish, Fish, and Madsen 1992).

Some form of institutionalized leadership almost certainly existed within the Marana community. This is suggested by the presence of a single platform mound, utilized by all members of the community. Additionally, administration above the village level would have been required to oversee the functioning of the irrigation canal. Because floods can wash out headgates and cause silt to accumulate (see Ackerly, Howard, and McGuire 1987; Haury 1976), mobilization of large crews would have been required to maintain the canal in working condition. Such leadership would also have been needed to oversee water allocation. Significantly, the platform mound village was located at the terminus of the canal. If those residents were to be assured of receiving water from the canal, they must have had some type of control over the amount of water that could be diverted upstream. The mechanisms by which the leaders maintained and developed their power are discussed in the following sections.

The Role of Monumental Architecture

Substantial debate has focused on the degree of social complexity indicated by platform mounds. Some archaeologists propose that the labor investments required to build the mounds could only have been met in a relatively complex society, characterized by strong leadership and subsistence surpluses (Doyel 1974; Neitzel 1991). Others have argued that because the mounds were built in stages, labor requirements would not have been particularly high (Craig, Elson, and Wood 1992). Regardless of the subsistence and leadership needs, the Marana platform mound almost certainly reflects the presence of some form of institutional leadership. Despite its relatively small size (900 cubic meters), the mound could only have been constructed through a group effort. Once the mound was constructed, most members of the group were excluded from direct access. The private nature of the mound is indicated by the presence of an encircling compound wall (Fish, Fish, Brennan, Gann, and Bayman 1992). Within this wall are several rooms used as domestic residences; this function is indicated by the nature of the midden refuse (see Bayman 1994:19; Bubemyre 1993).

There are several important points that can be drawn from this description of the Marana platform mound. Clearly, this feature was not available to all members of the community. Rather, access to the mound appears to have been reserved for the leaders residing within the mound compound. These leaders maintained exclusive control over an important symbol of societal power. Despite the fact that the mound could not be used directly by most members of the community, it almost certainly served an important community function. It is centrally located within both the mound village and the larger community and likely served as a ritual and/or political symbol for community members. By maintaining exclusive access to this symbol, the leaders could have solidified their social power (see Fish and Yoffee 1996; Preucel 1996; Yoffee, Fish, and Milner 1999).

Organization of Production, Distribution, and Consumption

CONSUMPTION OF HIGH VALUE ITEMS

Because high value goods can be used to attract followers and as symbols of power, they may be an important source of societal power. In this section, the distribution of four high value goods is examined. These are obsidian, shell, exotic pottery, and locally produced decorated pottery. Here, exotic pottery refers to that believed to have originated outside of the Tucson Basin and adjacent areas. Locally produced pottery includes that believed to have been produced in or adjacent to the Tucson Basin. The high value of these four types of goods is inferred from the costs associated with their procurement and/or their production.

Intersite Distributions.   A comparison of the distribution between sites of these goods is presented in Table 8.1. The data in this table derive from both surface and excavation data (see Bayman and Sanchez 1998 for information regarding the comparability of the data). Tanque Verde Red-on-brown is the predominant decorated ware produced locally. To compare the frequency of this ware recovered between sites, the proportion of Tanque Verde Red-on-brown in the recovered ceramic collection was calculated. The data in Table 8.1 indicate that these ceramics were most frequent at the Marana Mound site and Los Morteros. A third site, Huntington, is likely characterized by similarly high proportions, although the data are not quantified. A fourth site, Chicken Ranch, exhibits fewer of these ceramics but more than the remaining sites.

To compare the amount of exotic pottery, shell, and obsidian recovered, standardized counts were obtained by calculating the number of artifacts per thousand sherds. Where the data are available, they indicate that frequencies of these items follow that of Tanque Verde Red-on-brown ceramics. As before, the sites of Marana Mound and Los Morteros exhibit the highest proportion of high value goods. Together, these data indicate that the residents of the sites located near the top of the settlement hierarchy were able to consume a higher proportion of high value goods.

Intrasite Distributions. To determine whether residents of the platform mound compound consumed higher quantities of high value goods than other households in the same village, Bayman (1994) conducted an intrasite analysis of artifact distributions. Data were obtained from eighteen middens within the site, each located at varying distances from the platform mound. These data, presented in Bayman (1994: Figures 5.1 and 5.2), indicate that there exists little patterned variation in intrasite distributions of decorated sherds, shell, and obsidian. This suggests that there was little economic differentiation between the elite leaders living nearest the mound and other households within the village.

ORGANIZATION OF PRODUCTION AND DISTRIBUTION

It has been proposed that the Hohokam elite strengthened their political power through the economic control of production and distribution (Neitzel 1991; Rice 1987c; Teague 1984, 1985, 1989a). This conclusion, however, is generally based on indirect evidence such as settlement pattern or the differential distribution of artifact classes. In this section, direct evidence is examined to assess the organization of production and distribution for three types of goods: shell, obsidian, and Tanque Red-on-brown ceramics.

Shell. The production of shell artifacts is often inferred to have been centralized at platform mounds and to have been under elite control (Howard 1985; McGuire 1985; McGuire and Howard 1987; Teague 1989b). These inferences derive primarily from evidence of shell working at platform mound sites. Without comparative data from nonmound sites and from specific proveniences within mound sites, however, these conclusions remain speculative.

The data discussed above indicate that standardized shell-to-sherd ratios differ significantly between sites. Without additional data, it is impossible to determine whether these patterns reflect differential production or differential consumption of shell artifacts. Regardless, it is clear that the production of shell artifacts was not elite controlled. If this had been the case, shell should have been concentrated near the platform mound compound. Further evidence supporting this conclusion derives from a consideration

Table 8.2 CERAMIC AND OBSIDIAN COUNTS FROM MARANA COMMUNITY MIDDENS (DATA FROM BAYMAN 1995:TABLE 1).

Site(s)	Ceramics	Unmodified Nodule	Core/Split Cobble	Flake/ Shatter	Unfinished Point	Finished Point
Marana Mound	14,387	1	22	63	5	17
Muchas Casas/ Rancho Bajo/ Rancho Derrio	2,317	0	0	1	0	0
Sueño de Saguaro/Casa de Piedras	1,251	0	0	0	0	2
TOTAL	17,955	1	22	4	5	19

of the ratio of shell consumption to shell production artifacts (see Bayman 1996: Figure 11). Because consumption to production ratios do not vary with distance from the platform mound, the data support the interpretation that shell ornament production was not correlated with proximity to the platform mound and indicate that shell ornament production was spatially widespread at the platform mound settlement.

Obsidian. In a previous study, Bayman (1996) found that obsidian production debris was more frequent at the platform mound village than it was at other villages examined in the community (Table 8.2). This indicates that, relative to the residents of some other sites in the community, the inhabitants of the Marana Mound village emphasized the production of obsidian tools. Because comparative data are not available for other sites near the top of the settlement hierarchy, such as Los Morteros or Huntington, it is unknown whether these other settlements also emphasized obsidian production or whether it was restricted to the mound settlement. Significantly, however, within the mound village obsidian production debris was not concentrated near the mound vicinities (Bayman 1995:44).

To examine whether obsidian was centrally redistributed from the platform mound village, obsidian sourcing data are compared from different sites in the community. We propose that if distribution was centralized, then a similar proportion and diversity of compositional groups should be represented at different sites in the community (Alden 1982; Graves 1991; Longacre and Stark 1992; Pires-Ferreira 1975). Table 8.3 lists the obsidian

Table 8.3 GEOLOGIC SOURCES OF OBSIDIAN FROM THE MARANA MOUND SITE AND ASU SITES.

Source	Marana Mound Site		Muchas Casas / Rancho Bajo / Rancho Derrio	
	n	%	n	%
Sauceda	77	70.6	68	97.1
Vulture	8	7.3	—	—
Superior	4	3.7	2	2.9
Mule Creek	7	6.4	—	—
Cow Canyon	2	1.8	—	—
Unknown "A"	3	2.8	—	—
Unsourced	8	7.3	—	—
TOTAL	109	100	70	100

sourcing data available from the Marana community. This table shows that the residents of the Marana Mound site obtained obsidian from a greater number of sources than did the residents of Muchas Casas, Rancho Derrio, and Rancho Bajo. Furthermore, the diversity of sources differs between the two groups. In particular, the three nonmound sites are characterized by a higher proportion of Sauceda obsidian than the Marana Mound site. Although compositional data are not published for obsidian from other sites in the community, Bayman (1996) reports that one of two obsidian artifacts sourced from sites (i.e., from La Vaca Enferma and Casa de Piedras) in the upland area of the Marana community came from Mule Creek. Because Mule Creek obsidian is rare in the Marana Mound collection (6.4 percent) and is absent from the Muchas Casas, Rancho Bajo, and Rancho Derrio samples, Bayman tentatively interprets this as evidence that the upland residents emphasized interaction networks different from those of the residents of the lowland sites.

These compositional patterns support the interpretation that the residents of the nonmound sites obtained their obsidian through independent exchange rather than through redistribution mechanisms centered at the platform mound village. Because obsidian has not been sourced from other sites in the community, however, it is unknown whether the sites near the top of the settlement hierarchy obtained their obsidian though centralized exchange networks.

Tanque Verde Red-on-brown Ceramics. As a part of two larger studies (Harry 1997; Fish, Fish, Whittlesey, Neff, Glascock, and Elam 1992), sherds from the Marana community were compositionally analyzed. These sherds derive from Tanque Verde Red-on-brown vessels, the primary decorated ware found in the community. Mineralogical and chemical analyses were conducted on 416 sherds. The mineralogical study focused on the aplastic inclusions in the sherds and built upon more than a decade of petrographic research in the region. This study was conducted by researchers from the Center for Desert Archeology and is more fully reported by Harry (1997), Heidke and Wiley (1997), and Heidke and his colleagues (1997). The mineralogical analysis consisted of the binocular examination of all analyzed sherds, during which the sand temper in each sherd was identified as to tectonic origin and, when possible, to a specific petrofacies or area containing mineralogically distinct sands. No sherds were identified as containing sands from the Tortolita petrofacies, the petrofacies within which the Marana Mound site is located (Harry 1997; Harry, Fish, and Fish 1998; Heidke and Wiley 1997; Heidke et al. 1997). This suggests that few or no Tanque Verde Red-on-brown vessels were produced at the Marana platform mound village and that the production of these wares was neither conducted nor controlled by the community's elite.

The chemical analysis was conducted using neutron activation analysis at the Missouri University Research Reactor Facility and is more fully reported by Harry (1997). Data reduction was based on the concentration of thirty-two elements and involved the use of a variety of techniques, including cluster analysis, the examination of bivariate plots, principal components analysis, and the calculation of Mahalanobis distances. These procedures resulted in the identification of six compositional groups in the Marana community (Table 8.4). In Table 8.4, those habitation sites having a sample of at least twenty-nine analyzed sherds are presented individually; sherds from the remaining sites are combined and simply reported as deriving from "other habitation" or "other" site. The data from this table are graphically illustrated in Figure 8.2.

Four of the six habitation sites (Marana Mound, Los Morteros, Huntington, and Chicken Ranch) studied exhibit similar proportions of Tanque Verde Red-on-brown ceramics. These patterns suggest that the residents of the four sites maintained similar exchange networks. Elsewhere, Harry (1997; Harry, Fish, and Fish 1998) has suggested that the patterns most likely result from the exchange of Tanque Verde Red-on-brown vessels through some sort of centralized distribution network. To evaluate whether this

Table 8.4 NUMBER OF SHERDS, BY PROVENIENCE, ASSIGNED TO EACH CHEMICAL COMPOSITIONAL GROUP.

Provenience	A	BC	E	F	G	South Tucson	Unassigned	TOTAL
Marana Mound								
Mound proveniences	—	18	—	—	1	—	22	41
Nonmound proveniences	49	40	6	—	1	1	72	169
Total sites	*49*	*58*	*6*	—	*2*	*1*	*94*	*210*
Los Morteros	10	12	1	1	—	—	11	35
Huntington	8	7	1	—	—	—	13	29
Chicken Ranch	8	11	2	—	—	1	10	32
La Vaca Enferma/ Sueño de Saguaro	1	—	2	—	17	—	18	38
Muchas Casas	1	—	1	17	—	—	12	31
Other Habitation	3	4	1	—	1	—	16	25
Other[1]	3	1	4	—	2	—	6	16
TOTAL	83	93	18	18	22	2	180	416

[1] Refers to nonhabitation sites and sites of unknown function.

network was controlled by the residents living in the mound compound, ceramics from near the platform mound are compared against those from other proveniences (see Table 8.4). These data show that distribution was not elite controlled, an interpretation supported by the absence of some groups (especially Group A but also Group E) from the mound proveniences that are frequent in the collections from the other areas of Marana Mound, Los Morteros, Huntington, and Chicken Ranch.

Significantly, the four sites (Marana Mound, Los Morteros, Huntington, and Chicken Ranch) exhibiting similar compositional diversity are those sites in the Marana community having the highest proportion of Tanque Verde Red-on-brown ceramics. This suggests that sites near the top of the settlement hierarchy participated in centralized exchange networks from which the smaller sites were excluded. To obtain Tanque Verde Red-on-brown vessels, residents of the latter sites cultivated and maintained independent exchange ties. Both reciprocal and centralized exchange mecha-

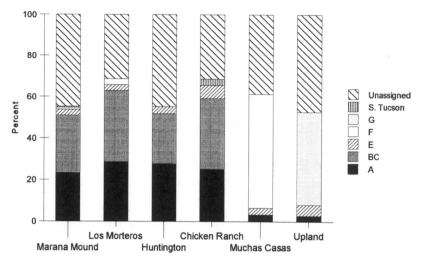

FIGURE 8.2. Graph of ceramic compositional group frequencies for various sites.

nisms, then, appear to have been responsible for the movement of Tanque Verde Red-on-brown ceramics within the Marana community. This information suggests that distribution mechanisms do not fall neatly into any one category. Sites near the top of the hierarchy participated in centralized exchange, but other sites were excluded from these networks and instead maintained independent trade ties.

Leadership Strategies in the Marana Community

The evidence indicates that a mixture of leadership strategies was used in the Marana community. As is so often the case with human behavior, the strategies do not neatly meet the expectations of any one model. Here, we summarize how the leaders used ritual and high value items to increase their social power, followed by an examination of why the leaders selected the particular mix of strategies that they did.

The nature of the platform mound indicates the use of exclusionary ritual by the elite. Access to the mound was not available to all in the community but, rather, was restricted to those living within its compound wall and presumably whoever else was invited to enter. This is in marked contrast to ritual indicated for other periods and areas of the Southwest. In the Pueblo region, kivas were the primary form of religious architecture. Unlike the Marana platform mound, these structures were intended to be used by all members of a clan or subgroup (see Fish and Fish, this volume). In the Preclassic Hohokam, the primary form of communal architecture was the ball court. The accessibility and public nature of these features suggest that they were intended to be used by all members of the community. The differences between these various forms of ritual architecture suggest that the Classic period Hohokam had a very different (more exclusionary) ritual power base than did other populations of the Greater Southwest. As Preucel (1996:126) has stated, "It is likely that the ritual practices performed in connection with ball courts publicly validated the status of the lineage head (men or women) in the eyes of commoners whereas the rituals performed in private in residential compounds upon platform mounds established and maintained special relationships between local and foreign elites."

In contrast to the exclusionary nature of the ritual activities, the economic system was characterized by both inclusionary and exclusionary aspects. If we define the "elite" as those individuals living within the platform mound compound, then they do not appear to have been significantly wealthier than other individuals in the same village. Wealth differences, however, did occur between the residents of the largest villages and those of smaller settlements, as indicated by the differential distribution of high value goods. How could high value goods have been manipulated to increase social or political power? None of these goods were inaccessible to the nonelite members of the community, thus they do not qualify as "luxury" or "elite" goods as typically conceived. The association of these artifacts with other status indicators, however, suggests that they functioned as wealth items and that their differential consumption reflects social and economic differences. Brumfiel and Earle (1987) refer to these items as *generalized wealth* and propose that these goods were used to meet social payments and to develop a body of supporters. Because the elite could "afford" to acquire more of these goods than could other people, they served to increase the social and political power of the wealthiest individuals.

As with consumption, production and distribution reflect a mixture of strategies. None of the artifact classes examined were produced exclusively or even primarily at the platform mound, indicating that production was not elite controlled. Yet there is some indication that production differences occurred between *villages*. Despite the high proportion (18.7 percent of the ceramic collection) of Tanque Verde Red-on-brown ceramics consumed at the Marana Mound site, virtually none of the 210 sherds examined from that site were produced there. This information implies that part-time pottery specialists who resided at other settlements met this demand. The production of other commodities, such as obsidian tools and perhaps shell ornaments, was partially centralized at the mound site, although still without elite intervention. Because few studies of production organization have been conducted that use direct measures, it is unknown to what degree these findings characterize the commodities and other communities. It is intriguing to speculate, however, that the residents of the platform mound villages emphasized the production of easily transportable, high value commodities over fragile and bulky goods such as pottery. Because the residents of the platform mound villages were economically and socially advantaged relative to other people, they would have been in a position to select part-time specializations with high returns.

There exists some evidence for centralized distribution between the largest sites, but this distribution was not elite controlled. The residents living within the platform mound compound did maintain more restricted trade ties than did other residents of the community (see Table 8.4). For example, Group A, frequent in the collections from the Los Morteros, Huntington, and Chicken Ranch sites, constitutes more than one fourth of the ceramics from the nonmound proveniences but is absent from the ceramics collected from the mound vicinity. Similarly, Group E is present in the collections from Los Morteros, Huntington, Chicken Ranch, and the nonmound proveniences of the Marana Mound site but is absent from the mound proveniences. Why the residents of the platform mound compound should have obtained their vessels from fewer sources is unknown, although this may reflect restricted allegiances maintained by the mound residents for social or political reasons.

The evidence suggests that there were several social tiers within the Marana community. At the top of the tier were those residents who lived within the platform mound compound. These residents undoubtedly held substantial social power, as indicated by their location within the community and their control over an important communal symbol, the platform mound. While economically advantaged relative to many residents of the community, they were not substantially better off than other residents of the same village, nor did they control production and distribution activities. An inferred second tier probably consisted of the remainder of the residents from the Marana Mound site, as well as those residents of other sites near the top of the settlement hierarchy. These residents were economically advantaged relative to those of the third social tier and participated in a distribution network from which the third-tier members were excluded.

Discussion

This essay has discussed the strategies used by the elite of the Marana community to solidify and increase their power within the community. To explain why leaders selected the particular mix of strategies that they did, however, requires an understanding of the local cultural sequence and the history of population shifts. The dual-processual model advanced by Blanton and his colleagues (1996a) and Feinman (1995) provides a useful framework for examining these issues.

The dual-processual model proposes that there are two types of leadership strategies that can be adopted: a *network-based* strategy, in which the leaders' prestige derives largely from the linkages they have with individuals from other regions, and a *corporate-based* strategy, in which the leaders' positions derive primarily from the support of kinship-based groups within the community. In the network mode, emphasis is placed on individual prestige and wealth accumulation. Kinship is de-emphasized, and long-distance trade and the acquisition of exotic wealth goods are pursued. Under this strategy, leaders maintain their status largely by excluding non-elite members of the community from trade networks. By contrast, the corporate mode is characterized by an emphasis on kinship affiliation and communal ritual. Societies dominated by this mode are characterized by the construction of public architecture and relatively suppressed economic differentiation. In a society dominated by a corporate model of leadership, all members of the community have more-or-less equal access to trade goods and trade networks (Feinman 1995).

Data presented in this paper indicate that elements of both strategies were present in the Marana community. As predicted by the network model, ritual was exclusionary and wealth differentials are evident between sites near the top of the settlement hierarchy and the lower-tier settlements. Other evidence, however, suggests the presence of corporate strategies. Such evidence includes a lack of economic differentiation between the residents of the platform mound site and shared access to exchange networks between the residents of the Marana Mound compound and those of the Marana Mound, Los Morteros, Huntington, and Chicken Ranch sites.

How are we to interpret these seemingly contradictory patterns? We suggest that they are not contradictory at all but indicate the use of different strategies in different social settings. The likelihood that these modes co-exist in most societies has been acknowledged by both Feinman (1995:264) and Blanton and his colleagues (1996b) and further emphasized by Demarest (1996) and Kolb (1996). To understand why a particular mode dominated in a particular social setting, however, requires an understanding of the local social and historical setting. In the Marana community, we argue that the use of these two very different types of leadership strategies was related to the population fluxes that characterized the area at the start of the Classic period.

Littler (1997) has proposed that in the Salt River region, Preclassic Hohokam communities were dominated by a corporate leadership mode. By the Classic period, however, he suggests that this pattern had undergone a shift toward a more network-oriented strategy. The patterns exhibited in the Marana community may reflect similar social changes. As already discussed, the sites of Los Morteros and Huntington exhibit evidence of lengthy Preclassic occupations. Settlement at these sites appears to have extended back to at least Colonial (A.D. 700–900) times. It is clear that the occupants of these sites had a long history of interaction. This history would have led to close social ties between the inhabitants that undoubtedly continued throughout the occupational sequence. It is even possible that these settlements were integrated through a corporate-based leadership strategy. If so, it seems likely that these ties and the corporate strategy would have continued into the Early Classic period.

Sometime near the end of the Preclassic period or the start of the Classic period, the sites of Marana Mound and Chicken Ranch were settled. Like those of Los Morteros and the other sites discussed above, the artifact assemblages from these sites are dominated by high proportions of Tanque Verde Red-on-brown sherds and other materials typically associated with the Tucson Basin tradition. The similarity of these assemblages to Tucson Basin sites suggests that the settlers may have originated from that area. In the case of the Marana Mound site, it seems further likely that the settlers may have come from Los Morteros or Huntington. As discussed above, a canal links the Marana Mound site with that of Los Morteros, indicating the integration of these two settlements. It is unlikely that outsiders would have been able to construct the platform mound and command leadership of these already established communities. Instead, it seems more likely that the people who lived at the base of the platform mound were already established elites who would have had kin ties with the residents of previously occupied sites such as Los Morteros and Huntington. These ties would have resulted in a continuation of the corporate strategy that characterized the Preclassic mode and would explain the shared exchange networks evident between these sites.

Other newly settled areas of the Marana community, however, appear to reflect population influxes from other areas. These sites are characterized by low frequencies of Tanque Verde Red-on-brown ceramics, distinguishing these sites from others in the Tucson Basin. These patterns suggest that the immigrants came from some other area than the Tucson Basin, one not characterized by a significant red-on-brown tradition. As newcomers, these settlers were excluded from the established trade networks. Lacking kin ties with the residents of sites such as Los Morteros, Huntington, Chicken Ranch, and Marana Mound, they were not a part of the established corporate group. To maintain their elite status over these residents, then, the preexisting leaders of the community were forced to adopt a new leadership strategy. The ceramic data suggest that the leaders of the Marana community adopted a network strategy when dealing with these newcomers. By excluding them from established exchange of networks, they were able to maintain social inequality and secure their social positions over these new immigrants.

Conclusion

This essay demonstrates the importance of examining leadership strategies on a case-by-case basis. Understanding why particular strategies were selected requires detailed understanding of local circumstances. Even within a single region or community, considerable variation may exist. In the Marana community, the dual-processual model provides a useful framework for examining the leadership strategies used, despite the fact that neither the corporate nor the network model predominated. Here, aspects of both strategies were found to have been employed (see Demarest 1996 for a similar view). We propose that the dual-processual model, like many other models of human behavior, may be more useful for understanding human behavior when used as a heuristic device rather than as a rigid typological model.

ACKNOWLEDGMENTS

Funding for this research was provided by the National Science Foundation (dissertation improvement grants #9311636 and 9400239), the Wenner-Gren Foundation for Anthropological Research (predoctoral grant #5722), Sigma Xi, the Missouri University Research Reactor, University of Arizona Graduate College, Arizona Archaeological and Historical Society, and Statistical Research, Inc. The authors would like to thank Paul Fish, Suzanne Fish, and Barbara Mills for discussion of many of the ideas contained in this essay. The senior author gratefully acknowledges the help of Tom Schable and Aina Dodge for their help in formatting this manuscript.

9

The Institutional Contexts of Hohokam Complexity and Inequality

SUZANNE K. FISH AND PAUL R. FISH

THE HOHOKAM AND other relatively complex prehistoric societies of the Southwest conform poorly to the dominant band-tribe-chiefdom-state classificatory scheme of the last several decades (Service 1962; Fried 1967). They cannot be adequately compartmentalized as tribes. They do not fit the variably defined criteria for chiefdoms nearly so well as do, for example, their North American contemporaries, the Mississippians. Furthermore, the comparatively abbreviated postagricultural trajectories of the Southwest never culminated in a prehistoric state, the preordained endpoint and proof of "mainstream" evolution. As a consequence, indigenous developments in the Southwest have not figured in theoretical formulations of the processes leading to complexity and inequality. Nevertheless, these Southwestern societies are undeniably middle range, organizationally intermediate between weakly integrated social entities referred to as tribes and those larger and internally differentiated ones known as states. Moreover, regional sequences on the whole exhibit increasingly large scale and complex societal configurations over time.

Factors internal to Southwestern archaeology also have contributed to a disjuncture from pandiscipline approaches to social evolution. Regional scholars have a strong propensity to rely on ethnographically derived kinship to reconstruct the organization of prehistoric societies. Current theories concerning trajectories that lead to early states, on the other hand, highlight an interplay among multiple and often competing sources of power (e.g., Runciman 1982; Yoffee 1993; Brumfiel 1992). Indeed, scholars of social evolution have suggested that political roles separated from real or fictive kinship are critical thresholds in advancing complexity (e.g., Yoffee 1993; Arnold 1996b:78).

The formulation of new approaches that do not entail comparison against poorly applicable ideal types offers a fresh opportunity for Southwestern prehistory to contribute significantly to the larger issues of social evolution and particularly to an understanding of the initial emergence of complexity and inequality in middle-range societies. A prominent theme in current alternative frameworks is an emphasis on agency—the motivations and machinations of existing and aspiring leaders and elites—to understand the forms and dynamics of increasing complexity. Such approaches run the risk of producing biased and potentially misleading perspectives, however, if they are not balanced by attention to the other social elements of prehistoric societies and the manner in which their members interfaced with the brokers of power and privilege.

Southwestern societies present a particular challenge to agent-based approaches because the pivotal actors, the leaders and elites, are not readily visible in the archaeological record. Although there is unequivocal evidence for strong centralization and massive coordinated effort in some spheres, leaders are not distinguished by easily recognized indicators such as lavish wealth, coercion toward personal ends, elaborate and exclusive insignia, or individualized prominence in art and iconography. The absence of powerholders demarcated in these ways has posed a problem in uniformly applying the chiefdom category to the highly variable configurations of middle-range societies in other regions of the world as well. Colin Renfrew (1974), for example, proposed a subdivision of the category between individualizing chiefdoms in which these anticipated markers of leadership were well represented and group-oriented chiefdoms in which they were not. He insightfully attributed these differing societal stances to contrastive rationales for institutions of centralized action and authority.

More recently, Blanton and others (1996a) and Feinman (1995) have discussed two polar modes in the rise of inequality and their societal consequences in terms of the predominant strategies by which leaders accrue and maintain power. In the networking strategy, prestige and influence depend primarily on ties external to a society and success in brokering goods and services as a result of those linkages. In the corporate strategy, leaders derive preeminence through elevated internal roles and manipulations of the corporate structures of their own societies. The corporate mode is characterized by relatively suppressed economic differentiation, in contrast to the networking mode, which emphasizes individual prestige and wealth accumulation (Feinman 1995:268).

Relating patterns of leadership and inequality to the cognitive codes and institutions that legitimate power and privilege provides the means for balancing a focus on agency with consideration of a society's structural solutions to the interface between leaders and the members of other social constituencies. The rationale for inequality and the conditions under which it is tolerated or supported are expressed in the corresponding institutions. The institutional context creates both the constraints and opportunities that shape the behavior of emerging leaders and aspiring elites.

Dual Developments in Societal Power

The archaeological sequences of the Southwest offer rich and detailed records of the differentiation of societal power within middle-range societies. We will examine the evidence for corporate structures and their relationship to leadership strategies among the Hohokam of southern Arizona. Although Feinman (1995:268) identifies the importance of kinship affiliation as a basic tenet of the corporate mode, kinship relations undoubtedly do not account for all significant corporate political behavior in Southwestern or other nonstate societies. We will focus on insights to be gained from examining dual developments in the archaeological expressions of kinship and another corporate realm that we term "civic-territorial." Civic-territorial roles and institutions represent a neglected but potentially important set of corporate structures with significant implications for inequality and social dynamics.

What are the social correlates of civic-territorial structure and relations? Familiar examples in the Southwest and worldwide include village membership with an attendant set of rights and obligations, larger-scale territorial affiliations, and broadly recruited councils of elders for individual villages or for related sets of settlements. Even though kinship may exert an influence on civic-territorial categories and institutions, it is not coterminous with them. In fact, the adjudication of relations between kin groups may be among the socially sanctioned functions of such institutions. Southwestern expressions of civic-territorial principles and organization are discernible, if not well recorded, in a regional ethnography preoccupied with kinship.

Parallel bodies of evidence document the dual development of Hohokam kinship and civic-territorial organization. Hohokam sequences illustrate processes of differentiation in these two potential sources of societal power from approximately A.D. 500 until the fifteenth century. This interval is divided between Preclassic times prior to A.D. 1150 and the subsequent Classic period.

Developments in Hohokam Kinship

EVIDENCE FOR KINSHIP THROUGH TIME

Beginning in early Hohokam village plans, the basic residential pattern involved from two to six houses opening onto a courtyard or common work area. Wilcox, McGuire, and Sternberg (1981) found this arrangement to become more formalized in the later Preclassic era. Other researchers have proposed that additional facilities are associated with the courtyard groups, such as trash deposits, ramadas, pits, and burials (Henderson 1987a, 1987b; Howard 1985; Gregory 1983; Sires 1985). There is widespread agreement on interpretation of the house cluster or courtyard group as a residential aggregate linked by kinship. Equation of individual structures with nuclear families and clusters of structures with an extended family is common (Wilcox and Sternberg 1983:136, 156, 168; Howard 1985; Elson 1986; Fish and Fish 1991; Henderson 1987a, 1987b; Gregory 1983; Doelle, Huntington, and Wallace 1987; Huntington 1986). Howard (1985) identified rules of residence as the social force promoting cluster persistence. Others (Doelle, Huntington, and Wallace 1987; Henderson 1987b) attribute the size and long-term continuity of many clusters to the success of a prominent household head in attracting and maintaining the cooperation of other nuclear families.

Larger residential groupings that incorporate several house clusters are designated by such terms as suprahousehold units or village segments (Henderson 1987a, 1987b; Howard 1985; Doyel 1991; Rice 1987a, 1987b; Doelle, Huntington, and Wallace 1987; Wilcox 1987b). Typical features shared by these suprahousehold units are a central open area of common use and joint facilities, including pit ovens, a trash mound, and a cemetery (Henderson 1987a, 1987b). Perhaps even more than residential patterns, the extended use of several separate cemeteries within many larger sites suggests generational continuity in lineages or other corporate kin groups. Cemeteries associated with subsets of village population and sometimes with specific sets of architecture span the Preclassic and Classic periods, although there are always alternative burial locations (e.g., Anderson 1986: 192; Gregory 1983).

There appears to be continuity in the constituents of social groups inhabiting Preclassic and Classic residential clusters. Preclassic pit houses were largely replaced by later adobe rooms, but in numerous instances, rooms were constructed over pit houses and generally reprise the arrangement of the previous structures (Sires 1987). Many Classic period room clusters and especially those at larger sites were enclosed by adobe walls. The resulting compounds contain sets of rooms that recall Preclassic courtyard groups. Sometimes compounds surround several such room clusters, separated by smaller internal walls, in arrangements recalling the higher order suprahousehold units or village segments.

If the composition of residential groups shows continuities through earlier and later occupations, other attributes reveal significant change between Preclassic and Classic times. The open layout of residential space was partitioned by compound enclosures that segregated and secluded household activities and possessions. The Classic period was a time of aggregation among the Hohokam and other populations throughout the Southwest (Fish and Fish 1993:100–101; Adler 1994). Increasing heterogeneity and higher densities in later societies must have strained the efficacy of kinship as a mechanism for comprehensively regulating social relations. Under such conditions, physical enclosure may have served to more emphatically demarcate coresidential groups and to reinforce the cohesiveness of members with dissimilar origins or competing kinship loyalties. Walled compounds also would have provided social and architectural opportunity for individualized economic motivations and accumulation.

KINSHIP IN HOHOKAM SOCIETY

In conjunction with the foregoing archaeological evidence, the role of kinship among the Hohokam can be addressed through the most relevant ethnographic analogies and in a comparative manner vis-à-vis other prehistoric middle-range societies. Southwestern ethnography is a rich resource for the first approach. The highly visible and influential kinship systems of the Puebloans are especially well publicized. Although similarly pervasive principles of unilineal descent were not encountered in the southern deserts of the Greater Southwest, early-twentieth-century ethnographers diligently sought unilineal structures. They could find only what they identified as "vestiges" of earlier but now-diminished unilineal organization (e.g., Underhill 1939:31; Russell 1975:197). It is not surprising that Puebloan styles of kinship often have been projected onto southern desert prehistory, despite the fact that Pimans and other *rancheria* peoples of the southern Southwest and adjacent northern Mexico tend toward more flexible, bilateral reckoning.

The imprint of kinship on residential layout and burial, and even the inference of unilineal forms, does not automatically identify the overriding principle of economic and political organization in Hohokam society. In the weakly unilineal kinship systems recorded by ethnographers in the southern part of the Greater Southwest (e.g., Beals 1943; Underhill 1939; Crumrine 1977), territorial affiliation was an additional social dimension in that village approval as well as kinship rights played a part in access to agricultural land. More to the point, participation in the initial construction of canals rather than clan membership was the mechanism for obtaining rights to irrigated land among the Pima, who succeeded the Hohokam in historic times (Russell 1975:88; Castetter and Bell 1942:126).

A similar sort of tenure for large-scale Hohokam irrigators would be in keeping with Netting's (1993:157–88) observation that farmers tend to exercise direct control over cultivated land in situations of intensive production and high investment in agricultural improvements. Indeed, individual rights to land are the cross-cultural norm in societies dependent on irrigation (Hunt and Hunt 1976). Fixed agricultural improvements also were central to intensive Hohokam production by other means such as the construction of extensive rockpile fields. Under such systems of tenure that are outside the immediate strictures of kinship, advantages in land quality or productive capacity could be manipulated as independent bases of economic power.

In the political arena, there is little evidence to identify ranked lineages, as in chiefdoms, as the unique or foremost framework for power and prestige in Hohokam society. Although cemeteries imply an importance for kinship, familial shrines and veneration of lineal ancestors are not evident, even during Preclassic times, when ritual artifacts such as figurines and censors were relatively widespread within and among sites (but see Wilcox and Sternberg 1983:229 for a proposed use of figurines in conjunction with an ancestor cult during the Pioneer period). This absence contrasts with practices in other middle-range societies that have been interpreted as ancestor oriented, such as the retention of plastered ancestral skulls in the Prepottery Neolithic of the Near East (Rollefson 1983; Simmons et al. 1990:108–9) and the display of the preserved bodies of lineal predecessors in charnel houses atop mounds of the contact-era Southeast (Brown 1985:104; Knight 1986; Shelby 1993:397–98).

Comparison with evidence from the Puebloan Southwest for the relative prominence of unilineal kinship in societal organization is also reveal-ing. Among the Hohokam, a comparable iconography of clans is un-known. A more significant contrast with northern neighbors is the absence in the Hohokam archaeological record of any functional equivalent for small kivas. Often associated with specific sets of domestic structures, small kivas are commonly seen as the architectural indicators of prehistoric kin-based ritual and political structure analogous to that of historic clans (Lipe and Hegmon 1989b).

If institutions of wider societal integration are generated by an extension of the principles that define kin groups at lower social levels, this may be indicated by a repetition or carryover in respective architectural symbols. For example, great kivas, which served inclusive populations of the north-ern Southwest, echo some architectural attributes of the small kivas that presumably were shared by clans. In the more overtly hierarchical chief-doms of the Southeast, prominent sites were composed of multiple archi-tectural units, each of which included mounds, cemeteries, and residences. These units have been interpreted as reflecting the social components of Mississippian society, with the size and relative location of the architec-tural complex expressing the relative status of the associated kin group (Knight 1990).

Developments in Civic-Territorial Organization

Having discussed indications for kinship and its role in Hohokam society, we turn our attention to parallel developments in civic-territorial organiza-tion. Elucidation of these trends is more directly dependent on the archaeo-logical record. Anthropologists are notoriously preoccupied with kinship; it is easier to find exhaustive treatments of genealogical constructs in the ethnographic literature of the Southwest than even passing mentions of civic-territorial institutions.

EVIDENCE FOR CIVIC-TERRITORIAL STRUCTURE OVER TIME

The most comprehensive body of evidence pertaining to civic-territorial phenomena is subsumed by the Southwestern concept of the community, which has archaeological expression in spatial patterns and symbols (e.g., Adler 1994; Doyel and Lekson 1992; P. Fish and Fish 1994; Rohn 1989; Wilcox and Sternberg 1983). A Hohokam community consists not of a single settlement but of a set of interrelated sites within a bounded commu-nity territory (S. Fish and Fish 1994). Such a community contains a center with public architecture of a kind and/or magnitude that is not duplicated in other community sites. These edifices are believed to be the focus of communal observances on behalf of all members. The interlinkage of population and settlements throughout is symbolically embodied in the communal structures.

The Southwestern ethnographic record offers some analogues for prehistoric communities and their centers. Both in the Puebloan north and in the southern deserts, centrally focused relationships occur among linked sets of sites. These examples involve the customary return by outlying populations to larger and more continuously occupied settlements for important ceremonial observances. Historic Laguna Pueblo in New Mexico typified such an arrangement (Eggan 1950:253–54; Parsons 1923:145). Likewise, residents of "daughter" villages formerly returned to a parent settlement for wikita ceremonies among the Tohono O'odham of Arizona (Underhill 1939:58). There are parallels for prehistoric communal architecture in the presence of kivas and plazas at main pueblos and specialized communal structures at central O'odham villages. A notable divergence in historic times, however, is the lack of investment in public architecture as a tangible symbol of settlement interlinkage at a level approaching that of even relatively modest prehistoric constructions.

Communities are usually defined and discussed in terms of constituent sites; canal networks are another referent in areas of major irrigation. An equally fundamental aspect of communities is the territory they encompassed and controlled. Community territory is also delimited by the distribution of member sites but incorporates a much greater area than was directly occupied by these concentrated loci of habitation, irrigation, or other activities. Community boundaries presumably demarcated the land and resources wherein primary use-rights were reserved to community members. Regularities in the size and spacing of territory circumscribed by Hohokam communities have been related to the demands and constraints of subsistence, communication, and integration (e.g., Crown 1987; Fish 1996; Fish, Fish, and Madsen 1992; Gregory 1991:97–106).

Archaeological definition of Southwestern communities is by one of two means: First, boundaries may be indicated by settlement fall off, when a cluster of settlements containing a central site is spatially discrete from other such settlement clusters (e.g., Adler 1994; Crown 1987; Breternitz, Doyel, and Marshall 1982; Fish, Fish, and Madsen 1992). This method necessitates comprehensive settlement data. Second, an array of community configurations also may be recognized through a replication of pattern elements at intervals. The distribution of central sites with public architecture is often considered a proxy for the distribution of communities, whether or not all the settlements associated with those centers have been located (Fish 1996; S. Fish and Fish 1994; Gregory and Nials 1985; Jewett 1989; Lekson 1991; Lightfoot and Most 1989; Upham 1982; Wilcox and Sternberg 1983).

Incipient Hohokam community organization is suggested by larger sites with unique constructions within groups of settlements. Small caliche-capped mounds were constructed about A.D. 600 at the prominent site of Snaketown on the Gila River (Haury 1976). Earthen-banked ball courts, the hallmarks of Preclassic public architecture, had been constructed at Hohokam sites in numerous locations by A.D. 750 (Wilcox and Sternberg 1983:193; McGuire 1987). Ball courts appeared at intervals along Phoenix area canals and in surrounding desert basins within the next two centuries. Relatively standardized organizational modes focused on community centers with public architecture can be recognized throughout the Hohokam domain at A.D. 1000, when sufficient data reveal fairly regularized spacing (Wilcox and Sternberg 1983). By that time, the multisite community had become firmly established as the principal territorial unit of the Hohokam (S. Fish and Fish 1994).

The transition to the Classic period is marked by a replacement of ball courts with platform mounds at community centers. This change in the dominant style of public architecture is usually attributed to a shift in the ideology and architectural symbols of community integration. The construction and use of ball courts may have ceased at variable times in different Hohokam subregions (Doelle and Wallace 1991). In the massively irrigated Hohokam core area around Phoenix, there appears to be at least a brief interval of coincidence between old and new forms of public architecture in some central sites (Gregory 1991). Territorial continuity in communities, probably reflecting the locational imperatives of existing canals, is indicated by the construction of platform mounds at many but not all previous ball court centers. In the Tucson Basin, with irrigation of lesser scale, platform mound sites do not coincide with former ball court centers, although there is overlap among the member settlements of Preclassic and Classic communities in the same general area.

CIVIC–TERRITORIAL STRUCTURE IN HOHOKAM SOCIETY

Several lines of evidence support the argument that the integrative rationale of civic-territorial entities among the Hohokam was not articulated along kinship lines. As noted previously, the public edifices of community centers do not repeat architectural elements or symbols associated with lower-order kin groups and their integration. Not only is there no indication of the celebration of kinship and genealogical rank as in ancestral cults, but there is a general dearth of evidence for ceremonial activity at the level of constituent units in Hohokam society, with the exception of Preclassic cremation rituals (McGuire 1992). Widely distributed portable artifacts of Preclassic times that may have functioned in individualized observances were no longer manufactured during the Classic period (Fish 1989; Gregory 1991). Thereafter, ritual was even more strongly centralized and spatially focused in the precincts of platform mounds at preeminent sites.

Ideologies attributed to Hohokam ball courts, the earlier form of public architecture in communities, have no recognized rationale in kinship organization. Recent researchers suggest that ball court activities served as maintenance mechanisms for social and spatial boundaries in Mesoamerican societies (e.g., Gillespie 1991; Kowalewski et al. 1991). Whether by reference to Mesoamerican ethnohistory, the persisting ethnographic ball games of northern Mexico, or the traditional courtless contests of Pimans, the primary social context of Hohokam ball court events was a competition between societal divisions defined by territorial affiliation at village or larger scales (Scarborough and Wilcox 1991). Ball court events only secondarily would have been amenable to kin-group agendas involving social or economic interchange and maneuvering.

The transition to the Classic period witnessed a major shift in integrative ideology and its architectural correlates, coupled with continuity in the community pattern of territorial organization. Hohokam ritual became more centralized than before, while the performers and observers of communal events in mound precincts also became a more exclusive subset of the population as a whole. In contrast to publicly approachable ball courts with berms that would have enhanced visibility for substantial audiences, platform mounds and their precincts were restricted first by palisades and finally by massive outer walls and internal divisions.

Symbols of commonality for territorial entities would have bestowed a unique status upon those who officiated in the associated activities. Such officiants probably played influential roles in both internal and external affairs and legitimately amassed and controlled local resources on behalf of the community. To the extent that Hohokam public architecture and an ideology linked to territory were highly centralized, the corresponding sources of societal power would have been potent as well. The largest and most elaborated architectural complexes occur in conjunction with mounds of the later Classic period. This architectural diversity corresponds to variety in ritual and other public functions, each of which would have entailed specialized knowledge, activities, resources, and participants. For example, at the Pueblo Grande platform mound in Phoenix, archaeological evidence suggests ritual, storage, communal preparation of foodstuffs, stockpiling of crafts and exotic materials, and calendrics, as well as domestic activities and burial (Bostwick and Downum 1994).

Mound rooms with potentially domestic attributes are usually interpreted as residences of community leaders (but see an opposing interpretation by Howard 1992). Limited numbers of individuals that include infants as well as adults were buried in and around mound precincts during later Classic times. Although there are no archaeological indications that communal roles and personae were generated through pervasive systems of ranked kin as in chiefdoms, the burials suggest that mound inhabitants established successional principles during at least the latest part of the Hohokam sequence. The limited number of such burials suggested that lineal succession was never firmly established.

In a theoretical field that has so strongly equated middle-range societies with kin-based chiefdoms, it is difficult to visualize alternative modes of centralized organization. The Mexican *comunidad* is one possible source of insight. It has been a unit of territory and local administration among agrarian and predominantly indigenous populations since early colonial times, with apparent continuities from precontact societal and territorial patterns in some regions (e.g., Chevalier 1970; Spores 1967; Whitecotton 1977). *Comunidades* typically incorporate more than one settlement but have an administrative center and a foremost church in a larger village. *Comunidad* boundaries guarantee continuing rights to agricultural land and access to natural resources beyond those available through membership in a single village. Such a territorially based organization would be likely to develop where, as among the Hohokam, structural improvements were crucial to agricultural success and the same land was cultivated over many years. Although kin groups may be strongly involved in political and economic machinations within the framework of a *comunidad,* territorial affiliation is the fundamental principle of membership and integration.

An implication of such centralized organization is that, unlike kin-based systems such as chiefdoms in the traditional sense, the architectural symbols of integration would be comprehensible within an ideology of community identity and territorial affiliation. Investment in public architecture would communicate the cohesiveness and prominence of the community (probably vis-à-vis neighbors) rather than the paramount position of a leader and his highly ranked lineage. In keeping with this sort of societal rationale and institutional context for power, Hohokam elites marked by obtrusive insignias of personal status or highly extravagant burial accompaniments have not been encountered (Mitchell 1991, 1994). A civic-territorial form of corporate integrative ideology is commensurate with Classic Hohokam burial regimes in which preeminent individuals were distinguished in death by a locational association with mounds, the architectural expression of community, more than by displays of genealogically prescribed wealth.

Dynamics of Hohokam Power

At this point it is appropriate to reiterate that we have presented a case for simultaneous developments in both kin-based and civic-territorial sources of societal power. If trajectories toward higher levels of complexity are characterized by an interplay among multiple and often competing sources of power, evolutionary processes among the Hohokam should be examined in this light. It is also true that integrative ideologies emphasizing territorial affiliation rather than pervasive genealogical ranking would not be immune to manipulation by kin groups or other competing subdivisions of Hohokam society.

Performers of rituals and other central functions on behalf of the entire community at platform mounds are the most obvious candidates for a group possessing ideological and economic power during the Classic period. Heads of kin groups also are probable political actors, with roles intensified and challenged by increasing Classic aggregation and social heterogeneity (Fish and Fish 1993; Fish et al. 1994). The coordinators of the most massive irrigation systems north of Peru (Doolittle 1990) and the leaders of other cooperative water-use associations would have occupied additional positions of considerable influence (Crown 1987; Gregory and Nials 1985; Nicholas and Feinman 1989). Indeed, these coordinators may have been designated and operated outside both kin and civic-territorial networks, in view of Piman acquisition of rights to irrigated plots through participation in canal construction. Prominent roles in the exchange of such goods as subsistence products, exotic raw materials, or ceramics (e.g., Abbott 1996; Fish and Donaldson 1991; Bayman 1995, 1996; Harry 1997) represent yet another source of influence and inequality.

Increasingly differentiated sources of societal power are evident within

Hohokam communities (or alliances of communities) during the Classic period. Domestic and public spaces were partitioned by the construction of physical and social barriers. Likewise, the specialization and number of roles in public functions increased with greater elaboration and specialization of public architecture at large, late centers. Competition and efforts to accrue, convert, or consolidate different sources of societal power may well have been the dynamic behind a convergence between platform mound precincts and resident family lines, as indicated by exclusive privileges of mound burial during the later Classic period.

A New Perspective on Hohokam and Southwestern Prehistory

The Hohokam trajectory toward complexity and inequality is marked by changing civic-territorial institutions that parallel developments in kinship structure. The civic-territorial corporate realm is not without analogues in the historic Southwest, despite an ethnographic record heavily biased toward accounts of kinship and preoccupied with unilineal forms. In addition to constituting the primary arena for political actors, Hohokam civic-territorial organization satisfied basic needs of society as a whole. Hohokam political ideology was compatible with highly centralized community functions such as the construction of unique public architecture, the performance of communal ritual, and other activities, including concentrated storage and probable coordination of external affairs. At the same time, the Hohokam cognitive code engendered limited societal tolerance or support for the aggrandizement of leaders as expressed through accumulation of individual wealth or durable symbols of personalized authority.

A trend toward increasing exclusivity in communal events can be traced from the end of the Preclassic era through Late Classic times. Direct participation and even observation of centralized activities became accessible to fewer and fewer society members, while roles became more diverse and specialized in the mound precincts of large, late centers. These trends toward exclusivity were not accompanied, however, by well-developed indications of the other hallmarks of exclusionary strategies as defined by Blanton and his colleagues (1996a:4–5) and Feinman (1995).

As in Preclassic times, there was lively Classic trade in exotic raw materials and finished craft items, but these remained widely dispersed among settlements and their residents. Efforts to detect material inequalities have been most successful in describing differentiation in terms of the upper tiers of sites in settlement hierarchies (and particularly mound centers) rather than in terms of restricted or unique consumption by a few privileged households or individuals (e.g., Bayman 1994; Harry 1997; Teague 1989b). Elaborated systems of prestige goods, circulating primarily among a regional network of elites and demarcating its members, are not readily apparent; however, it is possible that high value items were broadly manipulated to some degree to induce or reinforce obligations in goods and services. Likewise, extraordinarily wealthy burials and elaborate residences with unusually lavish domestic assemblages have not been encountered.

Thus, although both increasingly centralized and exclusionary tendencies appear over the course of the Classic period, the context of power and privilege remained primarily corporate and embodied in the institutions of civic-territorial organization. Attempts to implement and institutionalize exclusionary strategies culminated in the Late Classic period, likely in conjunction with efforts to interject principles of elevated heritage in order to justify lineal succession. Limited numbers of burials in Late Classic mound precincts imply a weak and perhaps discontinuous or contested establishment of these new rationales for leadership. The extent to which Late Classic trends reflect the concentration and consolidation of formerly disparate and competing sources of societal power is a pivotal issue in the ultimate episodes of the Hohokam political trajectory.

The archaeological record of the Southwest, and the Hohokam in particular, offers optimally well dated, detailed, and continuous histories of emergent complexity in middle-range societies. The completeness of this record is rarely duplicated in regions where states eventually arose because of the concomitant prehistoric and later destruction of older remains and the lower intensity of archaeological study for these early evolutionary intervals. Southwestern sequences illustrate trajectories that cumulatively produced increasingly complex forms. They represent a rich resource for understanding and comparing the components and processes of increasing social differentiation, integration, and inequality.

10

Leadership at Casas Grandes, Chihuahua, Mexico

MICHAEL E. WHALEN AND PAUL E. MINNIS

CASAS GRANDES, ALSO known as Paquimé, is located in northwestern Chihuahua, Mexico (Figure 10.1). With some two thousand rooms, it is one of the largest prehistoric or protohistoric pueblos known. Its huge room blocks, some of which still rise 10 meters high, and its Mesoamerican-style platform mounds and ball courts have impressed all who have seen them, from the first Spanish explorers to modern archaeologists. The community is best known through the monumental excavations of the Joint Casas Grandes Project, which was conducted between 1958 and 1961 (Di Peso 1974; Di Peso, Rinaldo, and Fenner 1974:vols. 5–8). Casas Grandes had its florescence during the Medio Period. Recent revisions of the site's chronology now date this period between about A.D. 1200 and 1450 (Dean and Ravesloot 1993).

Casas Grandes is generally acknowledged to have developed a significant level of sociopolitical complexity. In an overview of Southwestern organizational development, Gregory Johnson (1989:386), a Near Eastern archaeologist and theoretician, notes that "Casas looks elite—even to me." Another prominent Southwestern scholar characterizes Casas Grandes as "the largest and most complex prehistoric or protohistoric site in the Greater Southwest" (Wilcox 1995:287). Still others recognize Casas Grandes as the center of one of the major regional systems of the U.S. Southwest and northern Mexico (e.g., McGuire 1993:100; Nelson et al. 1994:64).

Despite its reputation, however, Casas Grandes is underrepresented in current discussions of sociopolitical evolutionary processes north of Mesoamerica. The problem is that Casas Grandes has for years existed in a sort of archaeological vacuum. There has been almost no excavation at neighboring communities, and, until recently, there had been no systematic survey to record these neighbors. Casas Grandes and its hinterland, then, have

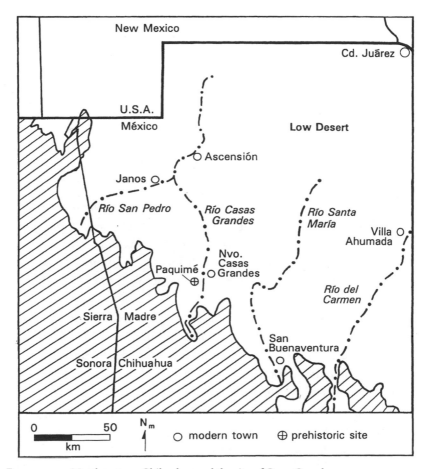

FIGURE 10.1. Northwestern Chihuahua and the site of Casas Grandes.

been studied at a level so far below what has been achieved in cases like the Chacoan and Hohokam that it can scarcely be discussed in the same terms. Accordingly, we begin this discussion of leadership at Casas Grandes by noting that there are sharp limitations on how far and in what detail the topic can be pursued. Nevertheless, old and new data can be used to make some observations on the nature and extent of leadership at Casas Grandes and in its environs in northwestern Chihuahua.

In the original and influential interpretation (Di Peso 1974:vol. 2), Casas Grandes was seen as a highly centralized polity governed by powerful, hereditary rulers of foreign descent. This scenario depended partly on archaeological observation and largely on ethnohistoric analogy. The community of Casas Grandes was large and elaborate, and it possessed monumental architecture in the form of platform mounds and ball courts, conspicuous

Mesoamerican-style elements in both architecture and artifacts, and large quantities of imported exotica, from macaws to copper ornaments and seashells. Some sort of links to Mesoamerica were apparent, and the descriptive writings of such sixteenth-century chroniclers as Sahagún and Durán provided a detailed body of Late Postclassic Mesoamerican social, economic, and religious data that were used to explain and interpret the archaeological observations.

Di Peso's well-known reconstruction of the origin and operation of the Casas Grandes polity has as its principal actors Late Postclassic Mesoamerican *pochteca,* or itinerant militarist merchants, to whom he refers as "the donors" of complex Mesoamerican cultural elements (Di Peso 1974:2:329). In the Casas Grandes valley, he theorized, these *pochteca* were able to establish themselves as professional rulers who organized local populations and had the city constructed to serve as a commercial outpost channeling raw materials and goods between Mesoamerica and the Pueblo societies of the Southwestern United States.

It was further assumed that Late Postclassic patterns of stratification and leadership accompanied the *pochteca* to Casas Grandes. These included a system of social hierarchy and hereditary inequality, plus highly centralized social, political, religious, and economic systems. Mesoamerican-style religious cults, particularly that of Quetzalcoatl, and craft guilds were also argued to have been brought by the *pochteca* and to have been important elements of their control over local populations and their mercantile economy. This concept of extensive centralization was extended beyond Casas Grandes itself, where, it was argued, "hundreds of mountain and valley satellite communities located within the Casas Grandes province bowed to the needs of the capital city" (Di Peso 1974:2:314–15). Di Peso's concept of the organization of Casas Grandes around craft guilds, religious cults, a high level of formalized social differentiation, and extensive centralization of control proposed a kind and level of leadership that are not usually thought of as characteristic of other prehistoric societies of the region, even in the elaborate Chacoan and Hohokam regional systems. Di Peso would have argued that this is precisely the point: the system was imported from Mesoamerica and adapted to the indigenous population.

Di Peso's *pochteca* and mercantile model has subsequently been heavily critiqued on a number of grounds, from the absence of convincing evidence for *pochteca* incursions anywhere in northern Mexico or the Southwestern United States to the paucity of evidence for sustained mercantile interactions between Casas Grandes and populations either to the north or south (e.g., Bradley 1993; McGuire 1980; Plog, Upham, and Weigand 1982; Ravesloot 1988). It has also been argued that there is little convincing evidence at Casas Grandes of the centralized large-scale production of exotica that was critical to the mercantile model (Minnis 1984, 1988). Instead, the presence of quantities of exotic materials such as shell and copper in some residential units is seen as more likely to represent elite hoards than the originally proposed craft guild warehouses. Other of the community's exotic items are dispersed throughout it, and there is evidence of decentralized, residential unit–level production of such exotica as shell jewelry and macaws (Bradley 1993; Minnis 1984, 1988).

Also noteworthy are the platform mounds at Casas Grandes. Up to eighteen solid-core mounds have been identified there, and it is further noted that none of them bore any traces of having been used as building platforms, although many were truncated (Di Peso, Rinaldo, and Fenner 1974:4:270). In size, these Chihuahuan mounds contained smaller volumes of fill than mounds at Pueblo Bonito in Chaco Canyon or the larger of the Hohokam mounds (Minnis 1989). Some of the Casas Grandes mounds were theorized to have been centers of ritual activities pertaining to Mesoamerican cults (Di Peso 1974:2:407). Not only are there many mounds at Casas Grandes, but there is considerable morphological variation among them, ranging from geometric shapes to a bird effigy. The mounds were characterized as public, ritual architecture built under centralized direction. There is no direct evidence of this latter assertion, however, and it might equally well be that the mounds were monuments commissioned by or for important individuals or family groups to emphasize or augment their social positions.

Finally, Schmidt and Gerald (1988) analyze water control systems of the eastern Sierra Madre, arguing convincingly that they were not built under centralized Casas Grandes direction as originally supposed (Di Peso, Rinaldo, and Fenner 1974:5:823) but instead were constructed by local social units to improve the productive capacities of their environs. Our own recent research on agriculture in the Casas Grandes core area also supports this argument for locally focused productive systems (Whalen and Minnis 1997).

All of these arguments suggest a lower level of centralized control than was originally proposed for Casas Grandes and its hinterland, and this line of thought has further implications. To argue against the existence of high levels of centralized control at and around the primate center raises fundamental doubts about the existence of the system of hereditary ranking that was assumed to have been imported from Mesoamerica to northwestern

Chihuahua. Hierarchical organization and centralization of control go hand in hand, so it is hard to conceive of one existing without the other. If centralization is found to be lacking, then, one is led to question the existence of extensive vertical, or hierarchical, differentiation. The preceding discussion points toward a less comprehensive kind of authority and leadership than was originally proposed for Casas Grandes and its hinterland.

Mortuary data offer a direct approach to the question of social differentiation and, indirectly, to patterns of leadership in extinct societies. The Casas Grandes Medio period burial population of nearly five hundred interments was described by Di Peso and his colleagues (Di Peso, Rinaldo, and Fenner 1974:vol. 8). It was later extensively analyzed by Ravesloot (1988), whose work focused on a basic, binary question: was there or was there not evidence of the presence of a hierarchical system of hereditary ranking at Casas Grandes? This was a reasonable approach at the time of writing (the mid-1980s) and against the backdrop of prevailing perceptions of the organizational structure of Casas Grandes.

Ravesloot used his results to argue for a system of ascriptive ranking within the community. His assumption was that societies organized on the basis of hereditary rank reflect this situation by placing what have been termed "symbols of authority" with a range of burials crosscutting age and sex distinctions. He also cites several opinions to the effect that perceptible, stepwise gradation from low to high in burial treatment and offerings is characteristic of ranked societies.

These are commonly held positions in mortuary analysis. A potential problem that we see with the Casas Grandes study, however, is unambiguous identification of the symbols of authority. Those postulated by Ravesloot (1988:51) at Casas Grandes include things like grave placement, presence of secondary burials, leg position of the primary interment, burial in a vault or simple tomb, offerings that include ceramic hand drums, polychrome pottery, jewelry made from nonlocal materials, and rare artifacts such as bone flutes. Many of these attributes seem to us to be questionably identified as symbols of authority. Almost all of the artifacts are objects of local manufacture (e.g., polychrome pottery). Other items seem as likely to be pieces of ritual paraphernalia as symbols of authority (e.g., hand drums, bone flutes). We readily concede that these latter items could be symbols of ritual authority of the sort that is seen as central to sociopolitical organization in the northern Southwest (e.g., Upham 1982:14) and that was probably significant in the Casas Grandes area as well. The precise linkage between possession of ritual paraphernalia and sociopolitical authority, however, remains unclear. The presence of jewelry in some burials, simple tombs in a few cases, and some well-accompanied infant burials might plausibly reflect only differences in personal or familial wealth, representing no more than claimed status in a context where social standing is a matter for negotiation rather than a firmly established rule. We do not argue that the objects just named could not be symbols of authority, only that they need not be so interpreted.

We also note that cross-tabulations of offerings by age and sex (Ravesloot 1988:55) show that every class of utilitarian and nonutilitarian mortuary offering occurs with practically every age and sex combination. The original study took this to mean that the symbols of authority crosscut age and sex differences. If we question the identification of these objects as symbols of authority, however, then we are simply left with mortuary goods of a wide range spread across the whole burial population.

Both Di Peso's (Di Peso, Rinaldo, and Fenner 1974:8:355–410) original description of the Medio period burials and Ravesloot's (1988) analysis of them show that the great majority of the Casas Grandes people were treated simply at death. Most were interred in simple pit graves under room or plaza floors. Less than half (42.5 percent) of Medio period burials had clearly associated mortuary offerings (Di Peso, Rinaldo, and Fenner 1974:8:363). Moreover, slightly less than half of these furnished grave pits contained only ceramic offerings, virtually all of which were common local types. Jewelry of shell, copper, and other minerals was present in about 42 percent of the furnished graves, but only a few burials had notable concentrations of these materials.

These arguments do not negate Ravesloot's conclusions about the existence of a system of hereditary ranking at Casas Grandes, and it is not our intention to argue that such a system did not exist. Rather, we suggest that if a system of hereditary status ascription existed at Casas Grandes, it likely was not a very elaborate one. Presently, for instance, the Casas Grandes burial sample contains nothing comparable to the wealth and variety of some Mississippian burials, where a well-established, widespread system of hereditary ranking is presumed (e.g., Pauketat 1994). Indeed, the Casas Grandes situation may ultimately be found to be more similar to the Emergent Mississippian culture described by Pauketat (1994:51–65), where ranking is argued to have been a simpler, less comprehensive phenomenon. Unfortunately, consideration of the relative position of Casas Grandes elites and such prominent people as may have existed in the outlying communities is still precluded by a complete lack of data.

To this point, we have questioned the traditional model of institutionalized and highly centralized local and regional leadership based on a formal, hierarchical set of statuses and roles and operating within the communal context of craft guilds and Mesoamerican-style religious cults at Casas Grandes. This may be described as a corporate political action strategy in Mesoamerican contexts (Blanton et al. 1996a:2), in which power is spread across a number of groups and parts of society according to a hierarchically graded set of roles and statuses that restrains individual power seeking. Corporate forms of political action, the authors explain, result in formal, static, noncompetitive systems of organization. As the preceding discussion questions the existence of corporate forms of political action at Casas Grandes, then the obvious alternative is some variant of less formalized, less hierarchical, less comprehensive, and more competitive leadership. We now turn to consideration of noncorporate leadership models for northwestern Chihuahua.

An Alternative Interpretation of Leadership at Casas Grandes

The contexts of leadership establishment in intermediate societies may be highly competitive, as would-be leaders and their factions constantly jockey for position with rivals, vying for resources, legitimacy, and followers and attempting to create social conditions to their own benefits. This sort of open, fluid, competitive activity has been termed "networking" (Feinman 1995:268), and it is included under the "exclusionary" political action strategy discussed by Blanton and his colleagues (1996a:2) as a potential alternative to corporate strategies.

For those who follow an exclusionary political action strategy, Blanton and his coauthors assert that there are two ways to keep ahead of the competition. One way is patrimonial rhetoric, or the manipulation of kinship ties to mobilize labor and resources. The alternative and higher capacity strategy is the use of prestige goods: valuable, nonlocal items that are increasingly substituted in midlevel societies for the food and utilitarian items exchanged in simpler systems. Prestige goods should be rare, exotic, and difficult to make or procure. Characteristically, elites obtain either the necessary raw materials or the items themselves through interregional trade networks. The elites control the supply of prestige goods through their management of foreign relations, labor, and production knowledge. At this point, it is important to emphasize that the term "elite" can have a variety of meanings in different cultural contexts. The ethnographic record shows that distributors of prestige goods may be anything from local "big men" to hereditary chiefs, the complexity and structure of the systems varying according to the power and stature of their managers.

A number of archaeologists (e.g., Bradley 1993; Whalen and Minnis 1996b) have argued that a prestige goods economic model covers the movement of nonlocal goods into and out of Casas Grandes better than does the previously proposed mercantile model. We have earlier (Whalen and Minnis 1996b) asserted that craft production at Casas Grandes likely took place within a kin-ordered mode (following Wolf 1982:88–99), where labor is organized by individual residential groups instead of being centralized. This means that production is also likely to be dispersed into residential units or into different communities, without large, centralized workshop or manufacturing activities. Every residential unit cannot be expected to show the same kinds or levels of productive effort, however, as the kin groups that they represent are usually of unequal wealth, position, and power. Moreover, while full-time craft specialization is sometimes found in complex kin-ordered economies, it is not characteristic of them. We note that these arguments are consistent with the presence of people or families at Casas Grandes who were elite enough to be successful political entrepreneurs but whose authority was not comprehensive enough to extend to the same degree into all spheres of life.

We see the same pattern in the region around Casas Grandes. We have argued elsewhere (Minnis 1984, 1989; Whalen and Minnis 1996c) that the Casas Grandes regional system did not extend more than about 130 kilometers from the primate center, making it about the same size as the Chaco and Hohokam regional systems (Crown and Judge 1991:2–3). At issue, then, seems to be an interaction sphere of a scale known from the Southwestern United States rather than one of Mesoamerican proportions. This observation alone implies that a Mesoamerican level of leadership would not have been required in the Casas Grandes case.

Moreover, our new settlement pattern data hint that the level of political centralization was not very high around Casas Grandes. Briefly, the area within about a day's walk (ca. 30 kilometers) around Casas Grandes was found to contain most of the ball courts known in the region (Whalen and Minnis 1996a). With our colleagues in Mesoamerica and the Hohokam world, we take ball courts to be ritual facilities where a wide range of political, economic, and social activities took place. This implies that the area near Casas Grandes saw the region's highest level of the integrative activities that focused on the ball courts. Mesoamerican ball courts have also been argued to have been stages where personal or factional rivalries were played out in ritualized contexts, and they are asserted to have been most common in regional systems that lacked strong, centralized political control and that were fragmented into competing units (Santley, Berman, and Alexander 1991). We have posited elsewhere (Whalen and Minnis 1996a) that if the Chihuahuan ball courts served similar ends, then their abundance within a day's walk of Casas Grandes itself may indicate a high level of factional rivalry among the elites of the core zone. This would, in turn, hint at a relatively low level of political centralization within that area. Both of these arguments are consistent with the open, fluid, competitive leadership earlier proposed for the area.

In addition, in the zone immediately around Casas Grandes were found almost all of the perforated, circular stones that we take to be the doors of macaw pens like those excavated at Casas Grandes. Significantly, these stones were as likely to be found at small, simple sites as at large, elaborate ones, and their presence reflects the practice of aviculture and the decentralized production of at least one important category of exotica (i.e., macaw plumes). Lastly, their distribution suggests much of this activity within around 30 kilometers of Casas Grandes and relatively little of it elsewhere, much like the ball court activity just described (Minnis et al. 1993).

Finally, we recorded some fifty of the features that we term "stone circles" in the area around Casas Grandes. Figure 10.2 shows an example. Upon excavation (Whalen and Minnis 1997), these proved to be unusually large roasting pits that were likely used in large-scale food preparation for feasting or for other large distributions. In the ethnographic record, this is another commonly encountered means of building factional support, particularly when combined with ritual and the distribution of prestige goods. Significantly, these facilities mirror the regional distribution of ball courts and macaw stones: common in the area around Casas Grandes and rare or absent elsewhere.

All of these observations are consistent with our present working hypothesis, which sees Casas Grandes as a "midlevel" (Feinman and Neitzel 1984; Lightfoot and Upham 1989; Upham 1990) or "intermediate" (Arnold 1996b) society. Midlevel or intermediate societies may be defined as those that developed beyond egalitarian, consensus-based decision making but that lack formal stratification, rigid decision-making hierarchies, and bureaucratic authority (e.g., Lightfoot and Upham 1989:16). These are societies in which emergent leaders lack the comprehensive, coercive power that characterized the highly developed complex societies of areas like

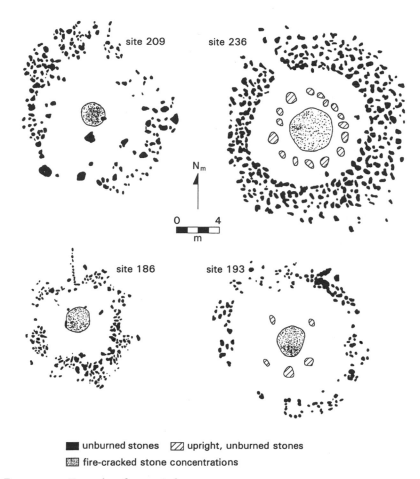

site 209   site 236

site 186   site 193

■ unburned stones   ▨ upright, unburned stones
▦ fire-cracked stone concentrations

FIGURE 10.2. Examples of stone circles.

Mesoamerica during the Classic and Postclassic periods. Emergent leaders in midlevel complex societies, lacking institutionalized power, operate by negotiating their statuses and by competing for positions of influence. We would, therefore, expect a society of intermediate complexity to be characterized by widespread factional competition and by alliance building done through competitive generosity, often involving nonlocal prestige goods perhaps given out in public or ritual contexts.

Accordingly, the combination of a number of ball courts, large quantities of prestige goods, and concentration of facilities for producing at least one class of exotica (macaws) in the inner zone around Casas Grandes leads us to hypothesize that a good deal of this sort of competitive activity took place there. Significantly, there seems to have been relatively little of it in neighboring areas. We reiterate that we do not suggest that the influence of

Casas Grandes extended no more than 30 kilometers. Rather, we raise the possibility that the level of Medio period political centralization may not have been very high in northwestern Chihuahua, whatever economic and social alliances existed among the region's communities. This, in turn, suggests an absence of strong, comprehensive leadership in the region.

One more piece of data also argues for a relatively low level of regional centralization. Our Arroyo la Tinaja survey unit is a populous valley that forms a major corridor for movement from the flat lands around Casas Grandes up into the Sierra Madre. Here we recorded a variety of large to small pueblos. Only the largest site had an associated ball court, but we recorded examples of isolated ball courts lying between several smaller sites. It is also notable that stone entryways for macaw cages were found on the large site, on the medium site, and on one of the small sites (Minnis et al. 1993). The Arroyo la Tinaja thus emerges as a localized area with its own site hierarchy, agricultural terrace systems, attached and isolated ritual structures, and production facilities for at least some exotica (i.e., macaws). The nearby El Alamito intensive survey unit, located above the Río Palanganus, seems to show a similar pattern of a site hierarchy, ritual facilities, and macaw production. Each of these presumed local polities lies less than 30 kilometers from Casas Grandes and, as far as can presently be determined, is contemporary with it.

These observations fit the settlement pattern that Blanton and his colleagues (1981) predict for decentralized regions. In a region lacking strong central control, they assert, competing settlement clusters, containing sites of all types and sizes, should be distributed across the landscape, and there may be empty "buffer" or "shatter" zones between them. In contrast, regions that are highly centralized under a primate center should show a more homogeneous site distribution, insofar as local conditions allow. This is because strong regional centralization results in suppression of peer polity competition, thus obviating the need for buffer zones.

Like the data from Casas Grandes itself, then, this regional information suggests a society at an intermediate level of sociopolitical organization. Although we still have far to go to achieve an adequate understanding of the organization of Casas Grandes and its hinterland, we tentatively see competing elites, long-distance trade, prestige goods, and the resulting "fragmented political landscape" that Blanton and his coauthors (1996a) describe under their "exclusionary" political action strategy.

Instead of the strictly hierarchical models that traditionally have been proposed for Casas Grandes and its environs, we suspect that more flexible concepts such as heterarchy (Ehrenreich, Crumley, and Levy 1995) will ultimately prove useful in the quest to understand the dynamics of leadership and power in northwestern Chihuahua. As argued in the above-cited volume: "The addition of the term heterarchy to the vocabulary of power relations reminds us that forms of order exist that are not exclusively hierarchical and that interactive elements in complex systems need not be permanently ranked relative to one another" (Crumley 1995:3). This concept is not advanced to the complete exclusion of hierarchy, however, and Crumley (1995:4) notes that both hierarchy and heterarchy are conditions that can exist to varying degrees in the same situation or over time.

This last point is particularly relevant to the case of Casas Grandes, where it is still impossible to date changes within the 250-year-long Medio period, a time that surely contained dynamic and even dramatic development. We cannot presently trace the political and economic processes that ultimately resulted in the formation of a primate center some eight to ten times the size of the next largest community in the region. We suggest, however, that Casas Grandes may not always have had the status of the primate community of its region. It is entirely possible that the political entrepreneurs of Casas Grandes may have been matched by their competitors elsewhere in the region during the Early Medio period, only solidifying their position at the primate center in the Late Medio period. In conclusion, we have put forward the concept of a kind and level of authority and leadership that are significantly different from what was originally proposed for Casas Grandes, but we assert that it is the model most consistent with both old data and new findings. Clearly, however, we still have far to go toward achieving an understanding of leadership and the organization of regional power in northwestern Chihuahua.

ACKNOWLEDGMENTS

The Paquimé Regional Survey project was funded by the National Science Foundation through grant SBR-9320007, made jointly to the authors at the Universities of Tulsa and Oklahoma, and a grant from the Kaplan Foundation. Portions of the work were also supported by a faculty research grant from the University of Oklahoma. Authorization for the project was provided by the National Institute of Anthropology and History of Mexico. All of this aid and support is gratefully acknowledged.

11

Reciprocity and Its Limits

Considerations for a Study of the Prehispanic Pueblo World

TIMOTHY A. KOHLER, MATTHEW W. VAN PELT,
AND LORENE Y. L. YAP

RECIPROCITY IS AN ancient and important social practice that evolved in very small scale societies. In this essay we present an abstract model of the way systems that are organized through balanced reciprocity work (Sahlins 1972:185–275). This model helps us understand the general nature of the problems that must be overcome by societies organized through reciprocity as they grow in size. We then suggest that the eastern and western Pueblo worlds took different paths to overcoming these difficulties. Finally, at the invitation of the editor, we discuss the other essays in this volume that deal with the prehispanic Pueblo world in light of this model.

The first part of the essay draws on theory from complex adaptive systems research, specifically the random Boolean network (RBN) model (Kauffman 1993 and elsewhere). Complex adaptive systems (CAS) research is the study of how many interacting and often adaptive agents, each of which may have access to only local information and each of which may be responding to quite simple rules, as an ensemble produce higher-order patterns and structures. Wills and his colleagues (1994) provide an overview of several major strands of CAS theory from a Southwestern archaeological perspective (see also Kohler 1993). Much recent anthropology attempts to generate thicker and more detailed descriptions of particular local societies to achieve a deeper understanding of their nature and operation. CAS approaches, on the other hand, are unabashedly abstract; they attempt to view adaptive systems of all kinds from a distance to perceive their similarities and differences. Typically, they locate causality in the manner in which entities simultaneously interact. Although such models strive for generality rather than for the realism or precision that are more traditionally honored in our field, we believe they can be used productively nonetheless.

Reciprocity Is Ancient and Fundamental

Some notion of reciprocity as a basic and structuring process is common in many theories of society and psyche. Lawrence Becker, a philosopher of the virtue-theoretic school, considers reciprocity to be a fundamental moral virtue because "its requirements have presumptive priority over many competing considerations. . . . [It] fixes the outline of our non-voluntary social life" (1986:5). Studies in experimental economics (Hoffman, McCabe, and Smith 1998) regularly find more reciprocal cooperation among humans than would be predicted by rational utility considerations. A number of explanations have been offered as to how practices that may have some immediate cost to the individual could become so widespread. A series of famous simulations by Axelrod (reviewed in Axelrod 1997:1–29) demonstrates that, given a sufficiently high initial density of cooperators, cooperation can spread and sustain itself within an interacting population playing the iterated Prisoner's Dilemma. It is also possible to explain the prevalence of reciprocity in societies even where direct interaction among reciprocators is rare through indirect reciprocity based on reputation (Nowak and Sigmund 1998). A third kind of explanation appeals to our intuition that groups with many cooperators ought to be more successful than groups lacking a high level of cooperation. Soltis, Boyd, and Richerson (1995) show that if the advantage that cooperative behaviors provide to the group outweighs their costs to individuals within the group, then norms specifying reciprocity can spread under certain circumstances, including strong between-group variation and significant group extinction rates. (For more discussion of cultural group selection models, see Sober and Wilson 1998.)

Evolutionary psychologists (Cosmides and Tooby 1992) claim that reciprocity is so ancient and central to hominid affairs that we have evolved specialized mental faculties that allow us to readily identify cheaters (i.e., defectors from reciprocity-based systems). More generally, the increased encephalization of *Homo sapiens sapiens* relative to earlier forms may be strongly related to selection for the ability to negotiate the burdens of achieving appropriately cooperative behavior in large groups (Dunbar 1998). The antiquity of food sharing is suggested by the fact that extensive

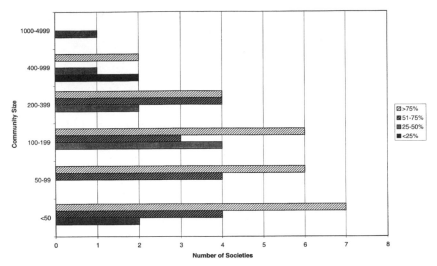

FIGURE 11.1. Percent of exchange activity involving reciprocity in sample of fifty-four nonhierarchical societies drawn from the Standard Cross-Cultural Sample.

transfers, helping to buffer daily variance in types of food acquired, is very common among living foragers (Hill and Hurtado 1989) and is visible in today's traditional village societies where risk sharing protects against crop, livestock, or fishing fluctuations (Coate and Ravallion 1993). Fiske (1991) has proposed that there are only four fundamental and universal "grammars" for social relationships: communal sharing (as in generalized reciprocity toward close kin); authority ranking (as in the relationship of chiefs with subordinates); equality matching (emphasizing balanced economic and social reciprocity); and market pricing (in which relationships are mediated by values determined by a market system).

However reciprocity achieved its centrality in human affairs, the key point is that noncentric reciprocal exchanges of goods (as defined by Pryor 1977) has played a critical role as a dominant economic exchange mechanism in small-scale societies both now and in prehistory. These exchanges are roughly what Sahlins (1972) termed balanced reciprocity, though Pryor's work has shown that such exchanges may be balanced more in ideal than in practice. Cultural evolutionary models of the 1950s and 1960s associated "egalitarian economies" characterized by reciprocity with egalitarian societies and predicted replacement of reciprocity by redistribution as the "paramount form" in rank societies (Fried 1967:116–17). Cross-cultural analyses by Pryor (1977:203–16) support the belief that reciprocal exchange of goods (much of which is food) is most characteristic of societies with low scores on his "economic development" scale. In Figure 11.1 we have tabulated data on the relative importance of reciprocal exchange in fifty-four nonhierarchical societies drawn from the Standard Cross-Cultural Sample (Murdock and White 1969). As is commonly believed, there is indeed a strong tendency for the importance of reciprocal exchanges to decline with increasing community size.[1] We now turn to an abstract model of the way such systems work in the hopes that it will help us understand why we see this pattern. Readers who are more interested in seeing how we apply this model than in how it works can skip the next section entirely and come back to it later if they wish. Others interested in still more detail than we provide should consult Wuensche (1998) and Kauffman (1993).

Boolean Networks as Models for Balanced Reciprocal Systems

Dynamics in general is the study of how things change through time, and discrete dynamics provides a body of approaches to systems that can be conceptualized as changing at discrete points in time (Sandefur 1990). Boolean networks (Kauffman 1993:181–91) are a class of discrete dynamical systems; cellular automata, which are more familiar to many, are a special subclass of these networks (Wuensche 1994:465). When Boolean networks have no exogenous inputs, as is the case for the networks we will discuss, they are called autonomous networks. The number of elements in a network is indexed by N, and the number of connections that each element has with other elements is indexed by K. Each element in the networks we shall be discussing is either active (has a value of 1) or inactive (has a value of 0) in any time step; elements have only these two possible states. The activity of each element depends on the activity or inactivity of the elements to which it is connected, plus the rules that govern those connections.

Here is an example to build your intuition of what we will be talking about. Figure 11.2a shows a tiny NK Boolean network where N=3 and K=2 (so there are three elements, each of which is connected to the other two). The activity of element 1 is governed by the "and" function; it becomes active at time t+1 only if both elements 2 and 3 are active at time t. The other two elements are governed by the "or" function and become active at time t+1 if at least one of their inputs is active at the previous step. Figure 11.2b shows each of the 2^3 possible states of this network at time t and its successor state at time t+1 (read along the rows). Figure 11.2c shows how the eight possible states for this network are divided into three basins

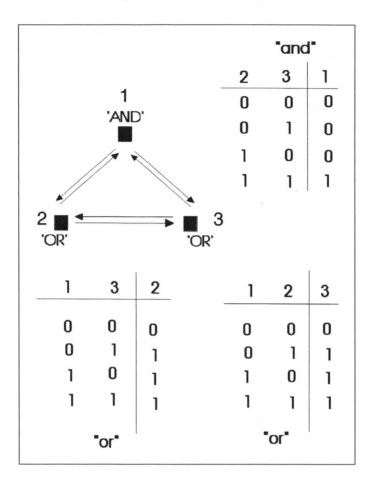

FIGURE 11.2A: A Boolean network with three elements (N=3) in which each element is connected to the other two (K=2); connections are governed by the Boolean "or" and "and" functions. B: The eight Boolean rules governing all possible states of each element in a transition from time t to time t+1. C: The three state cycles that represent the possible behaviors of the Boolean network represented in Figures 11.2a and 11.2b. (All after Kauffman 1993:fig. 5.6.)

1	T 2	3	1	T+1 2	3
0	0	0	0	0	0
0	0	1	0	1	0
0	1	0	0	1	1
0	1	1	1	1	1
1	0	0	0	1	1
1	0	1	0	1	1
1	1	0	0	1	1
1	1	1	1	1	1

I I.2B

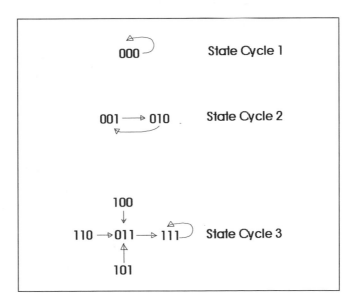

I I.2C

of attraction. The number of possible states in each basin of attraction (the state cycle length) varies from 1 to 5. Each attractor cycle (the repetitive stable behavior into which a network caught in any of these basins eventually settles) represents a permanent alternative behavior for the entire system. Without change in the wiring, or change in the rules, or some exogenous input, there is no way to jump from one to another. Notice that if each element begins with a value of 0, then the value for all elements will remain 0 forever (state cycle 1). If element 3 begins with a value of 1 while the other two elements have a value of 0, then in the next iteration of the network, element 2 will take on a value of 1, while the other two elements take on values of 0. By the third state transition, the network will return to its initial condition, and so forth, forever. This is state cycle 2. Any other initial condition for a network with these rules and connections will eventually result in all elements taking on the value of 1 (state cycle 3).

Boolean nets were designed by Stuart Kauffman and others, beginning in the late 1960s, to provide a computerizable approximation to genetic control circuitry, as an approach to answering questions like "what happens, in general, when the number of genes controlling other genes' activities increases?" In that analogy, genes are the N nodes in the network, and K is the number of epistatic interactions among the genes. If the rules governing these interactions are unknown for the empirical case, as they often will be, they can simply be modeled as random rules, in which case the system is a random Boolean network.

In this paper we will use autonomous RBNs as abstract models for exchange systems to examine what might happen in human communities governed by reciprocity as the number of elements (the exchanging units, here considered to be households) in the system increases and as the number of connections among those elements increases. Let a state of 1 for a particular household correspond to a gift of maize (or hospitality, or labor, or whatever) to the households with which it is connected and a state of 0 correspond to no gifting activity. In the example illustrated in Figure 11.2, the chosen wiring and rules result in three possibilities. State cycle 1 corresponds to no exchange, state cycle 2 to reciprocal exchange between "households" 3 and 2 in alternate periods, and state cycle 3 to continuous gifting by all households to each of the other two.

We wish to examine the notion that the systems of balanced reciprocity that, it is usual to believe, governed small-scale Neolithic communities become increasingly unwieldy in increasingly large communities, especially if K is allowed to scale along with N. If so, then it becomes useful to

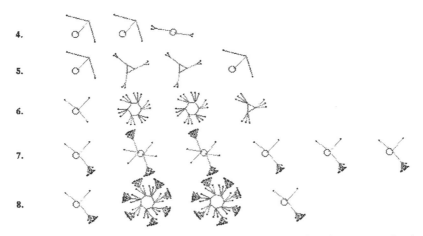

FIGURE 11.3. The basin of attraction fields for Boolean networks when K=2 under the majority rule, as N is scaled from 4 to 8. This and the next two figures are produced using DDLab (Wuensche 1998).

think about ways in which the size of K and N can be limited. We will show examples of networks with fixed wiring and a majority rule dictating that a household will be active (e.g., gifting in the present cycle) if and only if the majority of the households to which it is linked gifted in the previous time step.[2]

Let's first of all examine the case where K is quite small (K=2). Figure 11.3 shows the basins of attraction for example K=2 networks as we scale N from 4 to 8. These attractor fields are now shown in a more abstract way without labeling the values of the elements. Now lines instead of arrows represent transitions between possible states for the network, with the direction of time for the transitions being from the periphery toward the center and then clockwise around the attractor. This particular mapping of the basins of attraction represents only one of many possible wirings for systems of this size. The example corresponds to what might happen as small hamlets join together. In this illustration, chosen to be fairly typical, we see that the number of basins of attraction generally increases as N increases and that as N increases there is a tendency for the attractors to become quite "bushy" (though they remain symmetrical in appearance) and drain much larger basins (they spend a longer time going through transient states before settling into their stable behavior). Obviously there are many more possible states for the network when N=8 than when N=4.

What happens to networks of N=8 when we increase the connectivity so that each household is connected with the other seven? Figure 11.4

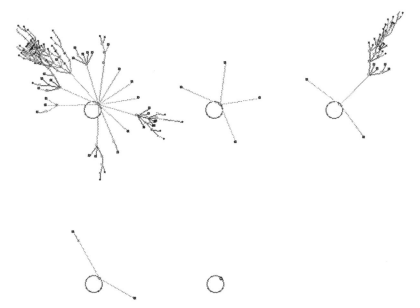

FIGURE 11.4. The basin of attraction fields for a Boolean network with K=7, N=8, under the majority rule.

shows the result, still applying the majority rule dictating that a household will gift in the current cycle if the majority of households with which it is linked gifted in the previous cycle. We see that there are more possible permanent behaviors and that two of these attractor cycles have a few long, straggly, sparsely branching subtrees. These represent long periods of transient behavior until a stable repetitive result is reached. By analogy with chaos theory developed for continuous dynamical systems, this behavior is called chaotic. In such networks many possible system states lie many transitions away from a stable repetitive pattern.

Increasing K slightly to 9 and N to 32—a small village!—we see that although the numbers of basins of attractions remains modest there is a huge number of possible states for the network (Figure 11.5). It is a surprising and intriguing result of the particular rule by which the elements are linked, the majority rule, that networks with this many linkages (K=9) do not appear more chaotic. Our brief explorations of the behavior of this rule show that compared with random rules for networks of the same N and K, it much more typically results in symmetrical, bushy state cycles in which a large number of different initial conditions rapidly settle into the same permanent stable behavior. Nevertheless, the state space (the ensemble of the possible states for the system and their organization into basins of attractions) is quite complicated compared to, say, the N=4 K=2 space.

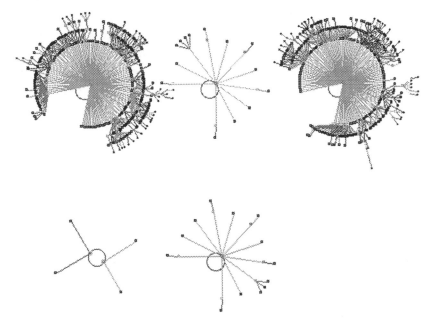

Figure 11.5. The basin of attraction fields for a Boolean network with K=9, N=32, under the majority rule.

In our analogy, the attractors represent alternative stable patterns of exchange or interaction that systems of various sizes and degrees of interconnectivity settle into and from which they cannot escape without some perturbation. When used to model gene networks, Kauffman has suggested, alternative attractors may represent alternative cell types in an organism. In the case of immune networks, alternative attractors might correspond to different immune states. For cardiac systems, alternative attractors might correspond to normal and abnormal rhythms (see Kauffman 1993:191).

We can't be sure that the majority rule provides the best or only possible rule for the way some specific economy based on balanced reciprocity actually worked. Fortunately, many general characteristics are known for Boolean networks with random rules and various settings for N and K (Kauffman 1993:181–224). When K=N (the case of the completely connected network), the number of state cycle attractors increases linearly as a function of N, and the state cycle lengths become very long. In fact, their length is an exponential function of N. For just four households, for example, median state cycle length is 8 (.5 × 2⁴) whereas for twenty-four households it is 2048 (.5 × 2¹²). There are relatively few basins of attraction in such systems, but they take a long time to traverse.

Significant changes in the properties of RBNs take place as K is reduced to 2. First, the number of attractors in these more sparsely connected networks increases much more slowly (as $\sqrt{N}$) as N increases than is the case in N=K networks. In these sparser networks the median state cycle length in each of the attractors also increases as a function of the $\sqrt{N}$ rather than as an exponential function of N. For four households, the median state cycle length is 2, and for twenty-four, about 10. Another important contrast between K=N and K=2 networks is their differing sensitivity to perturbation. Transient reversing of the activity of one element in a K=2 network usually does not cause the system to flow to a different attractor, whereas in K=N networks this almost always happens. That is why the basin of attraction portraits for the networks with higher K appears more leggy and asymmetrical than do the bushy symmetrical subtrees of K=2 networks.

Now, in this analysis we don't know which basins of attraction represent patterns of behavior that are advantageous to the systems and which represent disadvantageous patterns of behaviors. In the real world, of course, this is a primary consideration. We can ask a related question of our networks, however. Let's arbitrarily decide that one particular pattern of attractor represents the most fit pattern for a network. If we allow networks to change radically in their rules or their wiring of connections at each step and measure how long it takes populations of networks to improve the match of their attractors with this predetermined target, we find that when K=2, as N increases, it takes increasingly more generations to improve the fit of the networks' attractors with the arbitrarily defined target (Kauffman 1993:212). More simply, adaptation is more difficult and less likely as N gets larger even when K is small. We might roughly translate this to say that in our imagined community of reciprocators, even if mechanisms like strategic choice allowed people to change their sharing behaviors fairly radically in an attempt to achieve a desired outcome, movement toward an improved outcome will be increasingly difficult as the number of households in the community increases even if the number of other households with whom one is connected in a potential exchange relationship does not change. As K gets larger (that is, as the number of exchange connections among households increases), this difficulty of adaptation toward a specific target appears to get more severe.

We have not really done justice here to the richness and subtlety of RBN models and closely related NK landscape models as developed by Kauffman and others. To state things too simply, networks with high N and very small K (0 or 1) exhibit one kind of "complexity catastrophe" in that "fitness differentials between one-mutant neighbors dwindle below critical values and selection cannot overcome mutation" (Kauffman 1993:212). Such networks become frozen, and the states of their elements cease changing. However, a second kind of "complexity catastrophe" sets in when the components of a system are so richly coupled together (that is, have a high K) that the network exhibits chaotic behavior. Kauffman suggests that intermediate but rather low values of K (on the order of about 2–3) "poise" such networks near the transition between order and chaos, where selection has the greatest leverage in moving them toward higher fitness through the accumulation of useful variation.

Exploring Random Boolean Networks as a Metaphor

This model has some general implications for small-scale human organizations, if we are willing to take a generous perspective and not insist too much on the exactness of the metaphor (whose limitations we will soon consider). In general, increasing either the number of the interacting households or the density of their linkages may put stress on systems governed by balanced reciprocity. The nature of those stresses may include increased difficulty in predicting whether the system is headed toward a favorable pattern of interaction (what basin are we in?); the length of time it takes to arrive at a stable repetitive pattern (how long will this transition take?); an increased difficulty in changing system behavior toward a desired goal (how do we get to that specific attractor?); and increased difficulty in staying within a desirable attractor as households enter or leave the network or as rules of interaction change even slightly (how did we end up like this?).

This model suggests that reciprocity is most likely to be successful as the primary principle of economic organization in systems where N is small and K is in the region of 2–3.[3] In a system undergoing increases in N, one obvious way of preventing the dynamics from becoming chaotic is to increase the size of the basal units that constitute the N, for example, by moving the level at which exchange takes place from the household to the clan, sodality, moiety, or community. This may explain why something like reciprocity can structure large-scale exchange cycles such as the Te of the Mae Enga (e.g., Meggitt 1972), where prestations usually take place among units defined at the level of the phratry, clan, subclan, or patrilineage rather than at the level of the individual. Closer to home for this volume, a solution something like this is suggested by Richard Ford (1972) for the

Eastern Pueblos in historic times, where reciprocity as a principle remains important but has become impersonal and diffuse rather than personal, often structured as sodality-related transfers of food and hospitality during critical rites of passage or calendric observances.

It is also possible to construct RBNs with relatively high N and K and make them behave nonchaotically, as though these parameters were smaller. There are two main ways in which this can be done. The first is by biasing the internal homogeneity of the Boolean functions controlling the activities of the elements. If the Boolean functions governing whether an element will be on or off in the next period are unbiased, then a 1 or a 0 in the next period for each element is equally probable. But if most possible responses of an element to its input result in a 1 (or a 0), then those functions are said to be biased (Kauffman 1993:203–8). The majority rule we used above is slightly biased toward 0, which may be why we saw relatively orderly behavior even in moderately large networks.

Cultural norms (or at least social practice) are our closest analogy to the Boolean functions. Patterning of norms may make one type of output (behavior) much more common, given many different possible inputs. Very approximately, the corporate strategy of dual-processual theory (Blanton et al. 1996a) for achieving and maintaining power depends on the existence of norms patterned in such a way as to maintain group-oriented social formations given almost any input.

The other way in which more orderly dynamics can be achieved in networks with high N and K is through what are called "canalyzing functions" (Kauffman 1993:203–6). These are functions that force a specific result, as in the case where an element is connected to several others with the "or" function and will be forced on (or off) if any one of the elements to which it is linked is on (or off). The effect of such functions in causing orderly behavior is similar to the effect of biasing functions, although the analogy here may be with societies in which power is hierarchically distributed, such that one element by itself has the power to affect the values of other elements.

We find some intriguing correspondences between the conclusions derived from using RBNs as models for reciprocal exchange systems and earlier work based on different logics and currencies. Gregory Johnson (e.g., 1982) has shown that as the number of interacting decision makers in a society increases beyond a certain point (often about six), disputes erupt and decision performance degrades, presumably due to the stress of exceeding individual information-processing capacities. These stresses, he suggests, can be mitigated by formation of either sequential or simultaneous decision-making hierarchies that reduce the simultaneous communications load. Informal savings associations in developing countries, which are well documented in the anthropological literature, tend not to work as well as size increases, which also makes it less likely that the participants have close ethnic or social links.[4] Kent Flannery (1972:410) recognized situations in which there is "too great a coupling among institutions on various levels"; following Rappaport, he called this "the pathology of hyper-coherence." Johnson (1982:395) also suggested that decision performance decreases if the number of interacting individuals is too small.

In light of the preceding discussion, it is possible to place these suggestions in a larger context that may apply to all complex adaptive systems. Poor performance in very small groups or in societies with too few linkages among elements is an example of the complexity catastrophe at K=0; poor performance in groups with too many linkages and with insufficient structures for canalizing interaction, exchange, and decision making is an example of the high K complexity catastrophe. From this perspective it seems probable that societies are pushed—through processes of self-organization or selection, or both—into developing the structures associated with what we traditionally call "complex societies" as a way of avoiding the high-K complexity catastrophe when the population size of the interacting community passes certain thresholds (compare Kosse 1990).

The Limits of Metaphor

All metaphors have limits. Human communities are much more than very special cases of autonomous RBNs. Real societies have inputs from outside; those practicing "network-based" strategies (of dual-processual theory) are especially sensitive to outside exchange, whereas those practicing corporate strategies are especially sensitive to climatic inputs that affect level of activity in internal exchange networks (Kohler and Van West 1996). In real societies "wirings" among reciprocators are not random but are based on many factors, including friendship, propinquity, and kinship (e.g., Kent 1993), and exchange responses can be graded rather than simply on or off. Human societies are composed of not just one kind of exchange network but of many networks that are constructed through consanguineal, affinal, age-grade, and many other logics. Finally, real people can change their "Boolean functions" and connections with other households on the fly; human networks scarcely stand still long enough to be analyzed.

In fact, what would happen if the elements in the network could roam around and find exchange partners who had something they needed, and needed something they had, instead of being stuck in an inflexible web of reciprocal duties and obligations to kin and neighbors? What if one could pick an exchange partner for, say, obsidian, that was different from one for, say, corn or cotton? What if one did not need to use the same partner next time? What if one could find all these possibilities in a central place? All these are complications that are not easily accommodated by this model,[5] but we think these are precisely the factors that are critical to explaining the huge organizational changes we see in some areas of the late prehispanic Southwest. This is another pathway around the limitations on reciprocity, the one that societies fell into during the Classic period in the northern Rio Grande.

From Reciprocity to Markets

Many of the changes across the Late Coalition/Early Classic boundary in the northern Rio Grande are fundamentally due, we suggest, to the growing influence of a market economy. Our argument does not require the existence of centralized market*places,* although we suspect that these existed in or around the plazas of the largest towns; market exchanges may be dispersed. Following Pryor (1977:31–33), we define market exchanges as transactions in which there is high visibility of supply and demand forces. Such transactions can be negotiated through barter (and would have been, in our case) and need not require money. In markets, transactions can be accepted or rejected with few or no broad social repercussions, although trust and ongoing social interaction are sometimes important (Bowles 1998). There is openness to entering and leaving the market, and participation is voluntary. Finally, prices can be either fixed or fluctuating.

Markets are apparently quite ancient in the Americas. On the basis of the regional distribution of ceramics from local workshops, Feinman, Blanton, and Kowalewski (1984) infer the presence of markets in the Valley of Oaxaca by Monte Albán I times (500–200 B.C.).

Unfortunately, identification of markets—even in the context of marketplaces—is not entirely straightforward. The most recent and sophisticated attempt to develop indices of their presence is by Hirth (1998), who argues that a marketplace existed at the central Mexican site of Xochicalco in the Epiclassic (A.D. 650–900). His argument is based on the convergence of several criteria, including configurational data on the spatial and architectural characteristics of marketplaces; contextual data that identify the sorts of conditions (such as full-time craft specialists and large cities) under which marketplaces are virtually certain; and distributional data, at the household level, on obsidian and imported ceramics. Hirth (1998:456) argues that a key characteristic of market exchange is that "households provision themselves independently of one another and without regard to broader social and political relationships. . . . The result is an increase in the homogeneity of material culture assemblages between households of different social ranks."

Archaeologists have been strongly influenced by unilinear cultural evolutionary models that associate markets with states. States in turn should have precursors in chiefdoms with redistributive economies. Nevertheless, Wilk (1998:469) reminds us that "markets come in a variety of sizes and shapes . . . there is no single market principle . . . markets can be integrated into a remarkable variety of economic systems. Indeed, markets may best be seen as places where different kinds of economies—subsistence, specialized, simple-commodity-producing, elite gift-exchange—come together. From this perspective, they cannot be used as diagnostic markers of a single economic type or evolutionary grade."

Pryor (1977:110), who defines markets somewhat generously, argues that all societies have some market exchange, although the importance of these exchanges is correlated with his index of economic development. Interestingly for our argument here, Pryor (1977:112) suggests that markets are likely to become economically prominent earliest in societies that are characterized by monogamy and high participation of women in subsistence production, conditions that likely pertain to the northern Rio Grande of Late Coalition or Early Classic times. Our own tabulation of the importance of markets in the same sample of nonhierarchical societies used in Figure 11.1 shows that the percentage of exchange activity involving markets generally increases, as expected, with community size (Figure 11.6).[6] Market activity in this sample, which admittedly includes many societies in contact with states, becomes quite important at community sizes much lower than those achieved in the Classic northern Rio Grande.

Consider for a moment the social landscape of the Pajarito Plateau of north-central New Mexico around A.D. 1200, populated by dispersed, mostly mesa-top hamlets. (Many other areas could be substituted.) The three or four households in such units, probably related by consanguineal and affinal ties, certainly had dense internal linkages, on the order of $K=N$, and probably some sparser connections as well to other hamlets in the

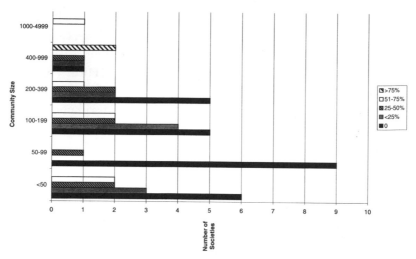

FIGURE 11.6. Percent of exchange activity involving markets in a sample of fifty-four nonhierarchical societies drawn from the Standard Cross-Cultural Sample.

neighborhood. Continued immigration onto the Pajarito in the 1200s was at first accommodated by adding additional hamlets of this size, but by about A.D. 1275 a larger class of site begins to appear, locally called plaza pueblos. Burnt Mesa Pueblo Area 1, the only one of these to have been investigated systematically, was two stories high along its western room block and the adjacent portions of its north and south room blocks and probably housed a maximum of about twenty households (Linse, Reilly, and Kohler 1992). This site class is short-lived and represents the final local acme of dry farming of mesa tops. By the mid-1300s, with the mesa tops possibly deforested (Huber and Kohler 1993) and eroding, most households further aggregate in or adjacent to well-watered valleys such as Frijoles Canyon. Farming becomes increasingly dependent on water-management techniques, and as these are worked out, they are most reliably and productively practiced along the Rio Grande itself, where, by the early 1500s, populations—by now in large aggregates—are almost exclusively residing.

Only an archaeologist can appreciate the richness and danger of the minefields negotiated in that brief summary, but let's not dwell on those, let's try to look at the big picture. The sudden appearance of sites in the plaza pueblo class almost certainly changed the N in the networks in which each household was embedded; what about the K? The plaza pueblo site plan, which is basically four small hamlets stuck together with a small plaza and a kiva in the middle (there is sometimes another outside to the southeast), suggests that the residents tried to maintain the older pattern of high connectivity within their modules (kin groups, room blocks) and sparser connectivity between. We may speculate, however, that the relatively low identification of each kin group with the village that would result from such patterns might put such aggregates at a disadvantage relative to other villages that had somehow discovered an organization that, without burdening households with a higher K, placed more of that connectivity among rather than within kin groups.

Tyuonyi-class towns of the Classic period represent the winners in this competition. Gone or at least submerged are the modular kin-based architectural units. Direct historical approaches and traditional thought among Southwestern archaeologists would suggest that households now have labor and exchange obligations within medicine and dance societies that crosscut kin lines, and sometimes pueblo lines, that are as salient as their obligations to kin. Our own analysis earlier in the chapter leads us to wonder if, in contrast to the earlier sites, balanced reciprocity at the level of the household could be effective as the dominant mode of exchange in communities of this size.

And yet Tyuonyi, with some three hundred ground-floor rooms, is only a small town by the standards of the northern Rio Grande Classic period. The multiple adobe room blocks and plazas of Sapawe, along the Rio Chama, may cover 29 hectares (Cordell 1997:404). Schroeder (1979b:246, 432) estimated that Acoma had six thousand inhabitants in Coronado's day and Pecos, two thousand.

There are abundant descriptions of the importance of trade among the protohistoric (Classic period) Pueblo people of the Southwest. Riley (1995:113–32), for example, emphasizes the variety and bulk of materials moving along corridors stretching from Hopi to Zuni and through the Tiguex province over to Pecos and from these areas to California, Sonora, Chihuahua, and the southern Plains. It is generally recognized that the volume and variety of materials moving along these routes and the distances they were moving represent a distinct and dramatic change from earlier periods. Snow (1981) provides a detailed account of the materials traded and cites historical records showing that in some instances the mechanism of movement was long-distance trading parties; he also documents an increasing emphasis on trade in bison and bison products for corn, cotton blankets, and ceramics between the northern Rio Grande pueblos and Plains people beginning around A.D. 1400 (see also Spielmann 1991a).

These exchanges are undoubtedly extremely important, especially since

Table 11.1 CONTRASTIVE TENDENCIES OF RECIPROCAL AND MARKET ECONOMIES.

Characteristic / Effect	Reciprocal Economic Systems	Small-scale Market Systems
Relationship among transactors	Social and personalized; exchange primarily within socially defined peer group; relationships enduring	Often anonymous, crossing lines of kinship or social group (Hirth 1998); relationships ephemeral (Weber 1978:636)
Nature of transactions	Transactions bundled with and channeled by social obligations (Mauss 1967)	Transactions more free from social obligations or considerations
How exchanged materials are matched	Like for like (dominated by food)	Unlike
Mode of production	Household mode of production dominant	Increasing importance of production for export and exchange
Ease of entry and exit	Low	High (Weber 1978)
Prices	Not widely known outside of a specific exchange system; often fixed	Generally known and often negotiable (Pryor 1977:32–33)
Household location	Access to subsistence resources a primary concern	Access to markets becomes a consideration (Smith 1976)
Household aggregation	May favor small aggregates under some circumstances (Kohler and Van West 1996)	Allows very large population concentrations (Muth 1975:28–31)
Volume of goods moved	Generally low (but see Allen 1984)	Higher
Variety of goods moved	Low	Greater
Distance goods move	Generally short, but somewhat dependent on level at which exchanging units are defined	Longer

some theories for the origins of markets (e.g., Polanyi 1944) require contact between different socioeconomic systems. We hear much less, however, about movements of goods within the Rio Grande. These are harder to see in the archaeological record, but even those that are visible are not adequately emphasized. Some time ago Snow (1981:364) noted that Shepard's 1930s discovery—that whole classes of pottery were being imported into some pueblos, while other pueblos specialized in making ceramic containers that ended up in the archaeological record at points both near and far—still had not been adequately digested by Southwestern archaeologists. This remains true today; what does the specialization in the production of a single commodity by whole communities tell us about the regional economic system? It is time to explore the probability that the northern Rio Grande economy of the Classic period was increasingly structured around and by market activity. Such activity would not have entirely displaced the older systems based on reciprocity, of course, but we contend that its consequences were nevertheless transformative. Markets thrive on and encourage very different kinds of relationships than do reciprocal exchange systems (Table 11.1).

A number of the characteristics of the late prehispanic period in the northern Rio Grande could be (and have been) explained individually without invoking markets. Aggregation could be due to defense; movement down into the Rio Grande trench and the Galisteo Basin could be explained by deforestation of the uplands, by climate change, or by the development of productive water-management techniques (as we did above); the presence of large plazas and the long-distance movement of some goods, by ceremonial demands; the apparent ease of accommodating new arrivals into the Rio Grande from the San Juan, by development of a new ritual system; and the apparent decreasing importance of kin-group affiliation, by new ceremonial organization.

Without invoking markets, however, it is somewhat less easy to explain the quite obvious new emphasis on production for exchange of ceramics, obsidian (Root and Harro 1992), and cotton (Herhahn and Hill 1998) that marks the Classic period. More important, *in their totality,* the constellation of changes that we see clearly by the late A.D. 1300s in this area is most simply and fundamentally explained by the effects of increasingly important market activity. Markets are transformative because they reduce the importance of kinship; they promote easier entry into and exit from communities; they ease acceptance of "stranger communities"; and they are stimulated by and in turn promote the development of craft specialization.

Furthermore, for at least two reasons, markets allow and promote the development of larger aggregates. Market exchange is usually more efficient than reciprocal exchange, enabling at least some (and possibly all) people to be better off without anyone suffering as a consequence. If by virtue of access to a market economy, a household with excess maize can exchange maize having low value (to it) for goods it needs (when it needs them) with another household that holds those in excess, then both have profited. Market access to goods may then raise the standard of living, which both favors internal population growth and attracts migrants from regions on the periphery of the market. We should consider the possibility that people come out of hinterlands like the Pajarito district in part because they are attracted to the higher standard of living promoted by the strong Rio Grande markets.

Of course we should not ignore the probability that Kachina dancers enlivened those large Classic period plazas. But let us not fail to consider that those spectacles also provided a wonderful opportunity for traders hawking everything from food to ceremonial paraphernalia at the plaza entrances. Toll (1985:370–89) summarizes the variety of economic activities surrounding current and historic Pueblo ritual gatherings.

Nor do we wish to propose that those traders somehow sponsored, even metaphorically, those festivals. More likely the new ceremonial system and new economic system were complementary and mutually reinforcing. (What better occasion to trade than a large gathering of people come to dance or watch the dancers? What better way to assure a large turnout for the dance than to make it also an occasion to trade?) Perhaps they even had a historical connection, and their local adoption was stimulated, however indirectly, by the same sources in Chihuahua and ultimately Mesoamerica via the densely occupied corridors of the Rio Grande and the Rio Conchos. That possibility lies, fortunately, beyond the scope of this essay. Our point in this last section is simply that the rapidly escalating importance and impact of market exchange in the late prehispanic Rio Grande have been virtually ignored in our conversations about the structural changes that we all recognize.

Some Remarks on the Essays

The economies of the Pueblo world up into the fourteenth century A.D. were probably dominated by reciprocal exchanges. This is neither a new nor a startling observation, but it may be that the structuring potential of such economic activity and the norms that tend to accompany it have been inadequately recognized.

For example, reciprocal economic systems would seem to resist the development of inequalities among members of the same network and would probably resist, though less immediately and successfully, the development of great inequalities between members of different networks. They would seem to enhance the power of kinship and perhaps, by their relative structural inflexibility, be resistant to change in general. They would seem to have a tendency to grow Lego-block style, by sticking similar poorly melded units together until the construction falls apart.

Even the Chaco phenomenon, despite its size and complexity, seems to be an example of this model of organization. We agree with Wills when he suggests in this volume that the organizational work getting done at Chaco represents an effort at communitas, a corporate-leadership-type effort to suppress competition. Even more specifically, we agree with his view that the great houses were metaphors for this inclusive emphasis in Chacoan society: "A specific household in the larger Chacoan world could conceptualize its relationships with very distant households as being 'like' its relationship with other households in its local pueblo. The religious elites of Chaco, then, were 'like' the respected elders of the pueblo, but with larger scope" (Kohler 1998:22).

How different seems the organizational basis of the protohistoric (Rio Grande) Salinas District sites considered by Graves and Spielmann in this volume. Absolutely rightly, in our view, they emphasize the appearance in this region of not just large pueblos but of clusters of pueblos that collectively house several thousand people. They remark on the notable increase in intensity of long-distance exchange of decorated ceramics, obsidian, and cotton. They note little evidence for individual prestige and wealth accumulation despite population sizes that would suggest the development of leadership positions based on personal persuasion and influence. They remark on an intriguing pattern in which Gran Quivira enjoyed much greater access to bison and bison products than the nearby Pueblo Colorado and had a greater diversity of nonlocal ceramic materials and much higher ceramic deposition rates. This pattern is interpreted, perhaps rightly, to indicate a pattern of competitive large-scale feasting that was more prevalent at Gran Quivira than at Pueblo Colorado.

We suggest an alternative (or possibly complementary) simple explanation for these patterns: Gran Quivira had the marketplace in the Jumanos cluster. The reason for the cluster of pueblos is that the other sites are located in positions of compromise between access to subsistence resources and access to the market (Table 11.1). Gran Quivira has more bison products and a greater variety of nonlocal ceramic materials because these materials were brought there from many neighboring localities for barter to people from Gran Quivira and people from the other pueblos in the Jumanos cluster. The higher ceramic deposition rate probably does indicate that people from neighboring pueblos were coming in to visit, but were they feasting, or bartering, or both? Is the pattern of little evidence for individual prestige and wealth accumulation due to the tendency noted by Hirth (1998) for market exchanges to crosscut socially defined groups?

Perhaps towns like Gran Quivira were not true central places for a completely integrated market system. More likely, they supported activities similar to the local markets that Smith (1976:46) reconstructs for the Tiv before they were connected to the Nigerian national system, when they seem to have been characterized by "few, poorly articulated trade gatherings whose locations and functions were variable and unstable" (though probably, in our case, linked to the ceremonial calendar).

It seems likely that the emerging market economy was weaker in the Zuni-Cibola region than in the Rio Grande and still more so in the Hopi region, and that as a consequence (or, perhaps, as a cause of the poor penetration of markets) these societies retained more elements of the older kin-group organization and more elements of the reciprocal economy and tended to solve the problems associated with growth through developing impersonal reciprocity based on exchange in accordance with role rather than in accordance with persona. (That is, the level at which the exchanging units were defined scaled up.) If roles were associated with kin groups, this of course leads to the possibility of some concentration of power, within the limits of economies basically structured along lines of reciprocity. Keith Kintigh (this volume) notes that burial data from Hawikuh tend to support the inference that power was concentrated in religious offices available to only a select few of the resident lineages. Potter and Perry's chapter (this volume) notes the development of quite uneven final distributions of highly valued fauna, the fruit of communal long-distance hunts, among residential units at the Pueblo de los Muertos.

In passing, we note (even though it is not closely related to our thesis) that the ritual-symbolic differentiation between the circular and the square site plans that Potter and Perry contrast in the El Morro Valley is very strongly paralleled by the same contrast in the shape of Hopewellian ceremonial enclosures noted by DeBoer (1997). DeBoer links this opposition to a winter-summer distinction, which he ultimately assimilates, through a structuralist argument, to Ortiz's (1969) interpretation of the Tewa as "nervously poised between an egalitarian ideal and the danger of tyranny" (DeBoer 1997:236). It's a small world after all.

Conclusions

We have devoted a great deal of effort in Southwestern archaeology to complicated models of political leadership and ceremonial organization. We do not deny that such considerations may illuminate certain aspects of the archaeological record. Our goal in this chapter, however, has been to introduce a model that suggests the sorts of problems that settlements or communities may encounter with growth if their economies are structured primarily along lines of reciprocity (as we suggest was the case throughout the Pueblo world through the thirteenth century A.D.). The RBN metaphor suggests that there should be fairly severe limits on the size of settlements operating through balanced reciprocity at the level of the household; we think these limits are in fact visible in community sizes cross-culturally and in the archaeological record.

We then proposed that the economies on the eastern periphery of the late prehispanic Puebloan world were increasingly emphasizing market processes. This is not an entirely new argument (although the word "market" is rarely used), but the consequences of this have not been appreciated. One of these is that markets reduce the importance of kinship. Several other aspects of the Classic period record in the northern Rio Grande that individually have been explained by resort to a variety of mechanisms may all be fundamentally connected to the increasing prominence of market activity.

Why should markets develop in the northern Rio Grande at this time but not earlier or not elsewhere in the Southwest? A complete explanation deserves a whole essay. The essential ingredients, however, appear to have been the influx during the 1200s of many new Pueblo peoples, accelerating in the late 1200s; the increasing contacts with Plains peoples who were even less definable within the reciprocal framework than the Pueblo immigrants; the simultaneous contact with new and possibly linked ceremonial and economic systems to the south, providing models for reorganization; and the increased time demands of the small-scale irrigation and water-harvesting techniques practiced along the Rio Grande. Blanton (1983:56–57) has suggested that the origin of market systems in Oaxaca should be understood "primarily as a consequence of the changing rhythm of work-time" as two-crop systems began to replace one-crop cycles. As a consequence, to use modern market jargon, households began to "outsource" activities such as ceramic manufacture to more efficient specialists as a strategy to preserve some nonwork time in spite of the new demands. In the northern Rio Grande case these demands also included the production of tobacco and cotton, difficult crops being grown either for the first time or in much greater quantities than before.

We were initially surprised to see that the chapters discussed above provide more evidence for unequal distributions of power and wealth in what we infer to have been the more traditional kin-based reciprocal systems to the west than in the societies increasingly dominated by markets to the east. Perhaps the power of market transactions to crosscut kin lines is initially a more powerful force than the ability of specific individuals to concentrate wealth in market economies. It may also be important that in our case, the economies dominated by markets were still quite young when they were disrupted by the Spanish. Apparently, reciprocal exchange can be manipulated by ambitious actors to create dependencies along kin lines.

At the beginning of this chapter we mentioned several mechanisms that might be responsible for the origins and maintenance of economic reciprocity in society. These included individual-level selection of reciprocators in small groups having a sufficient density of other reciprocators (by analogy with the increased payoffs to direct interaction among players having cooperative strategies in Prisoner's Dilemma games); individual selection through reputation building leading to future advantageous assortative interactions; or group-selection mechanisms. Interestingly, any of these mechanisms might have become less important in the contexts we describe for the Classic period northern Rio Grande. The presence of more players with a diversity of strategies would reduce the likelihood of interactions among reciprocators in the first case and increase the difficulty of building and maintaining a reputation in the second case. Too much mixing among groups would reduce the power of group selection to maintain highly cooperative strategies, as well as increasing the difficulty of identifying cheaters.

We hope that this chapter stimulates more attention to the powerful structuring role of changing fundamental economic patterns that we think has been unduly ignored in recent conversations about prehispanic Southwestern sociopolitical organization. It might also be worthwhile if it draws attention to the fainter lines of constraint that underlie all physical and living systems organized into networks.

ACKNOWLEDGMENTS

We thank Sam Bowles, Bill Lipe, and Barbara Mills for comments on an earlier version of this paper, Andy Wuensche for help navigating through DDLab, an anonymous reviewer for some constructive criticism and good leads, and, finally, Barbara Mills once more for her kind offer to participate in the symposium from which this volume grew.

NOTES

1. Relative importance of reciprocity refers to the relative percentage of extra-household procurement of goods and/or services conducted within the confines of reciprocity. Reciprocity is defined as obligatory (or quasi-obligatory) exchange of goods or services that is conducted regardless of demand existing on both sides. Reciprocity implies continued maintenance of the reciprocal exchange relationship and often implies previous interaction between exchange partners. In general, reciprocity here may be thought of as the obligatory two-way *social* exchange of goods and/or services, as opposed to one-way exchanges, as with a potlatch. Community size codes are from Murdock and Wilson (1980).

2. The majority rule provides the most exact model of a reciprocal dyadic system when $K=1$. In that case K will be "on" (1) in the current cycle when its partner was "on" in the previous cycle, and vice versa. For larger K, the majority rule is only an approximate rendering of a reciprocal system, since K will be "on" (or "off") for all its linked households at time $t+1$, even though a minority of those households may have been in the opposite state at time t. Such phenomena may happen, of course, in systems governed by delayed or indirect reciprocity.

3. We attempted to assess variables such as N, K, and the length of time by which gifts given were separated in time from gifts received, in various societies governed by reciprocity from materials in the HRAF, and in the Standard Cross-Cultural Sample (Murdock and White 1969). We were largely unsuccessful, because these variables are not emphasized by previous theories and are therefore not discussed or coded. Systematic work with primary materials is needed to assess the N and K parameters for a sample of societies.

4. In developing countries, informal associations designed to save enough for an exceptionally large purchase are a good example of the strengths, and limits, of small-scale reciprocal arrangements. Each participant puts a fixed amount of money into a pot at regular intervals, with the pot going to one member at a time, until each member receives the pot once. Default by members who receive their pots early are least likely when the associations are small (ten to twenty members) and the participants are known to each other (Besley, Coate, and Loury 1993).

5. Although one could say, in a general way, that they tend to keep effective N and K low by defining them through transactions rather than through social relationships or residency.

6. Relative importance of markets refers to the relative percentage of extra-household procurement of goods and services conducted within the confines of a market setting. Markets are defined as the immediate exchange of goods or services between individuals or groups in which such goods and/or services are valued and available according to demand. Market-based exchanges are ephemeral and do not imply long-term relationships (though some may in fact exist). In general, market activity may be thought of as the "free" two-way *economic* exchange of goods and/or services as opposed to one-way economic exchanges such as tribute or taxes. Community size codes are from Murdock and Wilson (1980). Presence or absence of money or "money-stuff" was disregarded in coding for reciprocity versus markets. Money was present in about half of the societies selected, but in general it consisted of either domestically useable goods or subsistence items. Where token money (indigenous coins, paper money, etc.) or the currency of a nearby state was used, it was often in conjunction with other items. Finally, the use of money does not change the *nature* of the relationships that are still either social-obligatory or "free"-economic. Thus when we speak of markets or reciprocity in nonstratified societies, we are not implying "barter" or exchange of nonmoney items/services alone.

12

Dual-Processual Theory and Social Formations in the Southwest

GARY M. FEINMAN

ANTHROPOLOGISTS LONG HAVE puzzled over how to characterize the socio-political organization of ancient Southwestern societies. Many researchers have viewed the majority of precontact Southwestern social formations as egalitarian (e.g., Ciolek-Torrello and Whittlesey 1996; Graves, Longacre, and Holbrook 1982:202; Johnson 1989; Vivian 1989:104). Others have emphasized greater variation in the past, recognizing that complex and hierarchical organizations were present at certain times in particular places (e.g., Cordell and Plog 1979; Upham 1982). Finally, a third group (e.g., Reid and Whittlesey 1990) claims to work from the bottom up, inductively interpreting the patterning recognized in archaeological data using insights derived from the direct application of specific Southwestern ethnographic analogies. Of course, the efficacy and tenability of this latter position entirely depend on a broad, analytical consensus concerning both the definitional criteria for hierarchical formations in the archaeological record and the nature of historic/ethnographic Southwestern social organization.

Although the proponents of these three opposing positions have uniformly agreed on very little, they did, until a decade or so ago, generally adhere to two basic and underpinning assumptions. First, they tended to see postcontact ethnographic or historic societies in the Southwest as largely egalitarian. And second, they shared a largely monolithic or unilinear (band-tribe-chiefdom-state) notion of how hierarchical social foundations are organized (e.g., Fried 1967; Service 1971) and how we might recognize them (or what indicators might be used to identify them) in the archaeological record (e.g., Wason 1994). In this essay, both of the above assumptions are questioned with principal attention given to the diverse cross-cultural nature of different hierarchical formations. Dual-processual theory (see Mills, this volume), which contrasts corporate and network forms of political action, is discussed, and some Southwestern social formations are argued to fit a less traditional corporate form of hierarchical organization. The implications of this argument are potentially significant, both for how we conceptualize ancient and historic Southwestern societies and also for broader comparative models of hierarchical formation.

I begin the remainder of this essay by briefly summarizing a theme of this collection: many examples of ancient Southwestern social organization do not fit traditional conceptions of tribes or chiefdoms (sensu Service 1971). These Southwestern social formations were neither entirely egalitarian in the sense of Morton Fried (1967), nor do they appear to have been characterized by the individualizing aggrandizers (Clark and Blake 1994) and competitive accumulators (Hayden 1990) that populate many current models of emergent sociopolitical complexity (see Wills, this volume). Following that discussion, dual-processual theory is briefly outlined, and the notion of corporately organized hierarchies is argued to have utility for understanding sociopolitical organization in the ancient and historic Southwest. I propose that political and social status inequalities need not always be directly manifest through stark discrepancies in individual or household wealth, and I discuss a comparative example from urban and hierarchically organized Teotihuacan (central Mexico). Subsequently, I address certain interpretive problems regarding the application of dual-processual theory and specific misconceptions that have been raised by previous essays in this volume. In a final segment, I look beyond the definition of corporate hierarchies in the precontact Southwest toward new insights and the definition of novel research questions that are raised by the application of dual-processual theory.

The Applicability of Service's Concepts to the Ancient Southwest

For much of the past half-century, the study of archaeological sociopolitical organization has relied heavily on the constructs of tribe and chiefdom (Service 1971). In Elman Service's evolutionary framework, tribes were viewed as egalitarian, having ephemeral and achieved positions of leadership. Alternatively, status was inherited in chiefdoms. In the latter formations, inequality was institutionalized and "pervasive" (Service 1971:145). For Service (1971:134), "chiefdoms are redistributional societies with a permanent central agency of coordination." This central agency (or the chief) comes to take on social, political, and religious functions as well as serving a nodal economic role for the society. Thus economic centrality is linked directly to political power and authority. Reflective of their name, chiefdoms also were seen to revolve around a specific individual (the chief), who generally was thought to have inherited his office through primogeniture (a highly linear system of descent) (Service 1971:147).

As outlined by Service (1971), the concept of chiefdom associated these hierarchical and unequal social formations with individualized power, a tight linkage between economic and sociopolitical inequality, and a high degree of centralization (focused on the chief and his lineal kin group). These associations in Service's framework have been fostered and amplified in a number of recent theoretical works that have stressed and broadly generalized the entrepreneurial tendencies of emergent leaders as well as the advantages in biological fitness that they are hypothesized to accrue (e.g., Hayden 1995; Maschner 1995). More broadly, the association of increasingly hierarchical social forms with the greater centralization of power and the concentration of economic wealth in the hands of specific individuals (and their immediate kin) is a basic notion that is found widely in archaeological thought (e.g., Flannery 1972; Haas 1982; Roscoe 1993).

Consequently, it is not really surprising that early perspectives on sociopolitical organization in the ancient Southwest coalesced around the cross-cultural models of tribes and chiefdoms. Those that adhered to an egalitarian or tribal view emphasized household autonomy and self-sufficiency. The constraints and implications of power, sociopolitical organization, and economic interdependency on individuals, households, and communities were rarely considered (e.g., Euler et al. 1979; see also Larson et al. 1996 for a contemporary example). Alternatively, the diametrically opposing expectations for nonegalitarian formations or chiefdoms included marked disparities in patterns of access (both during life and at death in burials) and the ostentatious display of personalized wealth (e.g., Grebinger 1973).

Yet, as noted in this collection (for example, see Fish and Fish; Kintigh), many precontact Southwestern societies do not easily conform to the complete set of indicators for either egalitarian tribes or hierarchical chiefdoms (see also McGuire 1992). For example, if a generalized picture of late precontact pueblos is considered (Table 12.1), one sees few marked intra-populational distinctions in burial furniture or treatment. In addition, great differences in access to wealth are rare, and there is little evidence for elaborate elite residences (that are distinct from more general domestic contexts). Representations of particular leaders or special personages are

Table 12.1 CHARACTERIZATION OF LARGE LATE PRECONTACT PUEBLOAN ORGANIZATION.

	Conforming Features	Apparent Anomalies
Egalitarian Formations	Rarity of princely burials	Monumental public construction
	Similar residential settings	Amassed labor efforts
	Damped household access differentials	Multimodal settlement pattern
	Lack of identifiable "rulers"	Marked disparities in storage
	Intrasettlement social segmentation	Restricted access to ceremonial features
		Specialized production and labor divisions
		Select differences in access/burial
		Large aggregated populations
Chiefly Polities	Monumental public construction	Rarity of princely burials
	Amassed labor efforts	Similar residential settings
	Multimodal settlement pattern	Damped household access differentials
	Marked disparities in storage	Lack of identifiable "rulers"
	Restricted access to ceremonial features	Intrasettlement social segmentation
	Specialized production and labor divisions	
	Select differences in access/burial	
	Large aggregated populations	

extremely uncommon (if not entirely absent). All of these findings are consistent with the egalitarian model and not with a traditional picture of chiefly organization.

Yet the later precontact Pueblos also do not conform to the traditional view of egalitarian societies (Table 12.1). As a number of papers in this volume illustrate (Graves and Spielmann; Wills; Kintigh), differential patterns of access have been noted between neighboring pueblos that were part of the same community and/or between different segments of the same pueblo. Monumental architecture was erected involving the coordination of a significant labor force, although the largest energy expenditures may have been devoted to domestic construction rather than public or elite space (Wills, this volume). Storage space was not evenly distributed across or between sites (Hantman 1989; Lightfoot 1984; Saitta 1991). And household economic self-sufficiency is no longer a widely accepted perception (Plog 1995). There is an increasing realization that interdependency, inequality, and elements of organizational complexity were part of many precontact (as well as historical) Southwestern sociopolitical systems, although the nature of that inequality and complexity may not always (or entirely) fit the wealth-based and individualizing aspects of our traditional models of socioeconomic behavior.

Corporate versus Network: An Alternative Comparative Dimension

As noted above, traditional neo-evolutionary models have tended to conflate increasing hierarchical complexity with ever greater degrees of centralization (Flannery 1972; Fried 1967; Service 1971). The development of hierarchical levels of leadership above the household group is seen as a coincident process with the consolidation of resources and power in the hands of a smaller and smaller coterie of people or even specific individuals. Yet it seems reasonable to question whether all hierarchical organizations are structured in the same fashion. From our own experiences, we know that some governing institutions are more democratic than others. At the same time, certain leaders stress more cooperative behaviors while others use their position in more self-serving ways. Even in complex and hierarchical institutions, the foundations and manifestations of power are highly variable (e.g., Lehman 1969). Consequently, when examining and comparing institutional and societal organizations, the adoption of a unilineal or monolithic perspective focused on hierarchical complexity alone would seem to be somewhat limiting or incomplete as illustrated for some of the social systems in the ancient Southwest.

Although I concur that a more multidimensional or heterarchical perspective is necessary to compare societal organization and decision making (see Crumley 1995), it also is useful to consider and build on prior studies that already have highlighted either different modes of leadership or distinct socioeconomic strategies (Table 12.2). This is the basis of the corporate/

Table 12.2 POLITICAL/ECONOMIC TYPOLOGIES THAT PARALLEL THE CORPORATE/NETWORK DISTINCTION.

Network/Exclusionary	Corporate	References
Individualizing chiefdoms	Group-oriented chiefdoms	Renfrew (1974), Drennan (1991)
Gumsa	*Gumlao*	Leach (1954), Friedman (1975)
Prestige-goods systems	Big-man competitive feasting	Friedman (1982)
Wealth-based	Knowledge-based	Lindstrom (1984)
Material-based	Magical-based	Harrison (1987)
Finance-based big man	Production-based big man	Strathern (1969)
Noncorporate organization	Corporate organization	Schneider, Schneider, and Hansen (1972)
Wealth finance	Staple finance	D'Altroy and Earle (1985)
Wealth distribution	Staple finance	Gilman (1987)
Twem exchange	*Sem* exchange	Lederman (1986)

network dimension (outlined below; see also Blanton 1998; Blanton et al. 1996a; Feinman 1995, 1997a, 1997b, 1998), which can be considered in conjunction with (and as orthogonal to) the analysis of hierarchical complexity. When studying the archaeological and historical record, there are numerous axes for possible comparison and various potential avenues for interpretation. Consequently, when expanding the cross-cultural analytical framework beyond the dimension of hierarchical complexity, it is prudent to define and construct comparative perspectives based on previously useful observations and constructions. In a general sense, such comparative insights are potentially important for the interpretation of the archaeological record, which in my opinion cannot speak for itself. At the same time, such an approach has advantages for the analysis of precontact and historic Southwestern social formations, which often have been left out of larger cross-cultural debates and considerations (Fish and Fish, this volume).

In contrast to a more monolithic perspective on hierarchies, this paper

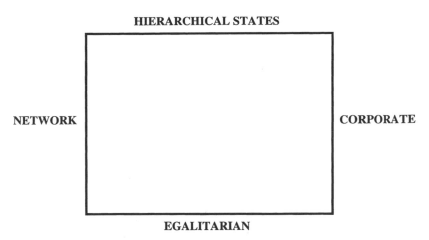

HIERARCHICAL STATES

NETWORK

CORPORATE

EGALITARIAN

FIGURE 12.1. Two orthogonal dimensions for the comparison of sociopolitical organization.

outlines a second comparative dimension that can be conceptualized as orthogonal to (or crosscutting) the familiar axis of hierarchical complexity (Figure 12.1). This second dimension defines a continuum between two modes or strategies of political-economic behavior that my colleagues and I (Blanton et al. 1996a; Feinman 1995) have referred to as the network or exclusionary mode, on the one hand, and the corporate mode, on the other. In proposing these modes and this analytical dimension, the aim is not to construct a new societal typology. Nor is concern with the corporate/network dimension meant to replace a focus on hierarchy. In principle, both the corporate and network modes can be envisioned at any degree or level of societal complexity. Rather, an expansion of the analytical frame is intended to improve our theoretical constructs and enhance our understanding of variation and change in historical cases (such as those described for the ancient Southwest) that do not easily conform to the traditional unilinear or unidimensional framework.

As noted above, the corporate/network continuum outlined here parallels similar distinctions in leadership strategies, organizational diversity, and political economy that have been noted in earlier comparative works (Table 12.2). These two general political-economic modes or paths of action (corporate-based and network-based) are envisioned as dual strategies of political-economic behavior (Table 12.3). To summarize what has been published by Richard Blanton, myself, and others, the corporate mode emphasizes staple food production, communal ritual, public construction, shared power, large cooperative labor tasks, social segments that are woven

Table 12.3 BASIC TENDENCIES OF THE NETWORK AND CORPORATE MODES.

Network	Corporate
Concentrated wealth	More even wealth distribution
Individual power	Shared power arrangements
Ostentatious consumption	More balanced accumulation
Prestige goods	Control of knowledge, cognitive codes
Patron/client factions	Corporate labor systems
Attached specialization	Emphasis on food production
Wealth finance	Staple finance
Princely burials	Monumental ritual spaces
Lineal kinship systems	Segmental organization
Power inherited through personal glorification	Power embedded in group association/affiliation
Ostentatious elite adornment	Symbols of office
Personal glorification	Broad concerns with fertility, rain

together through broad integrative ritual and ideological means, and suppressed economic differentiation. Despite the presence of large architectural spaces, individual leaders in such polities are relatively "faceless" and "anonymous" when it comes to representational art. In contrast, the network mode places greatest significance on personal prestige, wealth exchange, individualized power accumulation, elite aggrandizement, lineal patterns of inheritance and descent (e.g., patriarchy), particularizing ideologies, personal networks, princely burials, and the specialized (frequently attached) manufacture of status-related craft goods.

The corporate/network continuum bears some similarity to the distinction drawn by Johnson (1982) between societies having simultaneous and sequential-ritual hierarchies. Johnson's simultaneous hierarchies (which conform to the more traditional notion of hierarchies) are defined as social arrangements in which a few central individuals exercise integration and control over a larger population (they parallel the network mode). By contrast, sequential hierarchies are described as more consensual and egalitarian formations in which ritual and elaborate ceremonies are argued often to have key roles in the integration of modular social segments. However, unlike Johnson's sequential model, already widely applied to the precontact

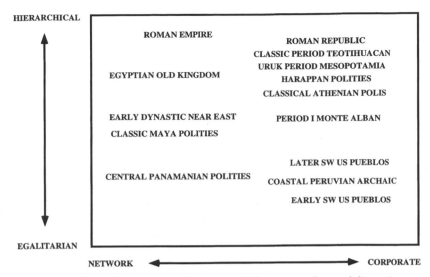

HIERARCHICAL

ROMAN EMPIRE

ROMAN REPUBLIC
CLASSIC PERIOD TEOTIHUACAN
URUK PERIOD MESOPOTAMIA
EGYPTIAN OLD KINGDOM   HARAPPAN POLITIES
CLASSICAL ATHENIAN POLIS

EARLY DYNASTIC NEAR EAST   PERIOD I MONTE ALBAN

CLASSIC MAYA POLITIES

LATER SW US PUEBLOS
CENTRAL PANAMANIAN POLITIES   COASTAL PERUVIAN ARCHAIC
EARLY SW US PUEBLOS

EGALITARIAN

NETWORK ⟵⟶ CORPORATE

FIGURE 12.2. Selected historic examples compared along two orthogonal dimensions.

Southwest, we have argued that corporate strategies are not restricted to nonstratified/nonhierarchical social formations (or "egalitarian societies" in the sense of Fried). A corporate organization is not by definition synonymous with egalitarian organization. Thereby, our framework challenges the unilinear proposition that cultural evolution necessarily moves either simply and directly from more consensual to simultaneous (individually focused) forms of organization or toward greater centralization. Corporate hierarchies may be characterized by more power sharing, greater depersonalization of rule, and less flaunting of wealth than is traditionally conceptualized for hierarchical or nonegalitarian societies. Yet corporate hierarchies should not be broadly equated with political or economic equality or utopian communalism. In corporate hierarchies, certain individuals may be more apt from birth to rise to ruling positions than others (based on kin or clan affiliations or other factors). And once in such positions, these agents or councils can make decisions that fundamentally affect the basic social and economic well-being of others. In contrasting corporate and network hierarchical formations, we believe that we have crafted a conceptual structure that will help us understand a key dimension of variation in ancient political economies.

In various historical and archaeological contexts (Figure 12.2), scholars have noted architectural and artifactual indicators of amassed labor and power, communal ritual, agricultural intensification, and demographic concentration but have not found the signs of wealth accumulation and ostentatious individualized display that otherwise might be predicted by the monolithic model. In many of these confounding cases (like the ancient Southwest), researchers have debated which "taxonomic box" (for example, egalitarian polity or chiefdom, chiefdom or state) is more appropriate. Yet, in so doing, informative behavioral differences have been ignored or assigned to local/unique/specific factors alone. Perhaps we must recognize that despite its urban setting there was not an all-powerful and individualizing king at Classic period Teotihuacan as we so clearly have for its distant neighbors, the Maya (Blanton et al. 1996a; Cowgill 1997; Feinman 1997c). Other scholars have inferred that the differences we have observed reflect the peculiarities of the archaeological record or the quirks of its preservation and recovery. Yet while such issues cannot be ignored, I suspect that ancient peoples were intimately aware of what would (and what would not) survive the tests of time in their local setting when they materialized their landscape.

The corporate/network dimension is defined as continuous because these organizational strategies may coexist in particular spatiotemporal contexts. Nevertheless, in certain ways these modes are antagonistic, and so in many situations one strategy or the other will have a tendency to predominate. That is, in a given social field, the ways that power can be implemented or people and resources put together may be limited and constrained. However, the relative predominance of a particular strategy can shift in a specific region or societal context over time with changes in the larger socio-environmental setting.

Corporate Hierarchies and Historic Southwestern Social Formations

Before turning to precontact Southwestern social formations, it is useful to consider briefly the organizations of the ethnographic and historic populations of this region. Here, I focus on the Pueblos (see Feinman 1997a for a fuller discussion) because their sociopolitical formations have been analyzed frequently and in detail.

The historic Pueblos are intricate social groupings that are themselves spatially and temporally diverse. Yet archaeologists often have liberally applied the direct historical approach and have used an egalitarian interpretation of the historic Pueblos as a template for understanding the precontact Plateau Southwest. For that reason, it is informative to summarize the recent scholarly interpretations of postcontact Puebloan organization that have been advanced by Brandt (1994), Levy (1992), Whiteley (1985), Watts

(1997), and others. The historic Pueblos are described as tightly interconnected and hierarchical societies that lack strong individualized leadership or extreme distinctions in wealth. Their perspectives closely correspond to what we would refer to as corporately organized hierarchical societies. Recent discussions of Pueblo organization describe (1) hierarchical offices that were not tied to great disparities of wealth or direct lineal descent, (2) shared power that was placed in the hands of ritual/political councils, (3) an emphasis on large public ceremonies, (4) the maintenance of order largely through rituals of fertility and the restricted control of sacred knowledge, (5) strong corporate codes that helped to reinforce order through ideological sanction and public ridicule, (6) ritual events that both maintained and integrated ranked societal segments, (7) faceless (even masked) rule and discipline with the power to allocate resources and even banish households from their means of production, (8) the economic importance of a communal organization of labor, and (9) an emphasis on staple finance/intensive food production rather than wealth distribution or a marked emphasis on prestige goods exchange.

Watts's (1997) recent analysis of Zuni is particularly apt since she argues that Zuni community organization is framed by the idioms of the house and familial links, providing an overarching structure that is both expandable and truly corporate. Yet the familial notions of seniority belie real inherited and ranked differences in status and decision making based largely on birthright and clan affiliation (as opposed to more linear patterns of direct descent). Historic Puebloan political organization often has been hierarchical, but individual competition and aggrandizement are not at the heart of their political process. In this regard it is significant that Fred Eggan, whose early work is often cited in traditional archaeological interpretations as indicative of the nonstratified and egalitarian nature of the ethnographic Pueblos, wrote only a few years before his death that "no modern ethnologist or social anthropologist believes that the modern Pueblo are egalitarian" (Eggan 1991:107).

If some of the historic Pueblos were organized as corporate hierarchies, then this construct also may prove informative for understanding the earlier Southwest (as a number of the authors in this collection suggest). Nevertheless, there are important differences between the ethnographic and precontact sociopolitical formations of this region (Wills, this volume). In addition, we also must give careful thought to the archaeological record and how corporate hierarchies can be defined. In this regard, it is crucial to remember that corporate organization is not synonymous with egalitarian formations. Consequently, as a guide, it is worth briefly considering an archaeologically known corporate formation (Blanton et al. 1996a; Feinman 1997c), the Classic period polity at Teotihuacan (central Mexico). Although urban Teotihuacan was much more hierarchically complex than the indigenous Southwestern social formations that are the focus here, there are some intriguing parallels.

Teotihuacan: A Corporately Organized State

Teotihuacan was an urban society (see Cowgill 1997 for a recent overview). The Classic period city is estimated to have had a population of at least 100,000 and to have been at the nexus of a preindustrial state. Nevertheless, the great size and well-known architectural monumentality of Teotihuacan (with its giant Pyramids of the Sun and Moon and numerous multifamily apartment compounds) often cloud other aspects of what we presently know about this ancient metropolis. At present, we have no named rulers at Teotihuacan, and we have few (if any) depictions or representations of specific ruling personages. At Teotihuacan, murals did sometimes depict lines or sets of priests or officeholders fulfilling certain ceremonial activities or other duties (Pasztory 1988), but these figures tended to be replicated images and certainly not distinctive portrayed individuals (often these figures wore masks that concealed their identity). Masks (as opposed to unique royal crowns) tend to diminish individuality, thereby indicating a less personalized manner of leadership (Steiner 1990).

At Teotihuacan, no known Classic period burials are highly elaborate or kingly in nature. Although differences in burial accompaniments do exist across the site, these distinctions are primarily manifest between multifamily residential complexes (referred to as "apartment compounds") and are rather subtle in degree (Sempowski and Spence 1994). Certainly, the known differences are much less extreme than one might expect for a site of this size and monumentality. Personal wealth and access distinctions also appear to be somewhat muted.

At Teotihuacan, monumental architecture focused on temples, plazas, platforms, and residential apartment compounds with less emphasis on princely tombs or truly palatial residences. The city layout with its basic grid plan, large plazas, and wide thoroughfares was more open and less exclusionary than many early cities. Teotihuacan also had a universalizing cosmovision, centered on the deity Tlaloc, rain, and fertility, that appears to have subsumed the differences in domestic customs and extraregional affiliations that have been noted between the various apartment compounds and barrios at the site (Manzanilla 1997).

Reflections Relevant to Social Formations in the Prehispanic Southwest

Urban Teotihuacan is far removed from the prehispanic Southwest. Marked differences in scale and hierarchical complexity are evident. Yet there are important parallels, including archaeological indications of organizational modularity (adjacent apartment compounds as compared to neighboring pueblos), the presence of multifamily domestic units, heavy architectural investments that defined open and significant ritual spaces, dampened economic differences in the face of other indicators of economic and sociopolitical complexity, the wearing of masks by influential persons, the rarity of lavish domestic assemblages or extraordinarily wealthy burials, and the existence of a broadly shared cosmovision or corporate code. Although the differences in complexity are great, the notion of corporate hierarchies helps us understand some apparent neo-evolutionary anomalies in the organizations of both the Teotihuacan state and many later Southwestern societies (Table 12.1).

Many of the authors in this volume highlight features in prehispanic Southwestern societies that conform to the notion of corporate hierarchies. For example, in discussing Chaco Canyon, Wills stresses the heavy and coordinated labor investment in collective domestic architecture and the noncompetitive nature of leadership. Graves and Spielmann, through their examination of the protohistoric Rio Grande, recognize the distinct political, ritual, and economic roles of different pueblos that were part of one polity. They, as well as Kintigh, emphasize the segmental yet interdependent and unequal nature of late Puebloan organization (see also Potter and Perry, this volume). The "mother-daughter" community model discussed for the Zuni area (Kintigh, this volume) conforms well with the notion of a corporate hierarchy in that political and ideological inequality would have been institutionalized on a long-term basis between settlements or component social segments rather than between entrepreneurial individuals. In the southern Southwest, Fish and Fish also note the corporate organization of the Classic Hohokam burial regimes in which key persons were distinguished at death through association with mounds, which they see as the architectural expression of a community as opposed to a genealogical display of personal networks and wealth. Indicators of ancestor veneration were generally rare in the prehispanic Southwest. As in the areas to the north, material inequalities were most evident between sites rather than in terms of restricted or unique consumption by a small number of privileged households or individuals (Fish and Fish, this volume).

Based on the discussions in this volume and in the wider literature, a number of later prehispanic Southwestern societies appear to have been hierarchical and corporate in organization. Such an interpretation would affect how we model and conceptualize Southwestern societies. For example, we might question whether it is appropriate to continue to interpret such formations as if they were composed of completely autonomous individual actors or households. Although these social systems may not have been led by competitive or accumulating individuals, individual and household decision making may still have been modified by the constraints and pulls of powerful hierarchical institutions and individuals, albeit ones who were acting in a less grandiose or self-serving manner.

Recognition of corporate hierarchies also requires us to expand and alter the indicators and expectations that guide our cross-cultural identifications of hierarchically organized societies. It is perhaps time to reconsider and expand the traditional archaeological indicators of complexity in the direction that Colin Renfrew (1974) outlined decades ago. Such broadening of interpretive and analytic frameworks of course renders pure bottom–up induction in archaeology all the more problematic.

Corporate / Network: Resolving Misunderstandings

Although the corporate/network dimension draws on and synthesizes related observations in earlier anthropological analyses (Table 12.2), its introduction to the literature is recent (Blanton et al. 1996a). Consequently, it is not surprising that this proposed continuum for modes of political-economic action has at times been misunderstood or misconstrued. Perhaps its exposition (Blanton et al. 1996a; Feinman 1995) has not always been as lucid as we might like. In this section, I aim to clarify certain key aspects of the corporate/network dimension so that these concepts can be employed both consistently and productively as we use them more broadly in the Southwest and elsewhere.

Most specifically, I endeavor to elucidate two points. First, corporate/ network is neither a stark dichotomy nor simply a new typology (Kintigh, this volume). As noted above, this dimension should be considered in conjunction with (rather than as a replacement for) variation in scale and hierarchical complexity (Kowalewski 1998). Second, the corporate/network continuum is not merely a trait list; rather, to be effective for archaeological interpretation it has to be used more subtly.

In discussions of the corporate/network continuum, we refer to strategies or the aims and practices of social actors. Social actors (people) implement these political-economic strategies based on their particular roles or positions. Our argument is that in a particular social field, these strategies are shaped and constrained by the specific role or status of the actors and that they may vary from highly corporate to highly network in character. In a specific spatiotemporal context, different or competing strategies may be employed simultaneously; sometimes the adoption of a new pathway to power becomes a way to challenge the existing leadership structure. Likewise, specific political-economic strategies are historical phenomena in themselves and so in certain contexts may fall between the extreme poles of the corporate/network continuum (despite the elements of antagonism between these two strategies). In sum, corporate/network is neither a typology nor a dichotomy since there is a large definable middle ground that can empirically be observed between these polar extremes. Rather, it is an axis or dimension on which modes of political-economic action may be compared and contrasted. The variability along this axis cannot be subsumed under the orthogonal dimension of hierarchical complexity (band-tribe-chiefdom-state), nor should it be trivialized as simply as idiosyncratic variation since there are so many cross-cultural parallels that have already been noted (Table 12.2; Blanton et al. 1996a).

To be analytically insightful, the corporate/network dimension also cannot be treated as a basic trait list. For example, in several of the essays in this volume, broad categories of behavior are attributed to either the corporate or network mode. For example, Graves and Spielmann imply that exchange (of any sort) is indicative of the network strategy, while Fish and Fish seem to think that we see any and all kinship relations as a basis of power in the corporate mode. In regard to both of these attributions, our original schema actually is more complex and contextualized.

In regard to exchange, our original formulations (Blanton et al. 1996a; Feinman 1995) did not intend that all the myriad kinds of exchange represent exemplars of a network strategy. Trade and exchange of different kinds may be the basis of power in either corporate or network strategies. Specifically, we (Blanton et al. 1996:5) proposed that prestige goods exchange, which generally involves items of portable wealth and adornment, would often be tied to network or exclusionary strategies that also were linked with personal accumulation and ornamentation. In the prehispanic Southwest, prestige goods exchange was generally rare (Graves and Spielmann, this volume), although exchange of other kinds was present and in some instances economically important. The varieties of exchange described (Graves and Spielmann, this volume), involving mainly food products and decorated ceramics (that may have been used as serving vessels), easily could have been part of corporate strategies, as the authors themselves seem to conclude at the end of their chapter.

Likewise, our original conception (Blanton et al. 1996a) of "kinship" is somewhat narrower than presumed (Fish and Fish, this volume) and very much in concert with the arguments made in this volume. We draw a distinction between kinship and descent-based strategies. We (Blanton et al. 1996a:5) associate patrimonial rhetoric, an emphasis on linear descent systems, and the primacy of descent from a common ancestor as indicative of network (as opposed to corporate) systems (much as Fish and Fish infer in their chapter). In contrast, corporate strategies often stress more fluid and looser kinship relations and associations. The bounds of descent and marriage are often transcended (fictively) through the establishment and maintenance of corporate codes that emphasize the collaborative solidarity of society as an integrated whole. Such solidarity often characterizes coresidents in a given territory or civically defined region as Fish and Fish (this volume) propose for the Hohokam. In short, I am comfortable with specific interpretations offered in the chapters above (Fish and Fish, this volume; Graves and Spielmann, this volume), but I do not think that the authors' interpretations require any significant modifications or expansions to the originally proposed corporate/network framework.

Looking Forward and Back:
New Questions Raised by the Corporate/Network Continuum

As we have noted above, consideration of Southwestern socioeconomic organization in the context of dual-processual theory helps provide an interpretive pathway out of the long, sometimes acrimonious debate (were certain Southwestern populations organized as egalitarian societies or traditional chiefdoms?) that has plagued Southwestern archaeology. Furthermore, such discussions serve to bring the investigation of the Southwest into a broader, cross-cultural theoretical and methodological framework. It is fitting that the consideration of Southwestern societies should have a pivotal role in such comparative dialogues, since our empirical perspective on these societies is so remarkably rich and multifaceted in relation to what we know about preliterate societies in almost every other global region.

At the same time, recognizing many ancient Southwestern societies as different kinds of corporate hierarchies represents only a small first step. The framework that we have introduced is measured most effectively by the questions that it raises and the research problems that it helps to address. For example, I concur that Casas Grandes was a hierarchical polity in which leadership and power were organized more along the network mode than many other precontact societies in the Southwest (Mills 1997; Whalen and Minnis, this volume). As noted (Whalen and Minnis, this volume), compared to its neighbors to the north, Casas Grandes was characterized by much greater quantities of portable wealth (turkey and parrot feathers, stone beads, shell ornaments). At the same time, some of these items were concentrated in a few select areas of the site (Minnis 1989:287), while others were differentially distributed in burials (Minnis 1989:288; Ravesloot 1988). Many of these goods appear to have been used as personal adornments and were exchanged over considerable distances (likely often serving as prestige goods). The degree of craft specialization and the extent of surplus accumulation have been judged to be unmatched for the Southwestern macroregion (Wilcox 1995:287). At the same time, the interment of selected individuals in tombs and vaults (sometimes with sizable quantities of burial furniture) is certainly unusual for the Greater Southwest. In addition, several residential compounds or houses are distinctive, having interior courtyards, ceremonial rooms, and areas of restricted access, and are thought to have been elite in nature (Di Peso 1974; LeBlanc 1989b:193).

The tacit indicators of economic differentiation, elite residences, craft production, and wealth accumulation (as well as its locational propinquity to Mesoamerica) probably account for the easier and wider recognition of Casas Grandes as "complex" and more hierarchically organized than other contemporaneous Southwestern societies (e.g., Johnson 1989:386). Hierarchical societies in which power is constituted through network or exclusionary strategies tend to conform more closely to traditional or monolithic conceptions of inequality based on personal accumulation and recognition. Yet following the discussion of the small spatial extent of the Casas polity (Whalen and Minnis, this volume) and the scale of its architecture, I would offer the hypothesis that Casas Grandes may not have been that much more hierarchically organized or "complex" than some of its contemporaries to the north, but the nature of its complexity was different (more network than corporate).

As Minnis (1989:278; Whalen and Minnis, this volume) has illustrated, the scale of the nonresidential architecture at Casas Grandes was markedly less in volume than estimated for the construction effort at Chaco Canyon and many Classic period Hohokam sites. Given the differences elaborated on above, this is not what would be expected if one ascribed to a unilinear model of social complexity in which all facets of social differentiation increased in concert. At the same time, the dimension of complexity alone cannot explain why the segmental and "cookie-cutter" pattern of its Puebloan contemporaries was not repeated at Casas Grandes, where architectural diversity was emphasized (Minnis 1989). Individual residential units at Casas Grandes appear to have had a greater degree of autonomy. Such architectural distinctions are just what would be expected if the basis of power at Casas Grandes was relatively more exclusionary or network in mode in comparison to the corporate hierarchies that appear to have been so prevalent in the later precontact Southwest.

This begs a few final questions that I bring forth in the hopes of stimulating future research initiatives along the lines discussed in this essay and throughout the collection. One may fairly query why corporate formations were so prevalent in the Greater Southwest, especially during the later precontact period, compared to other Native American regions. Like Wills (this volume), I (Feinman 1997b) have postulated that the prevalence of later corporate formations, as indicated in the northern Southwest by the pit house to pueblo transition, may be in part related to the frequency of migration and long-term propensity toward demographic fluidity. Corporate formations may have been more successful at the sociopolitical integration of diverse demographic groups that tended to share the sometimes economically marginal Southwestern landscape. Yet the frameworks employed here cannot alone explain how and why these diverse precontact sociopolitical formations in the American Southwest were themselves organized in such internally different ways. I hope the answers to this question will constitute the thematic basis for new investigations and publications in the not-too-distant future.

References Cited

Abbott, David R.

1994a   Hohokam Social Structure and Irrigation Management: The Ceramic Evidence from the Central Phoenix Basin. Ph.D. dissertation, Department of Anthropology, Arizona State University, Tempe.

1994b   Synthesis and Conclusions. In *The Pueblo Grande Project*. Vol. 3: *Ceramics and the Production and Exchange of Pottery in the Central Phoenix Basin,* ed. David R. Abbott, pp. 407–32. Publications in Archaeology 20. Phoenix: Soil Systems, Inc.

1996   Ceramic Exchange and a Strategy for Reconstructing Organizational Developments among the Hohokam. In *Interpreting Southwestern Diversity: Underlying Principles and Overarching Patterns,* ed. Paul R. Fish and J. Jefferson Reid, pp. 147–58. Arizona State University Anthropological Paper no. 48. Tempe.

2000   *Ceramics and Community Organization among the Hohokam.* Tucson: University of Arizona Press.

Abrams, Elliot M.

1989   Architecture and Energy: An Evolutionary Perspective. In *Archaeological Method and Theory,* vol. 1, ed. Michael B. Schiffer, pp. 47–88. Tucson: University of Arizona Press.

1994   *How the Maya Built Their World: Energetics and Ancient Architecture.* Austin: University of Texas Press.

Abu-Lughod, Lila

1986   *Veiled Sentiments: Honor and Poetry in a Bedouin Society.* Berkeley: University of California Press.

Ackerly, Neil W., Jerry B. Howard, and Randall H. McGuire

1987   *La Ciudad Canals: A Study of Hohokam Irrigation Systems at the Community Level.* Arizona State University Anthropological Field Studies no. 17. Tempe.

Adams, E. Charles

1988   The Case for Conflict during the Late Prehistoric and Protohistoric Periods in the Western Pueblo Area of the American Southwest. Paper presented at the Symposium "Conflict and the Archaeological Record," 20th Annual Chacmool Conference, University of Calgary, Alberta.

1989   Changing Form and Function in Western Pueblo Ceremonial Architecture from A.D. 1000 to A.D.1500. In *The Architecture of Social Integration in Prehistoric Pueblos,* ed. William D. Lipe and Michelle Hegmon, pp. 155–60. Crow Canyon Archaeological Center Occasional Paper no. 1. Cortez, Colo.

1991   *The Origin and Development of the Pueblo Katsina Cult.* Tucson: University of Arizona Press.

1994   The Katsina Cult: A Western Pueblo Perspective. In *Kachinas in the Pueblo World,* ed. Polly Schaafsma, pp. 35–46. Albuquerque: University of New Mexico Press.

Adler, Michael A.

1989   Ritual Facilities and Social Integration in Nonranked Societies. In *The Architecture of Social Integration in Prehistoric Pueblos,* ed. William D. Lipe and Michelle Hegmon, pp. 35–54. Crow Canyon Archaeological Center Occasional Paper no. 1. Cortez, Colo.

1994   Population Aggregation and the Anasazi Social Landscape: A View from the Four Corners. In *The Ancient Southwestern Community: Models and Methods for Study of Prehistoric Social Organization,* ed. W. H. Wills and R. D. Leonard, pp. 85–102. Albuquerque: University of New Mexico Press.

Akins, Nancy J.

1986   *A Biocultural Approach to Human Burials from Chaco Canyon, New Mexico.* Reports of the Chaco Center no. 9. Albuquerque: National Park Service.

1987   Faunal Remains from Pueblo Alto. In *Investigations at the Pueblo Alto Complex, Chaco Canyon,* vol. 3, pt. 2, ed. Frances Joan Mathien and Thomas C. Windes, pp. 445–650. Publications in Archeology 18F. Santa Fe, N.M.: National Park Service.

Alden, John R.

1982   Marketplace Exchange as Indirect Distribution: An Iranian Example. In *Contexts for Prehistoric Exchange,* ed. Jonathan E. Ericson and Timothy K. Earle, pp. 83–101. London: Academic Press.

Aldenderfer, Mark

1993   Ritual, Hierarchy, and Change in Foraging Societies. *Journal of Anthropological Archaeology* 12:1–40.

Allen, Jim

1984   Pots and Poor Princes: A Multidimensional Approach to the Role of Pottery Trading in Coastal Papua. In *The Many Dimensions of Pottery: Ceramics in Archaeology and Anthropology,* ed. Sander E. van der Leeuw and

Alison C. Pritchard, pp. 407–63. Cingula Series 7. Amsterdam: Universiteit van Amsterdam.

Allison, James R.

1993   Late Glaze-Paint Ceramics from Quarai and Gran Quivira: A Preliminary Analysis. In *The Evolution of Craft Specialization in Tribal Societies: Preliminary Report for the 1992 Excavation Season at Quarai Pueblo, New Mexico,* by Katherine Spielmann, pp. 60–83. Report submitted to the National Park Service, Southwestern Regional Office, Santa Fe, N.M.

Altschul, Jeffrey H.

1978   The Development of the Chacoan Interaction Sphere. *Journal of Anthropological Research* 34:109–46.

Ames, Kenneth M.

1995   Chiefly Power and Household Production on the Northwest Coast. In *Foundations of Inequality,* ed. T. Douglas Price and Gary M. Feinman, pp. 155–88. New York: Plenum Press.

Anderson, David G.

1994   *The Savannah River Chiefdoms: Political Change in the Late Prehistoric Southeast.* Tuscaloosa: University of Alabama Press.

Anderson, Keith

1986   Hohokam Cemeteries as Elements of Settlement Structure and Change. In *Anthropology of the Desert West: Essays in Honor of Jesse D. Jennings,* ed. Carol Condie and Don Fowler, pp. 179–201. Salt Lake City: University of Utah Press.

Anell, Bengt

1969   *Running Down and Driving of Game in North America.* Studia Ethnographica Uppsaliencia 30. Uppsala, Sweden: Berlingska Boktrijckereriel.

Anyon, Roger

1992   The Late Prehistoric and Early Historic Periods in the Zuni-Cibola Area, A.D. 1400–1680. In *Current Research on the Late Prehistory and Early History of New Mexico,* ed. Bradley J. Vierra, pp. 75–83. New Mexico Archaeological Council Special Publication vol. 1. Albuquerque.

Arnold, Jeanne E.

1996a   The Archaeology of Complex Hunter-Gatherers. *Journal of Archaeological Method and Theory* 3:77–126.

——, ed.

1996b   *Emergent Complexity: The Evolution of Intermediate Societies.* International Monographs in Prehistory, Archaeological Series 9. Ann Arbor, Mich.

Arthur, W. Brian

1988   Self-Reinforcing Mechanisms in Economics. In *The Economy as an Evolv-
        ing Complex System,* ed. P. Anderson, K. Arrow, and D. Pines, pp. 9–31.
        Reading, Mass.: Addison-Wesley.

Axelrod, Robert

1997   *The Complexity of Cooperation: Agent-based Models of Competition and Col-
        laboration.* Princeton Studies in Complexity. Princeton, N.J.: Princeton
        University Press.

Bandelier, Adolph F.

1892   Hemenway Southwestern Archaeological Expedition. I, An Outline of
        the Documentary History of the Zuni Tribe. *Journal of American Ethnology
        and Archaeology* 3:1–115.

1981   *The Discovery of New Mexico by the Franciscan Monk, Friar Marcos de Niza in
        1539,* ed. and trans. Madeleine Turrell Rodack. Tucson: University of
        Arizona Press.

Barth, Frederick

1975   *Ritual and Knowledge among the Baktaman of New Guinea.* New Haven,
        Conn.: Yale University Press.

Baxter, Michael

1994   *Exploratory Multivariate Analysis in Archaeology.* New Haven, Conn.: Edin-
        burgh University Press.

Bayman, James M.

1994   Craft Production and Political Economy at the Marana Platform Mound
        Community. Ph.D. dissertation, Department of Anthropology, Arizona
        State University, Tempe.

1995   Rethinking "Redistribution" in the Archaeological Record: Obsidian
        Exchange at the Marana Platform Mound. *Journal of Anthropological Re-
        search* 51:37–63.

1996   Shell Ornament Consumption in a Classic Hohokam Platform Mound
        Community Center. *Journal of Field Archaeology* 23:403–18.

Bayman, James M., and Maria Sanchez

1998   The Surface Archaeology of Classic Period Hohokam Community Orga-
        nization. In *Surface Archaeology,* ed. Alan P. Sullivan, pp. 75–88. Albuquer-
        que: University of New Mexico Press.

Beals, Ralph

1943   The Aboriginal Culture of the Cahita Indians. *Ibero-American* 6. Berkeley:
        University of California.

Becker, Lawrence C.

1986   *Reciprocity.* Chicago: University of Chicago Press.

Bell, Catherine

1992   *Ritual Theory, Ritual Practice.* Oxford: Oxford University Press.

1997   *Ritual: Perspectives and Dimensions.* Oxford: Oxford University Press.

Benavides, Fray Alonso de

1630   *The Memorial of Fray Alonso de Benavides,* trans. Mrs. Edward E. Ayer. Albuquerque: Horn and Wallace. (Originally published in 1916.)

Bender, Barbara

1985   Emergent Tribal Formations in the American Midcontinent. *American Antiquity* 50:52–62.

Besley, Timothy, Stephen Coate, and Glenn Loury

1993   The Economics of Rotating Savings and Credit Associations. *American Economic Review* 83:792–810.

Betancourt, Julio L., Jeffrey S. Dean, and Herbert M. Hull

1986   Prehistoric Long-Distance Transport of Construction Beams, Chaco Canyon, New Mexico. *American Antiquity* 51:370–74.

Blanton, Richard E.

1983   Factors Underlying the Origin and Evolution of Market Systems. In *Economic Anthropology: Topics and Theories.* Monographs in Economic Anthropology 1, ed. Sutti Ortiz, pp. 51–66. Lanham, Md.: Society for Economic Anthropology.

1998   Beyond Centralization: Steps toward a Theory of Egalitarian Behavior in Archaic States. In *Archaic States,* ed. Gary M. Feinman and Joyce Marcus, pp. 135–72. Santa Fe, N.M.: School of American Research Press.

Blanton, Richard E., Gary M. Feinman, Stephen A. Kowalewski, and Peter N. Peregrine

1996a   A Dual-Processual Theory for the Evolution of Mesoamerican Civilization. *Current Anthropology* 37:1–14.

1996b   Reply. *Current Anthropology* 37:65–68.

Blanton, Richard E., Stephen A. Kowalewski, Gary Feinman, and Jill Appel

1981   *Ancient Mesoamerica: A Comparison of Change in Three Regions.* New York: Cambridge University Press.

Blinman, Eric

1989   Potluck in the Protokiva: Ceramics and Ceremonialism in Pueblo I Villages. In *The Architecture of Social Integration,* ed. William D. Lipe and

Michelle Hegmon, pp. 113–24. Cortez, Colo.: Crow Canyon Archaeological Center.

Blitz, John H.

1993a   *Ancient Chiefdoms of the Tombigbee.* Tuscaloosa: University of Alabama Press.

1993b   Big Pots for Big Shots: Feasting and Storage in a Mississippian Community. *American Antiquity* 58:80–96.

Bloch, Maurice

1974   Symbols, Songs, Dance and Features of Articulation. *European Journal of Sociology* 15:55–81.

1975   *Political Language and Oratory in Traditional Society.* New York: Academic Press.

1992   *Prey into Hunter: The Politics of Religious Experience.* New York: Cambridge University Press.

Bostwick, Todd W., and Christian E. Downum, eds.

1994   *Archaeology of the Pueblo Grande Platform Mound and Surrounding Features.* Vol. 2: *Features in the Central Precinct of the Pueblo Grande Community.* Pueblo Grande Museum Anthropological Paper no. 1. Phoenix: City of Phoenix Parks, Recreation, and Library Department.

Bourdieu, Pierre

1977   *Outline of a Theory of Practice.* Cambridge Studies in Social Anthropology 16. New York: Cambridge University Press.

1990   *The Logic of Practice.* Stanford, Calif.: Stanford University Press.

Bowles, Samuel

1998   Endogenous Preferences: The Cultural Consequences of Markets and Other Economic Institutions. *Journal of Economic Literature* 36:75–111.

Bradley, Ronna J.

1993   Marine Shell Exchange in Northwest Mexico and the American Southwest. In *The American Southwest and Mesoamerica: Systems of Prehistoric Exchange,* ed. Jonathan E. Ericson and Timothy G. Baugh, pp. 121–58. New York: Plenum Press.

Brandt, Elizabeth A.

1977   The Role of Secrecy in a Pueblo Society. In *Flowers of the Wind: Papers on Ritual, Myth and Symbolism in California and the Southwest,* ed. T. Blackburn, pp. 11–28. Socorro, N.M.: Ballena Press.

1980   On Secrecy and Control of Knowledge: Taos Pueblo. In *Secrecy: A Cross-*

Cultural Perspective, ed. Stanton K. Tefft, pp. 123–46. New York: Human Sciences Press.

1985   Internal Stratification in Pueblo Communities. Revised version of a paper presented at the 84th Annual Meeting of the American Anthropological Association, December 4–9, 1985.

1994   Egalitarianism, Hierarchy, and Centralization in the Pueblos. In *The Ancient Southwestern Community: Models and Methods for the Study of Prehistoric Social Organization,* ed. W. H. Wills and Robert D. Leonard, pp. 9–23. Albuquerque: University of New Mexico Press.

Brandt, Elizabeth A., and Katherine A. Spielmann

1998   Manuscript in the possession of the authors. Department of Anthropology, Arizona State University, Tempe.

Braun, David P., and Stephen Plog

1982   Evolution of "Tribal" Social Networks: Theory and Prehistoric North American Evidence. *American Antiquity* 47:504–25.

Breternitz, Cory D., and David E. Doyel

1987   Methodological Issues for the Identification of Chacoan Community Structure: Lessons from the Bis Sa'ani Community Study. *American Archaeology* 6:183–89.

Breternitz, Cory D., David E. Doyel, and Michael P. Marshall, eds.

1982   *Bis Sa'ani: A Late Bonito Phase Community on Escavada Wash, Northwest New Mexico.* Navajo Nation Papers in Anthropology no. 14. Window Rock, Ariz.

Brody, J. J.

1977   *Mimbres Painted Pottery.* Albuquerque: University of New Mexico Press.

Brown, James A.

1985   The Mississippian Period. In *Ancient Art of the American Woodland Indians,* ed. David S. Brose, James A. Brown, and David W. Penny, pp. 169–200. New York: Harry N. Abrams.

Brumfiel, Elizabeth M.

1992   Breaking and Entering the Ecosystem: Gender, Class, and Faction Steal the Show. *American Anthropologist* 94:551–67.

1995   Heterarchy and the Analysis of Complex Societies: Comments. In *Heterarchy and the Analysis of Complex Societies,* ed. Robert M. Ehrenreich, Carole L. Crumley, and Janet E. Levy, pp. 125–31. Archeological Papers of the American Anthropological Association no. 6. Washington, D.C.

1996   Comments on A Dual-Processual Theory for the Evolution of Meso-
        american Civilization by Richard E. Blanton, Gary M. Feinman, Stephen
        A. Kowalewski, and Peter N. Peregrine. *Current Anthropology* 37:48–50.

Brumfiel, Elizabeth M., and Timothy K. Earle
1987   Specialization, Exchange, and Complex Societies: An Introduction. In
        Specialization, Exchange, and Complex Societies, ed. Elizabeth M. Brumfiel
        and Timothy K. Earle, pp. 1–9. New York: Cambridge University Press.

Brunson, Judy L.
1989   The Social Organization of the Los Muertos Hohokam: A Reanalysis of
        Cushing's Hemenway Expedition Data. Ph.D. dissertation, Department
        of Anthropology, Arizona State University, Tempe.

Bubemyre, Trixi D.
1993   Implications of Ceramic Variability at a Hohokam Platform Mound Vil-
        lage. M.A. thesis, Department of Anthropology, University of Arizona,
        Tucson.

Bunzel, Ruth L.
1992   *Zuni Ceremonialism.* Albuquerque: University of New Mexico Press.
        (Originally published Washington, D.C.: Smithsonian Institution Press,
        1932.)

Burns, Tom, and Charles D. Laughlin Jr.
1979   Ritual and Social Power. In *The Spectrum of Ritual: A Biogenetic Struc-
        tural Analysis,* by Eugine G. d'Aquili, Charles D. Laughlin, Jr., and John
        McManus, pp. 249–79. New York: Columbia University Press.

Bushnell, G. H. S.
1955   Some Pueblo IV Pottery Types from Kechipauan, New Mexico, U.S.A.
        Anais do XXXI Congresso Internacional de Americanistas, São Paulo 2:657–65.
        São Paulo: Editora Anhembi.

Bustard, Wendy Joy
1996   *Space as Place: Small and Great House Spatial Organization in Chaco Canyon,
        New Mexico, A.D. 1000—1150.* Ph.D. dissertation, Department of An-
        thropology, University of New Mexico. Ann Arbor, Mich.: University
        Microfilms International.

Cameron, Catherine M., ed.
1995   *Migration and Movement of Southwestern Peoples.* Special issue, *Journal of
        Anthropological Archaeology* 14(2).

Carlson, Roy L.
1970   White Mountain Redware: A Pottery Tradition of East-Central Arizona

and Western New Mexico. University of Arizona Anthropological Paper no. 19. Tucson: University of Arizona Press.

Castetter, E., and W. Bell

1942   *Pima and Papago Indian Agriculture.* Albuquerque: University of New Mexico Press.

Chapman, Richard C., Carolyn L. Daniel, and Jeanne A. Schutt

1997   Conclusions and Recommendations for Future Management. In *Cycles of Closure: A Cultural Resources Inventory of Fort Wingate Depot Activity, New Mexico,* ed. Jeanne Schutt and Richard Chapman, pp. 335–52. Office of Contract Archeology, Department of Anthropology, University of New Mexico, Albuquerque.

Chevalier, François

1970   *Land and Society in Colonial Mexico.* Berkeley: University of California Press.

Chowning, Ann

1979   Leadership in Melanesia. *Journal of Pacific History* 14:66–84.

Ciolek-Torrello, Richard S.

1985   A Typology of Room Function at Grasshopper Pueblo, Arizona. *Journal of Field Archaeology* 12:41–63.

1988   Conclusions. In *Hohokam Settlement along the Slopes of the Picacho Mountains.* Vol. 6: *Synthesis and Conclusions, Tucson Aqueduct Project,* ed. Richard S. Ciolek-Torrello and David R. Wilcox, pp. 300–14. Research Paper no. 35. Flagstaff: Museum of Northern Arizona.

Ciolek-Torrello, Richard S., Martha M. Callahan, and David H. Greenwald

1988   *Hohokam Settlement along the Slopes of the Picacho Mountains.* Vol. 2: *The Brady Wash Sites, Tucson Aqueduct Project.* Research Paper no. 35. Flagstaff: Museum of Northern Arizona.

Ciolek-Torrello, Richard S., and Stephanie M. Whittlesey

1996   A New Look at the Archaeology of Central Arizona. In *Debating Complexity: Proceedings of the 26th Annual Chacmool Conference,* ed. Daniel A. Meyer, Peter C. Dawson, and Donald T. Hanna, pp. 312–25. Archaeological Association and the Department of Archaeology, University of Calgary, Alberta.

Ciolek-Torrello, Richard S., Stephanie M. Whittlesey, and John R. Welch

1994   A Synthetic Model of Prehistoric Land Use. In *The Roosevelt Rural Sites Study.* Vol. 3: *Changing Land Use in the Tonto Basin,* ed. Richard S. Ciolek-Torrello and John R. Welch, pp. 437–72. Technical Series 28. Tucson: Statistical Research.

Ciolek-Torrello, Richard S., and David R. Wilcox, eds.

1988   *Hohokam Settlement along the Slopes of the Picacho Mountains, Tucson Aqueduct Project.* Vol. 6: *Synthesis and Conclusions.* Research Paper no. 35. Flagstaff: Museum of Northern Arizona.

Clark, Jeffery J.

1997   *Migration and Integration: The Classic Period Salado in the Tonto Basin.* Ph.D. dissertation, University of Arizona, Tucson. Ann Arbor, Mich.: University Microfilms International.

Clark, John E., and Michael Blake

1994   The Power of Prestige: Competitive Generosity and the Emergence of Rank Societies in Lowland Mesoamerica. In *Factional Competition and Political Development in the New World,* ed. Elizabeth M. Brumfiel and John W. Fox, pp. 17–30. New York: Cambridge University Press.

Coate, Stephen, and Martin Ravallion

1993   Reciprocity without Commitment: Characterization and Performance of Informal Insurance Arrangements. *Journal of Development Economics* 40:1–24.

Cooper, Laurel Martine

1995   *Space Syntax Analysis of Chacoan Great Houses.* Ph.D. dissertation, Department of Anthropology, University of Arizona, Tucson. Ann Arbor, Mich.: University Microfilms International.

Cordell, Linda S.

1982   The Pueblo Period in the San Juan Basin: An Overview and Some Research Problems. In *The San Juan Tomorrow: Planning for the Conservation of Cultural Resources in the San Juan Basin,* ed. Fred Plog and Walter Wait, pp. 59–83. Santa Fe, N.M.: National Park Service.

1997   *Archaeology of the Southwest.* New York: Academic Press.

Cordell, Linda S., and Fred Plog

1979   Escaping the Confines of Normative Thought: A Reevaluation of Puebloan Prehistory. *American Antiquity* 44:405–29.

Cosmides, Leda, and John Tooby

1992   Cognitive Adaptations for Social Exchange. In *The Adapted Mind,* ed. Jerome Barkow, Leda Cosmides, and John Tooby, pp. 163–228. New York: Oxford University Press.

Cowgill, George L.

1997   State and Society at Teotihuacan, Mexico. *Annual Review of Anthropology* 26:129–61.

Craig, Douglas B., and Jeffery J. Clark

1994   The Meddler Point Site, AZ V:5:4/26 (ASM/TNF). In *The Roosevelt Community Development Study.* Vol. 2: *Meddler Point, Pyramid Point, and Griffin Wash Sites,* by Mark D. Elson, Deborah L. Swartz, Douglas B. Craig, and Jeffrey J. Clark, pp. 1–198. Anthropological Paper no. 13. Tucson: Center for Desert Archaeology.

Craig, Douglas B., Mark D. Elson, and J. Scott Wood

1992   The Growth and Development of a Platform Mound in the Eastern Tonto Basin. In *Proceedings of the Second Salado Conference, Globe, Arizona, 1992,* ed. Richard C. Lange and Stephen Germick, pp. 22–30. Arizona Archaeological Society Occasional Paper. Phoenix.

Creamer, Winifred

1996   Developing Complexity in the American Southwest: Constructing a Model for the Rio Grande Valley. In *Emergent Complexity: The Evolution of Intermediate Societies,* ed. Jeanne E. Arnold, pp. 91–106. International Monographs in Prehistory, Archaeological Series 9. Ann Arbor, Mich.

Crown, Patricia L.

1987   Classic Period Hohokam Settlement and Land Use in the Casa Grande Ruins Area, Arizona. *Journal of Field Archaeology* 14:147–62.

1991   The Hohokam: Current Views of Prehistory and the Regional System. In *Chaco and Hohokam: Prehistoric Regional Systems in the American Southwest,* ed. Patricia L. Crown and W. James Judge, pp. 135–58. Santa Fe, N.M.: School of American Research Press.

1994   *Ceramics and Ideology: Salado Polychrome Pottery.* Albuquerque: University of New Mexico Press.

1996   Change in Ceramic Design Style and Technology in the Thirteenth- to Fourteenth-Century Southwest. In *Interpreting Southwestern Diversity: Underlying Principles and Overarching Patterns,* ed. Paul R. Fish and J. Jefferson Reid, pp. 241–48. Arizona State University Anthropological Research Paper no. 48. Tempe.

Crown, Patricia L., and Ronald L. Bishop

1994   Questions of Source. In *Ceramics and Ideology: Salado Polychrome Pottery,* by Patricia L. Crown, pp. 21–35. Albuquerque: University of New Mexico Press.

Crown, Patricia L., and W. James Judge, eds.

1991   *Chaco and Hohokam: Prehistoric Regional Systems in the American Southwest.* Santa Fe, N.M.: School of American Research Press.

Crumley, Carole L.

1979   Three Locational Models: An Epistemological Assessment for Anthropology and Archaeology. In *Advances in Archaeological Method and Theory,* vol. 2, ed. Michael B. Schiffer, pp. 141–73. New York: Academic Press.

1995   Heterarchy and the Analysis of Complex Societies. In *Heterarchy and the Analysis of Complex Societies,* ed. Robert M. Ehrenreich, Carole L. Crumley, and Janet E. Levy, pp. 1–5. Archeological Papers of the American Anthropological Association no. 6. Washington, D.C.

Crumley, Carole L., and William H. Marquardt

1987   Regional Dynamics in Burgundy. In *Regional Dynamics: Burgundian Landscapes,* ed. Carole L. Crumley and William H. Marquardt, pp. 609–23. New York: Academic Press.

Crumrine, N. Ross

1977   *The Mayo Indians of Sonora: A People Who Refuse to Die.* Tucson: University of Arizona Press.

Cushing, Frank Hamilton

1979   *Zuni, Selected Writings of Frank Hamilton Cushing,* ed. Jesse Green. Lincoln: University of Nebraska Press.

1988   *The Mythic World of the Zuni,* ed. and illustrated by Barton Wright. Albuquerque: University of New Mexico Press. (Originally published as 13th Annual Report of the Bureau of American Ethnology, Washington, D.C.: Smithsonian Institution Press, 1896.)

D'Altroy, Terence N., and Timothy K. Earle

1985   Staple Finance, Wealth Finance, and Storage in the Inka Political Economy. *Current Anthropology* 26:187–206.

Dean, Jeffrey S.

1993   Paleoenvironmental Variability in the American Southwest during the Last 2000 Years. Paper presented at the 58th Annual Meeting of the Society for American Archaeology, St. Louis.

Dean, Jeffrey S., William H. Doelle, and Janet D. Orcutt

1994   Adaptive Stress, Environment, and Demography. In *Themes in Southwest Prehistory,* ed. George J. Gumerman, pp. 53–86. Santa Fe, N.M.: School of American Research Press.

Dean, Jeffrey S., George J. Gumerman, Joshua M. Epstein, Robert Axtell, Alan C. Swedlund, Miles T. Parker, and Steven McCarroll

1999   Understanding Anasazi Culture Change through Agent-Based Modeling. In *Dynamics of Human and Primate Societies: Agent-Based Modeling of Social and Spatial Processes,* ed. T. A. Kohler and G. J. Gumerman. SFI Studies in the Sciences of Complexity. New York: Oxford University Press.

Dean, Jeffrey S., and John C. Ravesloot

1993   The Chronology of Cultural Interaction in the Gran Chichimeca. In *Culture and Contact: Charles C. Di Peso's Gran Chichimeca,* ed. Anne I. Woosley and John C. Ravesloot, pp. 83–103. Amerind Foundation, New World Studies Series 2. Dragoon, Ariz.: Amerind Foundation, and Albuquerque: University of New Mexico Press.

Dean, Jeffrey S., and William J. Robinson

1977   *Dendroclimatic Variability in the American Southwest,* A.D. 680 to 1970. Laboratory of Tree-Ring Research, University of Arizona, Tucson.

1978   *Expanded Tree-ring Chronologies for the Southwestern United States* (Chronology Series III). Laboratory of Tree-Ring Research, University of Arizona, Tucson.

Dean, Jeffrey S., and Richard L. Warren

1983   Dendrochronology. In *The Architecture and Dendrochronology of Chetro Ketl,* ed. Stephen H. Lekson, pp. 105–240. Reports of the Chaco Center no. 6. Albuquerque: National Park Service.

De Atley, Suzanne P.

1985   Mix and Match: Traditions of Glaze Paint Preparation at Four Mile Ruin, Arizona. In *Technology and Style,* ed. W. D. Kingery and E. Lense, pp. 297–329. Ceramics and Civilization 2. Columbus, Ohio: American Ceramic Society.

DeBoer, Warren R.

1997   Ceremonial Centers from the Cayapas (Esmeraldas, Ecuador) to Chillicothe (Ohio, U.S.A.). *Cambridge Archaeological Journal* 7:225–53.

Demarest, Arthur A.

1996   Comments. *Current Anthropology* 37:56.

DeMarrais, Elizabeth, Luis Jaime Castillo, and Timothy Earle

1996   Ideology, Materialization, and Power Strategies. *Current Anthropology* 37:15–31.

Dillehay, Tom D.

1990   Mapuche Ceremonial Landscape, Social Recruitment and Resource Rights. *World Archaeology* 22:223–41.

Di Peso, Charles C.

1974   *Casas Grandes: A Fallen Trading Center of the Gran Chichimeca,* vols. 1, 2, 3. Dragoon, Ariz.: Amerind Foundation, and Flagstaff, Ariz.: Northland Press.

Di Peso, Charles C., John B. Rinaldo, and Gloria J. Fenner

1974   *Casas Grandes: A Fallen Trading Center of the Gran Chichimeca,* vols. 4, 5, 6, 7, 8. Dragoon, Ariz.: Amerind Foundation, and Flagstaff, Ariz.: Northland Press.

Doelle, William H.

1995   Regional Platform Mound Systems: Background and Inventory. In *The Roosevelt Community Development Study: New Perspectives on Tonto Basin Prehistory,* ed. Mark D. Elson, Miriam T. Stark, and David A. Gregory, pp. 555–60. Anthropological Paper no. 15. Tucson: Center for Desert Archaeology.

Doelle, William H., David A. Gregory, and Henry D. Wallace

1995   Classic Period Platform Mound Systems in Southern Arizona. In *The Roosevelt Community Development Study: New Perspectives on Tonto Basin Prehistory,* ed. Mark D. Elson, Miriam T. Stark, and David A. Gregory, pp. 385–440. Anthropological Paper no. 15. Tucson: Center for Desert Archaeology.

Doelle, William, Frederick Huntington, and Henry Wallace

1987   Rincon Phase Reorganization in the Tucson Basin. In *The Hohokam Village: Site Structure and Organization,* ed. David Doyel, pp. 71–96. Glenwood Springs, Colo.: American Association for the Advancement of Science.

Doelle, William, and Henry Wallace

1991   The Changing Role of the Tucson Basin in the Hohokam Regional System. In *Exploring the Hohokam: Prehistoric Desert Peoples of the American Southwest,* ed. George J. Gumerman, pp. 279–346. Albuquerque: University of New Mexico Press.

Doolittle, William E.

1990   *Canal Irrigation in Prehistoric Mexico: The Sequence of Technological Change.* Austin: University of Texas Press.

Douglas, John E.

1995   Autonomy in the Late Prehistoric Southern Southwest. *American Antiquity* 60:240–57.

Doyel, David E.

1974   *Excavations in the Escalante Ruin Group, Southern Arizona.* Arizona State Museum Archaeological Series 37. University of Arizona, Tucson.

1981   *Late Hohokam Prehistory in Southern Arizona.* Contributions to Archaeology 2. Scottsdale, Ariz.: Gila Press.

1991   Hohokam Cultural Evolution in the Phoenix Basin. In *Exploring the Ho-hokam: Prehistoric Desert Peoples of the American Southwest,* ed. George J. Gumerman, pp. 231–79. Albuquerque: University of New Mexico Press.

Doyel, David E., Cory D. Breternitz, and Michael P. Marshall
1984   Chacoan Community Structure: Bis Sa'ani Pueblo and the Chaco Halo. In *Recent Research on Chaco Prehistory,* ed. W. James Judge and John D. Schelberg, pp. 37–54. Reports of the Chaco Center no. 8. Albuquerque: National Park Service.

Doyel, David E., and Stephen H. Lekson
1992   Regional Organization in the American Southwest. In *Anasazi Regional Organization and the Chaco System,* ed. David E. Doyel, pp. 23–35. Maxwell Museum of Anthropology Anthropological Paper no. 5. University of New Mexico, Albuquerque.

Dozier, Edward P.
1966   *Hano: A Tewa Indian Community in Arizona.* New York: Holt, Rinehart and Winston.
1970   *The Pueblo Indians of North America.* New York: Holt, Rinehart and Winston.

Drennen, Robert D.
1991   Pre-Hispanic Chiefdom Trajectories in Mesoamerica, Central America, and Northern South America. In *Chiefdoms: Power, Economy, and Ideology,* ed. Timothy Earle, pp. 263–87. New York: Cambridge University Press.

Driver, Jonathan
1990   Meat in Due Season: The Timing of Communal Hunts. In *Hunters of the Recent Past,* ed. Leslie B. Davis and Brian O. K. Reeves, pp. 11–33. London: Unwin Hyman.

Duff, Andrew
1998   The Process of Migration in the Late Prehistoric Southwest. In *Migration and Reorganization: The Pueblo IV Period in the American Southwest,* ed. Katherine A. Spielmann, pp. 31–52. Arizona State University Anthropological Research Paper no. 51. Tempe.

Dunbar, Robin I. M.
1998   The Social Brain Hypothesis. *Evolutionary Anthropology* 6:178–90.

Durand, Stephen Roland
1992   Architectural Change and Chaco Prehistory. Ph.D. dissertation, Department of Anthropology, University of Washington, Seattle.

Earle, Timothy

1990   Style and Iconography as Legitimation in Complex Chiefdoms. In *The Uses of Style in Archaeology*, ed. Margaret W. Conkey and Christine A. Hastorf, pp. 73–81. New York: Cambridge University Press.

1997   *How Chiefs Come to Power: The Political Economy in Prehistory.* Stanford, Calif.: Stanford University Press.

Eggan, Fred

1950   *Social Organization of the Western Pueblos.* Chicago: University of Chicago Press.

1991   Review of *The Sociopolitical Structure of Prehistoric Southwestern Societies,* ed. Steadman Upham, Kent G. Lightfoot, and Roberta A. Jewett. *Ethnohistory* 38(1):106–8.

Ehrenreich, Robert M., Carole L. Crumley, and Janet E. Levy, eds.

1995   *Heterarchy and the Analysis of Complex Societies.* Archeological Paper no. 6, American Anthropological Association, Washington, D.C.

Eighmy, Jeffery L.

1979   Logistic Trends in Southwest Population Growth. In *Transformations: Mathematical Approaches to Culture Change,* ed. Colin Renfrew and Kenneth L. Cooke, pp. 205–20. New York: Academic Press.

Elson, Mark D.

1986   *Archaeological Investigations at the Tanque Verde Wash Site, a Middle Rincon Settlement in the Eastern Tucson Basin.* Institute for American Research Anthropological Paper no. 7. Tucson.

1994   The Pyramid Point Site, AZ V:5:1/25 (ASM/TNF). In *The Roosevelt Community Development Study.* Vol. 2: *Meddler Point, Pyramid Point, and Griffin Wash Sites,* by Mark D. Elson, Deborah L. Swartz, Douglas B. Craig, and Jeffrey J. Clark, pp. 199–296. Anthropological Paper no. 13. Tucson: Center for Desert Archaeology.

1995   Assessment of Chronometric Methods and Dates. In *The Roosevelt Community Development Study: New Perspectives on Tonto Basin Prehistory,* ed. Mark D. Elson, Miriam T. Stark, and David A. Gregory, pp. 39–60. Anthropological Paper no. 15. Tucson: Center for Desert Archaeology.

1996   *An Ethnographic Perspective on Prehistoric Platform Mounds of the Tonto Basin, Central Arizona.* Ph.D. dissertation, University of Arizona, Tucson. Ann Arbor, Mich.: University Microfilms International.

1998   *Expanding the View of Hohokam Platform Mounds: An Ethnographic Perspective.* University of Arizona Anthropological Paper no. 63. Tucson: University of Arizona Press.

Elson, Mark D., Miriam T. Stark, and David A. Gregory

1996   Tonto Basin Local Systems: Implications for Cultural Affiliation and Migration. In *The Salado Culture of the American Southwest,* ed. Jeffrey S. Dean. Amerind Foundation New World Series. Albuquerque: University of New Mexico Press (in press).

Euler, Robert C., George J. Gumerman, Thor N. V. Karlstrom, Jeffrey S. Dean, and Richard H. Hevley

1979   The Colorado Plateaus: Cultural Dynamics and Paleoenvironment. *Science* 205:1089–101.

Feinman, Gary M.

1994   Boundaries and Social Organization: An Outside View on Debate in the Ancient American Southwest. In *The Ancient Southwestern Community: Models and Methods for the Study of Prehistoric Social Organization,* ed. W. H. Wills and Robert D. Leonard, pp. 241–47. Albuquerque: University of New Mexico Press.

1995   The Emergence of Inequality: A Focus on Strategies and Processes. In *Foundations of Social Inequality,* ed. T. Douglas Price and Gary M. Feinman, pp. 255–79. New York: Plenum Press.

1997a Corporate/Network: A New Perspective on Leadership in the American Southwest. Paper prepared for "Hierarchies in Action: Who Benefits?" 14th Annual Visiting Scholar Conference, organized by Michael Diehl at the Center for Archaeological Investigations, Southern Illinois University.

1997b Corporate/Network: New Perspectives on Models of Political Action and the Puebloan Southwest. Paper prepared for "Social Theory in Archaeology: Setting the Agenda Conference," organized by Michael B. Schiffer. University of Utah Press, Snowbird.

1997c Mesoamerican Political Complexity: The Corporate/Network Dimension. Paper prepared for "Leaders to Rulers: The Development of Political Centralization Conference," organized by Jonathan Haas. Field Museum, Chicago.

1998   Corporate Hierarchies: An Application to the American Southwest. Paper presented at the symposium "No Longer in the Whispers-Discussing Non-Hierarchically-Centralized Concepts of Cultural Evolution," organized by David Small, 63rd Annual Meeting of the Society for American Archaeology, Seattle.

1999   Rethinking Our Assumptions: Economic Specialization at the Household Scale in Ancient Ejutla, Oaxaca, Mexico. In *Pottery and People: Dynamic Interactions,* ed. James M. Skibo and Gary M. Feinman, pp. 81–98. Salt Lake City: University of Utah Press.

Feinman, Gary, Richard E. Blanton, and Stephen A. Kowalewski

1984   Market System Development in the Prehispanic Valley of Oaxaca, Mexico. In *Trade and Exchange in Early Mesoamerica,* ed. Kenneth Hirth, pp. 157–78. Albuquerque: University of New Mexico Press.

Feinman, Gary, and Jill Neitzel

1984   Too Many Types: An Overview of Sedentary Prestate Societies in the Americas. In *Advances in Archaeological Method and Theory,* vol. 7, ed. Michael B. Schiffer, pp. 39–102. New York: Academic Press.

Ferg, Alan

1982   14th Century Kachina Depiction on Ceramics. In *Collected Papers in Honor of J. W. Runyon,* ed. G. X. Fitzgerald, pp. 13–29. Papers of the Archaeological Society of New Mexico no. 7. Archaeological Society of New Mexico, Albuquerque.

Ferguson, T. J.

1989   Comment on Social Integration and Anasazi Architecture. In *The Architecture of Social Integration in Prehistoric Pueblos,* ed. William D. Lipe and Michelle Hegmon, pp. 169–74. Crow Canyon Archaeological Center Occasional Paper no. 1. Cortez, Colo.

1996   *Historic Zuni Architecture and Society: An Archaeological Application of Space Syntax.* University of Arizona Anthropological Paper no. 60. Tucson: University of Arizona Press.

Ferguson, T. J., and E. Richard Hart

1986   *A Zuni Atlas.* Norman: University of Oklahoma Press.

Fish, Paul R.

1989   The Hohokam: 1,000 Years of Prehistory in the Sonoran Desert. In *Dynamics of Southwestern Prehistory,* ed. Linda Cordell and George J. Gumerman, pp. 19–63. Washington, D.C.: Smithsonian Institution Press.

Fish, Paul R., and Suzanne K. Fish

1991   Hohokam Political and Social Organization. In *Exploring the Hohokam: Prehistoric Desert Peoples of the American Southwest,* ed. George J. Gumerman, pp. 151–76. Albuquerque: University of New Mexico Press.

1994   Southwest and Northwest: Recent Research at the Juncture of the United States and Mexico. *Journal of Archaeological Research* 2:3–44.

Fish, Paul R., Suzanne K. Fish, Curtiss Brennan, Douglass Gann, and James M. Bayman

1992   Marana: Configuration of an Early Classic Period Hohokam Platform Mound Site. In *Proceedings of the Second Salado Conference, Globe, Arizona,*

1992, ed. Richard C. Lange and Stephen Germick, pp. 62–68. Arizona Archaeological Society Occasional Paper. Phoenix.

Fish, Paul R., Suzanne Fish, George J. Gumerman, and J. Jefferson Reid

1994   Towards an Explanation of Southwestern Abandonments. In *Themes in Southwestern Prehistory,* ed. George J. Gumerman, pp. 135–64. Santa Fe, N.M.: School of American Research Press.

Fish, Paul R., Suzanne K. Fish, Stephanie Whittlesey, Hector Neff, Michael D. Glascock, and J. Michael Elam

1992   An Evaluation of the Production and Exchange of Tanque Verde Red-on-brown Ceramics in Southern Arizona. In *Chemical Characterization of Ceramic Pastes in Archaeology,* ed. Hector Neff, pp. 233–54. Monographs in World Archaeology no. 7. Madison, Wis.: Prehistory Press.

Fish, Suzanne K.

1996   Dynamics of Scale in the Southern Deserts. In *Interpreting Southwestern Diversity: Underlying Principles and Overarching Patterns,* ed. Paul R. Fish and J. Jefferson Reid, pp. 107–14. Arizona State University Anthropological Research Paper no. 48. Tempe.

Fish, Suzanne K., and Marcia Donaldson

1991   Production and Consumption in the Archaeological Record: A Hohokam Example. *Kiva* 56:255–76.

Fish, Suzanne K., and Paul R. Fish

1992   The Marana Community in Comparative Context. In *The Marana Community in the Hohokam World,* ed. Suzanne K. Fish, Paul R. Fish, and John H. Madsen, pp. 97–105. University of Arizona Anthropological Paper no. 56. Tucson: University of Arizona Press.

1993   An Assessment of Classic Period Hohokam Abandonment Processes in the Tucson Basin. In *The Abandonment of Settlements and Regions,* ed. Catherine M. Cameron and Steve Tomka, pp. 99–109. New York: Cambridge University Press.

1994   Multisite Communities as Measures of Hohokam Aggregation. In *The Ancient Southwestern Community,* ed. W. H. Wills and Robert D. Leonard, pp. 119–30. Albuquerque: University of New Mexico Press.

Fish, Suzanne K., Paul R. Fish, and John H. Madsen, eds.

1989   Differentiation and Integration in a Tucson Basin Classic Period Hohokam Community. In *The Sociopolitical Structure of Prehistoric Southwestern Societies,* ed. Steadman Upham, Kent G. Lightfoot, and Roberta A. Jewett, pp. 237–67. Boulder, Colo.: Westview Press.

1992   *The Marana Community in the Hohokam World.* University of Arizona Anthropological Paper no. 56. Tucson: University of Arizona Press.

Fish, Suzanne K., and Norman Yoffee

1996   The State of the Hohokam. In *Debating Complexity: Proceedings of the 26th Annual Chacmool Conference,* ed. Daniel A. Meyer, Peter C. Dawson, and Donald T. Hanna, pp. 290–96. Archaeological Association and the Department of Archaeology, University of Calgary, Alberta.

Fiske, Alan Page

1991   *Structures of Social Life: The Four Elementary Forms of Human Relations.* New York: Free Press.

Flanagan, James G.

1989   Hierarchy in Simple "Egalitarian" Societies. *Annual Review of Anthropology* 18:245–66.

Flannery, Kent V.

1972   The Cultural Evolution of Civilizations. *Annual Review of Ecology and Systematics* 3:399–426.

Ford, Richard I.

1968   *An Ecological Analysis Involving the Population of San Juan Pueblo, New Mexico.* Ph.D. dissertation, Department of Anthropology, University of Michigan. Ann Arbor, Mich.: University Microfilms International.

1972   An Ecological Perspective on the Eastern Pueblos. In *New Perspectives on the Pueblos,* ed. Alfonso Ortiz, pp. 1–17. Albuquerque: University of New Mexico Press.

Foucault, Michel

1980   *Power/Knowledge: Selected Interviews and Other Writings 1972–77,* ed. C. Gordon. New York: Pantheon.

Fowler, Andrew P., and John R. Stein

1992   The Anasazi Great House in Space, Time, and Paradigm. In *Anasazi Regional Organization and the Chaco System,* ed. David E. Doyel, pp. 101–22. Maxwell Museum of Anthropology Anthropological Paper no. 5. University of New Mexico, Albuquerque.

Freidel, David, and Linda Schele

1988   Symbol and Power: A History of the Lowland Maya Cosmogram. In *Maya Iconography,* ed. Elizabeth P. Benson and Gillett G. Griffen, pp. 44–93. Princeton, N.J.: Princeton University Press.

Fried, Morton H.

1967   *The Evolution of Political Society: An Essay in Political Anthropology.* New York: Random House.

Friedman, Jonathan

1975   Tribes, States, and Transformations. In *Marxist Analyses in Social Anthro-pology,* ed. Maurice Bloch, pp. 161–202. London: Malaby Press.

1982   Catastrophe and Continuity in Social Evolution. In *Theory and Explana-tion in Archaeology: The Southampton Conference,* ed. Colin Renfrew, Mi-chael J. Rowlands, and Barbara A. Segraves, pp. 175–96. New York: Academic Press.

Garrett, Elizabeth

1992   A Petrographic Analysis of Glaze Sherds from Gran Quivira. In *Subsistence and Exchange at Gran Quivira Pueblo,* pt. 2, by Katherine Spielmann, pp. 110–28. Report submitted to the National Park Service, Southwestern Regional Office, Santa Fe, N.M.

Geertz, Clifford

1966   Religion as a Cultural System. In *Anthropological Approaches to the Study of Religion,* ed. Michael Banton, pp. 1–46. London: Tavistock.

Giddens, Anthony

1984   *The Constitution of Society: Outline of the Theory of Structuration.* Berkeley: University of California Press.

Gillespie, Susan

1991   Ballgames and Boundaries. In *The Mesoamerican Ballgame,* ed. Vernon L. Scarborough and David R. Wilcox, pp. 317–46. Tucson: University of Arizona Press.

Gilman, Antonio

1987   Unequal Exchange in Copper Age Iberia. In *Specialization, Exchange, and Complex Societies,* ed. Elizabeth M. Brumfiel and Timothy K. Earle, pp. 22–29. New York: Cambridge University Press.

1991   Trajectories towards Social Complexity in the Later Prehistory of the Mediterranean. In *Chiefdoms: Power, Economy, and Ideology,* ed. Timothy Earle, pp. 146–68. New York: Cambridge University Press.

Glascock, Michael D.

1992   Neutron Activation Analysis. In *Chemical Characterization of Ceramic Pastes in Archaeology,* ed. Hector Neff, pp. 11–26. Monographs in World Ar-chaeology no. 7. Madison, Wis.: Prehistory Press.

Gluckman, Max

1954   *Rituals of Rebellion in South-east Africa.* Manchester: Manchester Univer-sity Press.

Gnabasik, Virginia

1981   Faunal Utilization by the Pueblo Indians. M.A. thesis, Eastern New Mex-ico University, Portales.

Godelier, Maurice

1982   Social Hierarchies among the Baruya of New Guinea. In *Inequality in New Guinea Highland Societies,* ed. Andrew Strathern, pp. 3–34. New York: Cambridge University Press.

1991   *Big Men and Great Men: Personifications of Power in Melanesia.* New York: Cambridge University Press.

Gordon, Deborah

1995   The Development of Organization in an Ant Colony. *American Scientist* 83:50–57.

Gramsci, Antonio

1971   *Selections from the Prison Notebooks,* trans. and ed. Q. Hoare and G. N. Smith. London: Lawrence and Wishart.

Graves, Michael W.

1991   Pottery Production and Distribution among the Kalinga: A Study of Household and Regional Organization and Differentiation. In *Ceramic Ethnoarchaeology,* ed. William A. Longacre, pp. 112–43. Tucson: University of Arizona Press.

Graves, Michael W., William A. Longacre, and Sally J. Holbrook

1982   Aggregation and Abandonment at Grasshopper Pueblo, Arizona. *Journal of Field Archaeology* 9:193–206.

Graves, William M.

1996   Social Power and Prestige Enhancement among the Protohistoric Salinas Pueblos, Rio Grande Valley, New Mexico. M.A. thesis, Department of Anthropology, Arizona State University, Tempe.

Grebinger, Paul

1973   Prehistoric Social Organization in Chaco Canyon, New Mexico: An Alternative Reconstruction. *Kiva* 39:3–23.

Green, Jesse, ed.

1979   *Selected Writings of Frank Hamilton Cushing.* Lincoln: University of Nebraska Press.

Gregory, David A.

1983   Excavations at the Siphon Draw Site (AZ U:10:6). In *Hohokam Archaeology along the Salt-Gila Aqueduct, Central Arizona Project.* Vol. 4: *Village Sites on Queen Creek and Siphon Draw,* ed. Lynn S. Teague and Patricia L. Crown. Arizona State Museum Archaeological Series 150. University of Arizona, Tucson.

1987   The Morphology of Platform Mounds and the Structure of Classic Period Hohokam Sites. In *The Hohokam Village: Site Structure and Organization,* ed. David E. Doyel, pp. 183–210. Glenwood Springs, Colo.: American Association for the Advancement of Science.

1988   *The 1982–1984 Excavations at Las Colinas.* Vol. 3: *The Mound 8 Precinct.* Arizona State Museum Archaeological Series 162. University of Arizona, Tucson.

1991   Form and Variation in Hohokam Settlement Patterns. In *Chaco and Hohokam: Prehistoric Regional Systems in the American Southwest,* ed. Patricia L. Crown and W. James Judge, pp. 159–93. Santa Fe, N.M.: School of American Research Press.

Gregory, David A., and Fred L. Nials

1985   Observations Concerning the Distribution of Classic Period Hohokam Platform Mounds. In *Proceedings of the 1983 Hohokam Symposium,* pt. 2, ed. Alfred E. Dittert Jr. and Donald E. Dove, pp. 373–88. Arizona Archaeological Society Occasional Paper no. 2. Phoenix.

Griffen, P. Bion

1967   A High Status Burial from Grasshopper Ruin, Arizona. *Kiva* 33:37–53.

Gumerman, George J., and Murray Gell-Mann, eds.

1994   *Understanding Complexity in the Prehistoric Southwest.* SFI Studies in the Sciences of Complexity Proceedings 16. Reading, Mass.: Addison-Wesley.

Gumerman, George J., Murray Gell-Mann, and Linda Cordell

1994   Introduction. In *Understanding Complexity in the Prehistoric Southwest,* ed. George J. Gumerman and Murray Gell-Mann, pp. 3–14. SFI Studies in the Sciences of Complexity Proceedings 16. Reading, Mass.: Addison-Wesley.

Haas, Jonathan

1982   *The Evolution of the Prehistoric State.* New York: Columbia University Press.

Haas, Jonathan, and Winifred Creamer, eds.

1993   *Stress and Warfare among the Prehistoric Kayenta Anasazi of the Thirteenth Century.* Fieldiana: Anthropology, n.s. 21. Field Museum of Natural History, Chicago.

Habicht-Mauche, Judith A.

1988   Town and Province: Regional Integration among the Classic Period Rio Grande Pueblos. Paper presented at the 53rd Annual Meeting of the Society for American Archaeology, Phoenix.

1995   Changing Patterns of Pottery Manufacture and Trade in the Northern Rio Grande Region. In *Ceramic Production in the American Southwest,* ed. Barbara J. Mills and Patricia L. Crown, pp. 167–99. Tucson: University of Arizona Press.

Hantman, Jeffrey L.

1989   Surplus Production and Complexity in the Upper Little Colorado Province, East Central Arizona. In *The Sociopolitical Structure of Prehistoric Southwestern Societies,* ed. Steadman Upham, Kent G. Lightfoot, and Roberta A. Jewett, pp. 419–45. Boulder, Colo.: Westview Press.

Hardin, Margaret A.

1984   Models of Decoration. In *The Many Dimensions of Pottery: Ceramics in Archaeology and Anthropology,* ed. S. E. van der Leeuw and A. C. Pritchard, pp. 575–601. Amsterdam: Universiteit van Amsterdam.

Harrison, Simon

1985   Ritual Hierarchy and Secular Equality in a Sepik River Village. *American Ethnologist* 12:413–26.

1987   Magical and Material Polities in Melanesia. *Man* 24:1–20.

1991   The Commerce of Cultures in Melanesia. *Man* 28:139–58.

Harry, Karen G.

1997   Ceramic Production, Distribution, and Consumption in Two Classic Period Hohokam Communities. Ph.D. dissertation, Department of Anthropology, University of Arizona, Tucson.

Harry, Karen G., Paul R. Fish, and Suzanne K. Fish

1998   Ceramic Production and Distribution in Two Classic Period Hohokam Communities. Draft manuscript submitted to *Neutron Activation Analysis of Prehistoric Pottery from the Greater Southwest,* ed. Donna M. Glowacki and Hector Neff. UCLA Institute of Archaeology (under review).

Haury, Emil

1934   The Canyon Creek Ruin and the Cliff Dwellings of Sierra Ancha. *Medallion Paper* no. 14. Gila Pueblo, Globe, Ariz.

1958   Evidence at Point of Pines for Prehistoric Migration from Northern Arizona. In *Migrations in New World Culture History,* ed. Raymond H. Thompson. University of Arizona Bulletin 29(2), Social Science Bulletin 27. Tucson: University of Arizona Press.

1976   *The Hohokam: Desert Farmers and Craftsmen.* Tucson: University of Arizona Press.

Haury, Emil W., and Lyndon L. Hargrave

1931   *Recently Dated Pueblo Ruins in Arizona.* Smithsonian Miscellaneous Collections, vol. 82, no. 11, Publication 3069. Washington, D.C.: Government Printing Office.

Hayden, Brian

1990   Nimrods, Piscators, Pluckers, and Planters: The Emergence of Food Production. *Journal of Anthropological Archaeology* 9:31–69.

1995   Pathways to Power: Principles for Creating Socioeconomic Inequalities. In *Foundations of Social Inequality,* ed. T. Douglas Price and Gary M. Feinman, pp. 15–86. New York: Plenum Press.

Hayes, Alden C.

1981   *The Excavation of Mound 7.* National Park Service Publication in Archaeology 16. Washington, D.C.

1982   The Jumanos Pueblos. In *Salinas: Archaeology, History, Prehistory, Exploration,* Annual Bulletin of the School of American Research, pp. 11–15. Santa Fe, N.M.

Hays, Kelley A.

1989   Katsina Depictions on Homol'ovi Ceramics: Toward a Fourteenth-Century Pueblo Iconography. *Kiva* 54:297–313.

1994   Kachina Depictions on Prehistoric Pueblo Pottery. In *Kachinas in the Pueblo World,* ed. Polly Schaafsma, pp. 47–62. Albuquerque: University of New Mexico Press.

Hegmon, Michelle

1989   Social Integration and Architecture. In *The Architecture of Social Integration in Prehistoric Pueblos,* ed. William D. Lipe and Michelle Hegmon, pp. 5–14. Crow Canyon Archaeological Center Occasional Paper no. 1. Cortez, Colo.

1996   Variability in Food Production, Strategies of Storage and Sharing, and the Pithouse-to-Pueblo Transition in the Northern Southwest. In *Evolving Complexity and Environmental Risk in the Prehistoric Southwest,* ed. Joseph A. Tainter and Bonnie Bagley Tainter, pp. 223–50. SFI Studies in the Sciences of Complexity Proceedings 24. Reading, Mass.: Addison-Wesley.

Heidke, James M., Elizabeth J. Miksa, Diane C. Kamilli, and Michael K. Wiley

1997   Appendix Five: Desert Archaeology Letter Report. In Ceramic Production, Distribution, and Consumption in Two Classic Period Hohokam Communities, by Karen G. Harry, pp. 363–72. Ph.D. dissertation, Department of Anthropology, University of Arizona, Tucson.

Heidke, James M., and Michael K. Wiley

1997   Appendix Four: Petrographic and Qualitative Analysis of Tanque Verde Red-on-brown Sherds. In Ceramic Production, Distribution, and Consumption in Two Classic Period Hohokam Communities, by Karen G. Harry, pp. 302–63. Ph.D. dissertation, Department of Anthropology, University of Arizona, Tucson.

Henderson, T. Kathleen

1987a   The Growth of a Hohokam Village. In *The Hohokam Village: Site Structure and Organization,* ed. David E. Doyel, pp. 97–126. Glenwood Springs, Colo.: American Association for the Advancement of Science.

1987b   *Structure and Organization at La Ciudad.* Arizona State University Anthropological Field Studies 18. Tempe.

1993   Perspectives on the Classic Period Occupation of the Santa Cruz Flats. In *Classic Period Occupation on the Santa Cruz Flats: The Santa Cruz Flats Archaeological Project,* ed. T. Kathleen Henderson and R. J. Martynec, pp. 579–96. Tempe, Ariz.: Northland Research.

Herdt, Gilbert
1990   Secret Societies and Secret Collectives. *Oceania* 60:360–81.

Herhahn, Cynthia L.
1998   Glaze Ware Petrographic Analysis Descriptive Report for Gran Quivira (LA 120), Quarai (LA 95), Pueblo Colorado (LA 476), and Pueblo Blanco (LA 51). Manuscript on file, Department of Anthropology, Arizona State University, Tempe.

Herhahn, Cynthia L., and J. Brett Hill
1998   Modeling Agricultural Production Strategies in the Northern Rio Grande Valley, New Mexico. *Human Ecology* 26:469–87.

Herr, Sarah A.
1999   The Organization of Migrant Communities on a Pueblo Frontier. Ph.D. dissertation, Department of Anthropology, University of Arizona, Tucson.

Hill, Kim, and A. Magdalena Hurtado
1989   Hunter-Gatherers of the New World. *American Scientist* 77:437–43.

Hillier, Bill, and Julienne Hanson
1984   *The Social Logic of Space.* New York: Cambridge University Press.

Hirth, Kenneth G.
1998   The Distributional Approach: A New Way to Identify Marketplace Exchange in the Archaeological Record. *Current Anthropology* 39:451–76.

Hodder, Ian, and Clive Orton
1976   *Spatial Analysis in Archaeology.* New York: Cambridge University Press.

Hodge, Frederick Webb
1920   The Age of the Zuni Pueblo of Kechipauan. In *Museum of the American Indian, Heye Foundation, Indian Notes and Monographs* 3(2):41–60. New York: Museum of the American Indian.

1937   *History of Hawikuh, New Mexico, One of the So-called Cities of Cibola.* Los Angeles: Southwest Museum.

Hoffman, Elizabeth, Kevin A. McCabe, and Vernon L. Smith
1998   Behavioral Foundations of Reciprocity: Experimental Economics and Evolutionary Psychology. *Economic Inquiry* 36:335–52.

Hogan, Patrick, and Joseph C. Winter, eds.

1983   *Economy and Interaction along the Chaco River.* Office of Contract Archeology, Department of Anthropology, University of New Mexico, Albuquerque.

Howard, Ann V.

1985   A Reconstruction of Hohokam Interregional Shell Production and Exchange within Southwestern Arizona. In *Proceedings of the 1983 Hohokam Symposium,* pt. 2, ed. Alfred E. Dittert Jr. and Donald E. Dove, pp. 459–72. Arizona Archaeological Society Occasional Paper no. 2. Phoenix.

Howard, Jerry B.

1985   Courtyard Groups and Domestic Cycling: A Hypothetical Model of Growth. In *Proceedings of the 1983 Hohokam Symposium,* pt. 2, ed. Alfred E. Dittert Jr. and Donald E. Dove, pp. 311–26. Arizona Archaeological Society Occasional Paper no. 2. Phoenix.

1987   The Lehi Canal System: Organization of a Classic Period Community. In *The Hohokam Village: Site Structure and Organization,* ed. David E. Doyel, pp. 211–22. Glenwood Springs, Colo.: American Association for the Advancement of Science.

1990   Paleohydraulics: Modeling the Operation of Prehistoric Hohokam Irrigation Systems. M.A. thesis, Department of Anthropology, Arizona State University, Tempe.

1991   System Reconstruction: The Evolution of an Irrigation System. In *The Operation and Evolution of an Irrigation System: The East Papago Canal Study,* by Jerry B. Howard and Gary Huckleberry, pp. 5.1–5.33. Publications in Archaeology 18. Phoenix: Soil Systems, Inc.

1992   Architecture and Ideology: An Approach to the Functional Analysis of Platform Mounds. In *Proceedings of the Second Salado Conference, Globe, Arizona, 1992,* ed. Richard C. Lange and Stephen Germick, pp. 69–77. Arizona Archaeological Society Occasional Paper. Phoenix.

Howard, Jerry B., and Gary Huckleberry

1991   *The Operation and Evolution of an Irrigation System: The East Papago Canal Study.* Publications in Archaeology 18. Phoenix: Soil Systems, Inc.

Howell, Todd L.

1994   Leadership at the Ancestral Zuni Village of Hawikku. Ph.D. dissertation, Department of Anthropology, Arizona State University, Tempe.

1995   Tracking Zuni Gender and Leadership Roles across the Contact Period. *Journal of Anthropological Research* 51:25–147.

1996   Identifying Leaders at Hawikku. *Kiva* 62:61–82.

Howell, Todd L., and Keith W. Kintigh

1996   Archaeological Identification of Kin Groups Using Mortuary and Biological Data: An Example from the American Southwest. *American Antiquity* 61:537–54.

Huber, Edgar K., and Timothy A. Kohler

1993   Pollen Analysis, Kiva Area 1, Burnt Mesa Pueblo (LA 60372). In *Papers on the Early Classic Period Prehistory of the Pajarito Plateau, New Mexico,* ed. Timothy A. Kohler and Angela R. Linse, pp. 121–29. Department of Anthropology Reports of Investigations 65. Washington State University, Pullman.

Hudson, Charles

1990   *The Juan Pardo Expeditions: Explorations of the Carolinas and Tennessee, 1566–1568.* Washington, D.C.: Smithsonian Institution Press.

Hunt, Robert C., and Eva Hunt

1976   Canal Irrigation and Local Social Organization. *Current Anthropology* 17:389–411.

Huntington, Frederick W.

1986   *Archaeological Investigations at the West Branch Site: Early and Middle Rincon Occupation in the Southern Tucson Basin.* Institute for American Research Anthropological Paper no. 5. Tucson.

Irwin-Williams, Cynthia, and Philip Shelley

1980   Investigations at the Salmon Site: The Structure of Chacoan Society in the Northern Southwest. Manuscript on file, National Park Service, University of New Mexico, Albuquerque.

Jacobs, David

1994   *Archaeology of the Salado in the Livingston Area of Tonto Basin, Roosevelt Platform Mound Study.* Roosevelt Monograph Series 3, Anthropological Field Studies 32. Office of Cultural Resource Management, Arizona State University, Tempe.

Jacobs, David, and Glen E. Rice

1994   Summary. In *Archaeology of the Salado in the Livingston Area of Tonto Basin, Roosevelt Platform Mound Study,* by David Jacobs, pp. 923–26. Roosevelt Monograph Series 3, Anthropological Field Studies 32. Office of Cultural Resource Management, Arizona State University, Tempe.

1997   The Function of U:4:33/132, the Cline Terrace Mound. In *A Salado Platform Mound on Tonto Creek: Roosevelt Platform Mound Study, Report on the Cline Terrace Mound, Cline Terrace Complex,* by David Jacobs, pp. 577–85. Roosevelt Monograph Series 7, Anthropological Field Studies 36. Office of Cultural Resource Management, Arizona State University, Tempe.

Jewett, Roberta A.

1989   Distance, Interaction, and Complexity: The Spatial Organization of Pan-Regional Settlement Clusters in the American Southwest. In *The Socio-political Structure of Prehistoric Southwestern Societies,* ed. Steadman Upham, Kent G. Lightfoot, and Roberta A. Jewett, pp. 363–88. Boulder, Colo.: Westview Press.

Johnson, Allen W., and Timothy K. Earle

1987   *The Evolution of Human Societies.* Stanford, Calif.: Stanford University Press.

Johnson, Gregory A.

1982   Organizational Structure and Scalar Stress. In *Theory and Explanation in Archaeology: The Southampton Conference,* ed. Colin Renfrew, Michael J. Rowlands, and Barbara A. Segraves, pp. 389–421. New York: Academic Press.

1989   Dynamics of Southwestern Prehistory: Far Outside, Looking In. In *Dynamics of Southwestern Prehistory,* ed. Linda S. Cordell and George J. Gumerman, pp. 371–89. Washington, D.C.: Smithsonian Institution Press.

Judd, Neil M.

1925   Everyday Life in Pueblo Bonito. *National Geographic* 48:227–62.

1959   *Pueblo del Arroyo, Chaco Canyon, New Mexico.* Smithsonian Institution Miscellaneous Collections 138, no. 1.

1964   *The Architecture of Pueblo Bonito.* Smithsonian Institution Miscellaneous Collections 147, no. 1.

Judge, W. James

1989   Chaco Canyon—San Juan Basin. In *Dynamics of Southwestern Prehistory,* ed. Linda S. Cordell and George J. Gumerman, pp. 209–62. Washington, D.C.: Smithsonian Institution Press.

1992   Chaco: Current Views of Prehistory and the Regional System. In *Chaco and Hohokam: Prehistoric Regional Systems in the American Southwest,* ed. Patricia L. Crown and W. James Judge, pp. 11–30. Santa Fe, N.M.: School of American Research Press.

1993   Resource Distribution and the Chaco Phenomenon. In *The Chimney Rock Archaeological Symposium,* ed. James Malville and Gary Matlock, pp. 35–36. USDA Forest Service General Technical Report RM-227. Fort Collins, Colo.: Rocky Mountain Forest and Range Experiment Station.

Judge, W. James, William B. Gillespie, Stephen H. Lekson, and H. Wolcott Toll

1981   *Tenth Century Developments in Chaco Canyon.* Papers of the Archaeological Society of New Mexico no. 6. Archaeological Society of New Mexico, Albuquerque.

Kantner, John

1996   Political Competition among the Chaco Anasazi of the American Southwest. *Journal of Anthropological Archaeology* 15:41–105.

Kauffman, Stuart

1993   *The Origins of Order: Self-Organization and Selection in Evolution.* New York: Oxford University Press.

1995   *At Home in the Universe: The Search for the Laws of Self-Organization and Complexity.* New York: Oxford University Press.

Keen, Ian

1994   *Knowledge and Secrecy in an Aboriginal Religion.* Oxford: Clarendon Press.

Keesing, Roger M.

1982   *Kwaio Religion: The Living and the Dead in a Solomon Island Society.* New York: Columbia University Press.

Kent, Susan

1993   Sharing in an Egalitarian Kalahari Community. *Man* n.s. 28:479–514.

Kintigh, Keith W.

1985   *Settlement, Subsistence, and Society in Late Zuni Prehistory.* University of Arizona Anthropological Paper no. 44. Tucson: University of Arizona Press.

1990   Protohistoric Transitions in the Western Pueblo Area. In *Perspectives on Southwestern Prehistory,* ed. Paul E. Minnis and Charles L. Redman, pp. 258–75. Boulder, Colo.: Westview Press.

1994   Chaco, Communal Architecture, and Cibolan Aggregation. In *The Ancient Southwestern Community: Models and Methods for the Study of Prehistoric Social Organization,* ed. W. H. Wills and Robert D. Leonard, pp. 131–40. Albuquerque: University of New Mexico Press.

1996   The Cibola Region in the Post-Chacoan Era. In *The Prehistoric Pueblo World,* A.D. 1150–1350, ed. Michael A. Adler, pp. 131–44. Tucson: University of Arizona Press.

Kintigh, Keith W., Todd L. Howell, and Andrew Duff

1996   Post-Chacoan Social Integration at the Hinkson Site, New Mexico. *Kiva* 61:257–74.

Knight, Vernon

1986   The Institutional Organization of Mississippian Religion. *American Antiquity* 51:675–87.

1990   Social Organization and the Evolution of Hierarchy in Southeastern Chiefdoms. *Journal of Anthropological Research* 46:1–23.

Kohler, Timothy A.

1992   Field Houses, Villages and the Tragedy of the Commons in the Early Northern Anasazi Southwest. *American Antiquity* 57:617–34.

1993   News from the Northern American Southwest: Prehistory on the Edge of Chaos. *Journal of Archaeological Research* 1:267–321.

1998   Public Architecture and Power in Pre-Columbian North America. Paper presented at the symposium "Power, Monuments, and Civilization," Nara, Japan. Santa Fe Institute Working Paper 98-03-022.

Kohler, Timothy J., and Carla Van West

1996   The Calculus of Self-Interest in the Development of Cooperation: Sociopolitical Development and Risk among the Northern Anasazi. In *Evolving Complexity and Environmental Risk in the Prehistoric Southwest,* ed. Joseph A. Tainter and Bonnie Bagley Tainter, pp. 169–96. SFI Studies in the Sciences of Complexity Proceedings 24. Reading, Mass.: Addison-Wesley.

Kolb, Michael J.

1994   Monumentality and the Rise of Religious Authority in Precontact Hawai'i. *Current Anthropology* 34:521–47.

1996   Comments. *Current Anthropology* 37:59–60.

Kosse, Krisztina

1990   Group Size and Societal Complexity: Thresholds in Long-term Memory. *Journal of Anthropological Archaeology* 9:275–303.

1996   Middle Range Societies from a Scalar Perspective. In *Interpreting Southwestern Diversity: Underlying Principles and Overarching Patterns,* ed. Paul R. Fish and J. Jefferson Reid, pp. 87–96. Arizona State University Anthropological Research Paper no. 48. Tempe.

Kovacik, Joseph J.

1996   A Social/Contextual Archaeology of Chaco Canyon, New Mexico: Collective Memory and Material Culture amongst the Chaco Anasazi. Ph.D. dissertation, Faculty of Archaeology and Anthropology, Cambridge University.

Kowalewski, Stephen A.

1998   Cyclical Transformation in North American Prehistory. Paper prepared for "Concepts of Humans and Behavior Patterns in the Cultures of the East and the West: Interdisciplinary Approach," Russian State University for Humanities, Institute of Cultural Anthropology, Moscow.

Kowalewski, Stephen A., Gary M. Feinman, Laura Finsten, and Richard E. Blanton

1991   Pre-Hispanic Ballcourts from the Valley of Oaxaca, Mexico. In *The Mesoamerican Ballgame,* ed. Vernon L. Scarborough and David R. Wilcox, pp. 25–44. Tucson: University of Arizona Press.

Kroeber, Alfred L.

1917   *Zuni Kin and Clan.* Anthropological Papers of the American Museum of Natural History, vol. 18. New York.

1957   *Style and Civilizations.* Ithaca, N.Y.: Cornell University Press.

Kus, Susan

1996   Archaeologist as Anthropologist: Much Ado about Something After All? *Journal of Anthropological Method and Theory* 4:199–211.

Ladd, Edmund J.

1979   Zuni Social and Political Organization. In *Handbook of North American Indians.* Vol. 9: *Southwest,* ed. Alfonso Ortiz, pp. 482–91. Washington, D.C.: Smithsonian Institution Press.

Larson, Daniel O., Hector Neff, Donald A. Graybill, Joel Michaelsen, and Elizabeth Ambos

1996   Risk, Climatic Variability, and the Study of Southwestern Prehistory: An Evolutionary Perspective. *American Antiquity* 61:217–41.

Leach, Edmund R.

        Political Systems of Highland Burma. London: Athlone Press.

LeBlanc, Steven A.

1989a   Cibola: Shifting Cultural Boundaries. In *Dynamics of Southwestern Prehistory,* ed. Linda S. Cordell and George J. Gumerman, pp. 337–69. Washington, D.C.: Smithsonian Institution Press.

1989b   Cultural Dynamics in the Southern Mogollon Area. In *Dynamics of Southwestern Prehistory,* ed. Linda S. Cordell and George J. Gumerman, pp. 179–207. Washington, D.C.: Smithsonian Institution Press.

1999   Regional Interaction and Warfare in the Late Prehistoric Southwest. In *The Archaeology of Regional Interaction: Religion, Warfare, and Exchange across the Southwest and Beyond,* ed. Michelle Hegmon. Niwot: University Press of Colorado.

Lederman, Rena

1986   *What Gifts Engender: Social Relations and Politics in Mendi, Highland Papua New Guinea.* New York: Cambridge University Press.

Lehman, Edward W.

1969   Toward a Macrosociology of Power. *American Sociological Review* 34:453–65.

Lekson, Stephen H.

1984a   *Great Pueblo Architecture of Chaco Canyon.* Publications in Archeology 18B, Chaco Canyon Series. Santa Fe, N.M.: National Park Service.

1984b   Standing Architecture at Chaco Canyon and the Interpretation of Local and Regional Organization. In *Recent Research on Chaco Prehistory,* ed.

W. James Judge and John Schelberg, pp. 55–74. Reports of the Chaco Center no. 8. Albuquerque: National Park Service.

1988   The Idea of the Kiva in Anasazi Archaeology. *Kiva* 53:213–34.

1990   Sedentism and Aggregation in Anasazi Archaeology. In *Perspectives on Southwestern Prehistory,* ed. Paul E. Minnis and Charles L. Redman, pp. 333–40. Boulder, Colo.: Westview Press.

1991   Settlement Patterns and the Chaco Regional System. In *Chaco and Hohokam: Prehistoric Regional Systems in the American Southwest,* ed. Patricia L. Crown and W. James Judge, pp. 31–56. Santa Fe, N.M.: School of American Research Press.

1997   Anasazi Communities in Context. In *Anasazi Architecture and American Design,* ed. B. Morrow and V. B. Price, pp. 27–35. Albuquerque: University of New Mexico Press.

———, ed.

1983   *The Architecture and Dendrochronology of Chetro Ketl, Chaco Canyon, New Mexico.* Reports of the Chaco Center no. 6. Albuquerque: National Park Service.

Lekson, Stephen H., and Peter J. McKenna

1983   Excavation Notes. In *The Architecture and Dendrochronology of Chetro Ketl, Chaco Canyon, New Mexico,* ed. Stephen H. Lekson, pp. 11–49. Reports of the Chaco Center no. 6. Albuquerque: National Park Service.

Lekson, Stephen H., Thomas C. Windes, John R. Stein, and W. James Judge

1988   The Chaco Canyon Community. *Scientific American* 256:100–109.

Leonard, Robert D., and Heidi E. Reed

1993   Population Aggregation in the Prehistoric American Southwest: A Selectionist Model. *American Antiquity* 58:648–61.

Levy, Jerrold E.

1992   *Orayvi Revisited: Social Stratification in an "Egalitarian" Society.* Santa Fe, N.M.: School of American Research Press.

1994   Ethnographic Analogs: Strategies for Reconstructing Archaeological Cultures. In *Understanding Complexity in the Prehistoric Southwest,* ed. George J. Gumerman and Murray Gell-Mann, pp. 223–44. SFI Studies in the Sciences of Complexity Proceedings 16. Reading, Mass.: Addison-Wesley.

Lewin, Roger

1992   *Complexity: Life at the Edge of Chaos.* New York: Macmillan.

Lightfoot, Kent G.

1984   *Prehistoric Political Dynamics: A Case Study from the American Southwest.* DeKalb: Northern Illinois University Press.

Lightfoot, Kent G., and Gary M. Feinman

1982   Social Differentiation and Leadership Development in Early Pithouse Villages in the Mogollon Region of the American Southwest. *American Antiquity* 47:64–86.

Lightfoot, Kent G., and Rachel Most

1989   Interpreting Settlement Hierarchies: A Reassessment of Pinedale and Snowflake Settlement Patterns. In *The Sociopolitical Structure of Prehistoric Southwestern Societies,* ed. Steadman Upham, Kent G. Lightfoot, and Roberta A. Jewett, pp. 389–418. Boulder, Colo.: Westview Press.

Lightfoot, Kent G., and Steadman Upham

1989   Complex Societies in the Prehistoric American Southwest: A Consideration of the Controversy. In *The Sociopolitical Structure of Prehistoric Southwestern Societies,* ed. Steadman Upham, Kent G. Lightfoot, and Roberta A. Jewett, pp. 3–30. Boulder, Colo.: Westview Press.

Lightfoot, Ricky R.

1988   Roofing an Early Anasazi Great Kiva: Analysis of an Architectural Model. *Kiva* 53:253–72.

Lightfoot, Ricky R., and Kristin Kuckelman

1994   Warfare and the Pueblo Abandonment of the Mesa Verde Region. Paper presented at the 59th Annual Meeting of the Society for American Archaeology, Anaheim, Calif.

Lindauer, Owen

1995   *Where the Rivers Converge: Report on the Rock Island Complex, Roosevelt Platform Mound Study.* Roosevelt Monograph Series 4, Anthropological Field Studies 33. Office of Cultural Resource Management, Arizona State University, Tempe.

1996   *The Place of the Storehouses: Report on the Schoolhouse Point Mound, Pinto Creek Complex, Roosevelt Platform Mound Study.* Roosevelt Monograph Series 6, Anthropological Field Studies 35. Office of Cultural Resource Management, Arizona State University, Tempe.

Lindstrom, Lamont

1984   Doctor, Lawyer, Wise Man, Priest: Big-Men and Knowledge in Melanesia. *Man* 19:291–309.

Linse, Angela R., Michael V. Reilly, and Timothy A. Kohler

1992   Excavations in Area 1 of Burnt Mesa Pueblo. In *Bandelier Archaeological Excavation Project: Summer 1990 Excavations at Burnt Mesa Pueblo and Casa del Rito,* ed. Timothy A. Kohler and Matthew J. Root, pp. 45–90. Department of Anthropology Reports of Investigations 64. Washington State University, Pullman.

Lipe, William D.

1989   Social Scale of Mesa Verde Anasazi Kivas. In *The Architecture of Social Integration in Prehistoric Pueblos,* ed. William D. Lipe and Michelle Hegmon, pp. 53–72. Crow Canyon Archaeological Center Occasional Paper no. 1. Cortez, Colo.

Lipe, William D., and Michelle Hegmon

1989a   Historical Perspectives on Architecture and Social Integration in the Prehistoric Pueblos. In *The Architecture of Social Integration in Prehistoric Pueblos,* ed. William D. Lipe and Michelle Hegmon, pp. 15–34. Crow Canyon Archaeological Center Occasional Paper no. 1. Cortez, Colo.

——, eds.

1989b   *The Architecture of Social Integration in Prehistoric Pueblos.* Crow Canyon Archaeological Center Occasional Paper no. 1. Cortez, Colo.

Littler, Mathew L.

1997   Canal Irrigation and the Emergence of Hohokam Inequality. Manuscript in possession of the author, Department of Anthropology, University of Arizona.

Longacre, William A., and Miriam T. Stark

1992   Ceramics, Kinship, and Space: A Kalinga Example. *Journal of Anthropological Archaeology* 11:125–36.

Mahoney, Nancy

1998   Redefining the Scale of Chacoan Communities. Paper presented at the 63rd Annual Meeting of the Society for American Archaeology, Seattle.

Manzanilla, Linda

1997   Teotihuacan: Urban Archetype, Cosmic Model. In *Emergence and Change in Early Urban Societies,* ed. Linda Manzanilla, pp. 109–31. New York: Plenum Press.

Marinakis, Yorgos

1995   A Phase Transition in a Prehistoric Human Population. Ph.D. dissertation, Department of Biology, University of New Mexico, Albuquerque.

Marshall, Michael P., John R. Stein, Richard W. Loose, and Judith E. Novotny

1979   *Anasazi Communities of the San Juan Basin.* Albuquerque: Public Service Company of New Mexico.

Maschner, Herbert D. G.

1995   Review of *A Complex Culture of the British Columbia Plateau: Traditional Stl'atl'imx Resource Use,* ed. Brian Hayden. *American Antiquity* 60:378–80.

Mathien, Frances Joan

1997   Ornaments of the Chaco Anasazi. In *Ceramics, Lithics and Ornaments of Chaco Canyon,* ed. Frances Joan Mathien, pp. 1119–220. Publications in Archeology 18G, Chaco Canyon Series. Santa Fe, N.M.: National Park Service.

Mathien, Frances Joan, and Thomas C. Windes

1988   *Historic Structure Report: Kin Nahasbas Ruin, Chaco Culture National Historical Park, New Mexico.* Santa Fe, N.M.: National Park Service.

Mauss, Marcel

1967   *The Gift: Forms and Functions of Exchange in Archaic Societies.* New York: Norton. (Originally published in 1925.)

McCulloch, Warren S.

1945   A Heterarchy of Values Determined by the Topology of Neural Nets. *Bulletin of Mathematical Biophysics* 7:89–93.

McGuire, Randall H.

1980   The Mesoamerican Connection in the Southwest. *Kiva* 46:3–38.

1985   The Role of Shell Exchange in the Explanation of Hohokam Prehistory. In *Proceedings of the 1983 Hohokam Symposium,* pt. 2, ed. Alfred E. Dittert Jr. and Donald E. Dove, pp. 473–79. Arizona Archaeological Society Occasional Paper no. 2. Phoenix.

1986   Economies and Modes of Production in the Prehistoric Southwestern Periphery. In *Ripples in the Chichimec Sea,* ed. Frances Joan Mathien and Randall H. McGuire, pp. 243–69. Carbondale: Southern Illinois University Press.

1987   A Gila Butte Ballcourt at La Ciudad. In *The Hohokam Community of La Ciudad,* ed. Glen Rice, pp. 69–110. Office of Cultural Resource Management Report 69. Department of Anthropology, Arizona State University, Tempe.

1992   *Death, Society, and Ideology in a Hohokam Community.* Boulder, Colo.: Westview Press.

1993   The Structure and Organization of Hohokam Exchange. In *The American Southwest and Mesoamerica: Systems of Prehistoric Exchange,* ed. Jonathan E. Ericson and Timothy G. Baugh, pp. 95–120. New York: Plenum Press.

McGuire, Randall H., and Dean J. Saitta

1996   Although They Have Petty Captains, They Obey Them Badly: The Dialectics of Prehispanic Western Pueblo Social Organization. *American Antiquity* 61:197–216.

McGuire, Randall H., and Ann Valdo Howard

1987   The Structure and Organization of Hohokam Shell Exchange. *Kiva* 52:113–46.

McKenna, Peter J., and Marcia L. Truell

1986   *Small Site Architecture of Chaco Canyon, New Mexico.* Publications in Archeology 18D, Chaco Canyon Series. Santa Fe, N.M.: National Park Service.

Meggitt, Mervyn

1972   System and Subsystem: The Te Exchange Cycle among the Mae Enga. *Human Ecology* 1:111–23.

Mendelssohn, Kurt

1971   A Scientist Looks at the Pyramids. *American Scientist* 59:210–20.

Mera, H. P.

1934   *A Survey of the Biscuit Ware Area in Northern New Mexico.* Laboratory of Anthropology Technical Series Bulletin no. 6. Santa Fe, N.M.

1940   *Population Changes in the Rio Grande Glaze-Paint Area.* Laboratory of Anthropology Technical Series Bulletin no. 9. Santa Fe, N.M.

Mills, Barbara J.

1995   The Organization of Protohistoric Zuni Ceramic Production. In *Ceramic Production in the American Southwest,* ed. Barbara J. Mills and Patricia L. Crown, pp. 200–30. Tucson: University of Arizona Press.

1997   Gender, Craft Production, and Inequality in the American Southwest. Paper prepared for the School of American Research Advanced Seminar "Sex Roles and Gender Hierarchies in the American Southwest," organized by Patricia L. Crown.

1998   Migration and Pueblo IV Community Reorganization in the Silver Creek Area, East-Central Arizona. In *Migration and Reorganization: The Pueblo IV Period in the American Southwest,* ed. Katherine A. Spielmann, pp. 65–80. Arizona State University Anthropological Research Paper no. 51. Tempe.

1999   Ceramics and the Social Contexts of Food Consumption in the Northern Southwest. In *Pottery and People: Dynamic Interactions,* ed. James Skibo and Gary Feinman, pp. 99–114. Salt Lake City: University of Utah Press.

Mills, Barbara J., and Patricia L. Crown, eds.

1995   *Ceramic Production in the American Southwest.* Tucson: University of Arizona Press.

Mills, Barbara J., Sarah A. Herr, and Scott Van Keuren, eds.

1999   *Living on the Edge of the Rim: Excavation and Analysis by the Silver Creek Archaeological Research Project, 1993–1998.* Arizona State Museum Archaeological Series 192. University of Arizona, Tucson.

Minnis, Paul E.

1984   Peeking under the Tortilla Curtain: Regional Interaction and Integration on the Northeastern Periphery of Casas Grandes. *American Archaeology* 4(3):181–93.

1988   Four Examples of Specialized Production at Casas Grandes, Northwestern Chihuahua. *Kiva* 53:181–94.

1989   The Casas Grandes Polity in the International Four Corners. In *The Sociopolitical Structure of Prehistoric Southwestern Societies,* ed. Steadman Upham, Kent G. Lightfoot, and Roberta A. Jewett, pp. 269–305. Boulder, Colo.: Westview Press.

Minnis, Paul E., Michael E. Whalen, Jane H. Kelley, and Joe D. Stewart

1993   Prehistoric Macaw Breeding in the North American Southwest. *American Antiquity* 58:270–76.

Mitchell, Douglas R.

1991   An Investigation of Two Classic Period Hohokam Cemeteries. *North American Archaeologist* 12:109–27.

——, ed.

1994   *The Pueblo Grande Project.* Vol. 7: *An Analysis of Classic Period Mortuary Patterns.* Publications in Archaeology 20. Phoenix: Soil Systems, Inc.

Mobley-Tanaka, Jeanette L.

1998   Craft and Ritual on the Rio Grande: Ideology and the Development and Maintenance of Specialized Production in the American Southwest. Manuscript on file, Department of Anthropology, Arizona State University, Tempe.

Montgomery, Barbara K., and J. Jefferson Reid

1990   An Instance of Rapid Ceramic Change in the American Southwest. *American Antiquity* 55:88–97.

Moore, Sally F., and Barbara G. Myerhoff

1977   Introduction: Secular Ritual: Forms and Meaning. In *Secular Ritual,* ed. Sally F. Moore and Barbara G. Myerhoff, pp. 3–24. Amsterdam: Van Gorcum.

Morris, Craig

1995   Symbols to Power: Styles and Media in the Inka State. In *Style, Society, and Person: Archaeological and Ethnological Perspectives,* ed. Christopher Carr and Jill E. Neitzel, pp. 419–36. New York: Plenum Press.

Morrow, Baker H., and V. B. Price

1997   *Anasazi Architecture and American Design.* Albuquerque: University of New Mexico Press.

Murdock, George P., and Douglas R. White

1969   Standard Cross-Cultural Samples and Codes. *Ethnology* 8:329–63.

Murdock, George P., and Suzanne F. Wilson

1980   Settlement Patterns and Community Organization, Cross-Cultural Codes. In *Cross-Cultural Samples and Codes,* ed. Herbert Barry III and Alice Schlegel, pp. 75–116. Pittsburgh: University of Pittsburgh Press.

Muth, Richard F.

1975   *Urban Economic Problems.* New York: Harper and Row.

Neitzel, Jill

1989   The Chacoan Regional System: Interpreting the Evidence for Sociopolitical Complexity. In *The Sociopolitical Structure of Prehistoric Southwestern Societies,* ed. Steadman Upham, Kent G. Lightfoot, and Roberta A. Jewett, pp. 509–54. Boulder, Colo.: Westview Press.

1991   Hohokam Material Culture and Behavior: The Dimensions of Organizational Change. In *Exploring the Hohokam: Prehistoric Desert Peoples of the American Southwest,* ed. George J. Gumerman, pp. 177–230. Amerind Foundation Publication. Albuquerque: University of New Mexico Press.

Neitzel, Robert

1965   *Archaeology of the Fatherland Site: The Grand Village of the Natchez.* Anthropological Papers of the American Museum of Natural History, vol. 51, pt. 1. New York.

Nelson, Ben A.

1995   Complexity, Hierarchy, and Scale: A Controlled Comparison between Chaco Canyon, New Mexico, and La Quemada, Zacatecas. *American Antiquity* 60:597–618.

Nelson, Ben A., Debra L. Martin, Alan C. Swedlund, Paul R. Fish, and George J. Armelagos

1994   Studies in Disruption: Demography and Health in the Prehistoric Southwest. In *Understanding Complexity in the Prehistoric Southwest,* ed. George J. Gumerman and Murray Gell-Mann, pp. 59–112. SFI Studies in the Sciences of Complexity Proceedings 16. Reading, Mass.: Addison-Wesley.

Netting, Robert McC.

1990   Population, Permanent Agriculture, and Polities: Unpacking the Evolutionary Portmanteau. In *The Evolution of Political Systems: Sociopolitics in Small-Scale Sedentary Societies,* ed. Steadman Upham, pp. 21–61. New York: Cambridge University Press.

1993   *Smallholders, Householders: Farm Families and the Ecology of Intensive, Sustainable Agriculture.* Stanford, Calif.: Stanford University Press.

Nicholas, Linda, and Gary Feinman

1989   A Regional Perspective on Hohokam Irrigation in the Lower Salt River

REFERENCES   263

Valley. In *The Sociopolitical Structure of Prehistoric Southwestern Societies,* ed. Steadman Upham, Kent G. Lightfoot, and Roberta A. Jewett, pp. 199–236. Boulder, Colo.: Westview Press.

Nowak, Martin A., and Karl Sigmund
1998   Evolution of Indirect Reciprocity by Image Scoring. *Nature* 393:573–77.

Nyerges, A. Endre
1992   The Ecology of Wealth-in-People: Agriculture, Settlement, and Society on the Perpetual Frontier. *American Anthropologist* 94:860–81.

Ortiz, Alfonso
1969   *The Tewa World: Space, Time, Being and Becoming in a Pueblo Society.* Chicago: University of Chicago Press.

Ortman, Scott
1998   Corn Grinding and Community Organization in the Late Prehistoric Pueblo Southwest, A.D. 1150–1550. In *Migration and Reorganization: The Pueblo IV Period in the American Southwest,* ed. Katherine A. Spielmann, pp. 165–92. Arizona State University Anthropological Research Paper no. 51. Tempe.

Ortner, Sherry B.
1984   Theory in Anthropology since the Sixties. *Comparative Studies in Society and History* 26:126–66.

Pandey, Triloki Nath
1994   Patterns of Leadership in Western Pueblo Society. In *North American Indian Anthropology: Essays on Society and Culture,* ed. Raymond J. DeMallie and Alfonso Ortiz, pp. 328–39. Norman: University of Oklahoma Press.

Parsons, Elsie
1920   Notes on Isleta, Santa Ana, and Acoma. *American Anthropologist* 23:149–69.
1923   *Laguna Genealogies.* Anthropological Papers of the American Museum of Natural History, vol. 19. New York.
1939   *Pueblo Indian Religion.* 2 vols. Chicago: University of Chicago Press.
1996   *Pueblo Indian Religion.* Lincoln: University of Nebraska Press. (Originally published Chicago: University of Chicago Press, 1939.)

Pasztory, Esther
1988   A Reinterpretation of Teotihuacan and Its Mural Painting Tradition. In *Feathered Serpents and Flowering Trees: Reconstructing the Murals of Teotihuacan,* ed. Kathleen Berrin, pp. 45–77. San Francisco: Fine Arts Museum of San Francisco.

Pauketat, Timothy R.

1994   *The Ascent of Chiefs: Cahokia and Mississippian Politics in Native North Amer-ica.* Tuscaloosa: University of Alabama Press.

1996   The Foundations of Inequality within a Simulated Shan Community. *Journal of Anthropological Archaeology* 15:219–36.

Pauketat, Timothy R., and Thomas E. Emerson

1991   The Ideology of Authority and the Power of the Pot. *American Anthropologist* 93(4):919–41.

Paynter, Robert

1989   The Archaeology of Equality and Inequality. *Annual Review of Anthropology* 18:369–99.

Pepper, George H.

1920   *Pueblo Bonito.* Anthropological Papers of the American Museum of Natural History, vol. 27. New York.

Peregrine, Peter

1991   Some Political Aspects of Craft Specialization. *World Archaeology* 23(1):1–11.

Pires-Ferreira, Jane W.

1975   *Formative Mesoamerican Exchange Networks with Special Reference to the Valley of Oaxaca.* Memoirs of the Museum of Anthropology no. 7. University of Michigan, Ann Arbor.

Plog, Fred

1989   Studying Complexity. In *The Sociopolitical Structure of Prehistoric Southwestern Societies,* ed. Steadman Upham, Kent G. Lightfoot, and Roberta A. Jewett, pp. 103–25. Boulder, Colo.: Westview Press.

Plog, Fred, Steadman Upham, and Phil C. Weigand

1982   A Perspective on Mogollon-Mesoamerican Interaction. In *Mogollon Archaeology: Proceedings of the 1980 Mogollon Conference,* ed. Patrick Beckett and Kira Silverbird, pp. 227–38. Ramona, Calif.: Acoma Books.

Plog, Stephen

1989   Ritual, Exchange, and the Development of Regional Systems. In *The Architecture of Social Integration in Prehistoric Pueblos,* ed. William D. Lipe and Michelle Hegmon, pp. 143–54. Crow Canyon Archaeological Center Occasional Paper no. 1. Cortez, Colo.

1990   Sociopolitical Implications of Southwestern Stylistic Variation. In *The Use of Style in Archaeology,* ed. Margaret Conkey and Christine Hastorf, pp. 61–72. New York: Cambridge University Press.

1995   Equality and Hierarchy: Holistic Approaches to Understanding Social

Dynamics in the Pueblo Southwest. In *Foundations of Social Inequality,* ed. T. Douglas Price and Gary M. Feinman, pp. 189–206. New York: Plenum Press.

1997   *Ancient Peoples of the American Southwest.* London: Thames and Hudson.

Plog, Stephen, and Julie Solemeto

1996   Alternative Pathways in the Evolution of Western Pueblo Ritual. In *Debating Complexity: Proceedings of the 26th Annual Chacmool Conference,* ed. Daniel A. Meyer, Peter C. Dawson, and Donald T. Hanna, pp. 326–32. Archaeological Association and the Department of Archaeology, University of Calgary, Alberta.

Polanyi, Karl

1944   *The Great Transformation: The Political and Economic Origins of Our Time.* New York: Holt.

Pollock, Susan

1983   Style and Information: An Analysis of Susiana Ceramics. *Journal of Anthropological Archaeology* 2:354–90.

Potter, James M.

1995   The Effects of Sedentism on the Processing of Hunted Carcasses in the Southwest: A Comparison of Two Pueblo IV Sites in Central New Mexico. *Kiva* 60:411–28.

1997a   Communal Ritual and Faunal Remains: An Example from the Dolores Anasazi. *Journal of Field Archaeology* 24:353–64.

1997b   *Communal Ritual, Feasting, and Social Differentiation in Late Prehistoric Zuni Communities.* Ph.D. dissertation, Arizona State University. Ann Arbor, Mich.: University Microfilms International.

1998   The Structure of Open Space in Late Prehistoric Settlements in the Southwest. In *Migration and Reorganization: The Pueblo IV Period in the American Southwest,* ed. Katherine A. Spielmann, pp. 137–63. Arizona State University Anthropological Research Paper no. 51. Tempe.

2000   Ritual, Power, and Social Differentiation in Small-Scale Societies. In *Hierarchies in Action: Cui Bono,* ed. Michael W. Diehl. Center for Archaeological Investigations Occasional Paper, Southern Illinois University at Carbondale.

Powers, Robert P., William B. Gillespie, and Stephen H. Lekson

1983   *The Outlier Survey: A Regional View of Settlement in the San Juan Basin.* Reports of the Chaco Center no. 3. Albuquerque: National Park Service.

Preucel, Robert W.

1996   Cooking Status: Hohokam Ideology, Power, and Social Reproduction. In *Interpreting Southwestern Diversity: Underlying Principles and Overarching Pat-*

terns, ed. Paul R. Fish and J. Jefferson Reid, pp. 125–31. Arizona State University Anthropological Research Paper no. 48. Tempe.

Price, T. Douglas, and Gary M. Feinman, eds.

1995   *Foundations of Social Inequality.* New York: Plenum Press.

Pryor, Frederic L.

1977   *The Origins of the Economy: A Comparative Study of Distribution in Primitive and Peasant Economies.* New York: Academic Press.

Rappaport, Roy

1979a   *Ecology, Meaning, and Religion.* Richmond, Calif.: North Atlantic Books.

1979b   The Obvious Aspects of Ritual. In *Ecology, Meaning, and Religion,* ed. Roy Rappaport, pp. 173–221. Richmond, Calif.: North Atlantic Books.

Rautman, Alison E.

1998   Hierarchy and Heterarchy in the American Southwest: A Comment on McGuire and Saitta. *American Antiquity* 63:325–33.

Ravesloot, John C.

1988   *Mortuary Practices and Social Differentiation at Casas Grandes, Chihuahua, Mexico.* University of Arizona Anthropological Paper no. 49. Tucson: University of Arizona Press.

Reff, Daniel T.

1990   Contact Shock and the Protohistoric Period in the Greater Southwest. In *Perspectives on Southwestern Prehistory,* ed. Paul E. Minnis and Charles L. Redman, pp. 276–88. Boulder, Colo.: Westview Press.

Reid, J. Jefferson

1985   Measuring Social Complexity in the American Southwest. In *Status, Structure and Stratification: Current Archaeological Reconstructions,* ed. M. Thompson, M. T. Garcia, and F. J. Kense, pp. 167–74. Archaeological Association, University of Calgary, Alberta.

1989   A Grasshopper Perspective on the Mogollon of the Arizona Mountains. In *Dynamics of Southwestern Prehistory,* ed. Linda S. Cordell and George J. Gumerman, pp. 65–98. Washington, D.C.: Smithsonian Institution Press.

1998   Return to Migration, Population Movement, and Ethnic Identity in the American Southwest: A Peer Reviewer's Thoughts on Archaeological Inference. In *Vanishing River: Landscapes and Lives of the Lower Verde Valley,* ed. Stephanie M. Whittlesey, Richard S. Ciolek-Torrello, and Jeffrey H. Altschul, pp. 629–38. Tucson: SRI Press.

Reid, J. Jefferson, H. David Tuggle, John R. Welch, Barbara K. Montgomery, and Maria Nieves Zedeño

1996   A Demographic Overview of the Late Pueblo III Period in the Mountains of East-Central Arizona. In *The Prehistoric Pueblo World,* A.D. 1150–1350, ed. Michael A. Adler, pp. 73–85. Tucson: University of Arizona Press.

Reid, J. Jefferson, and Stephanie M. Whittlesey

1982   Households at Grasshopper Pueblo. *American Behavioral Scientist* 25(6): 687–703.

1990   The Complicated and the Complex: Observations on the Archaeological Record of Large Pueblos. In *Perspectives on Southwestern Prehistory,* ed. Paul E. Minnis and Charles L. Redman, pp. 184–95. Boulder, Colo.: Westview Press.

Renfrew, Colin

1974   Beyond a Subsistence Economy: The Evolution of Social Organization in Prehistoric Europe. In *Reconstructing Complex Societies: An Archaeological Colloquium,* ed. Charlotte B. Moore, pp. 69–95. Supplement to the American School of Oriental Research, no. 20. Cambridge.

Reyman, Jonathan

1987   Priests, Power and Politics: Some Implications of Socioceremonial Control. In *Astronomy and Ceremony in the Prehistory Southwest,* ed. J. Carlson and W. James Judge, pp. 121–48. Maxwell Museum of Anthropology Anthropological Paper no. 2. University of New Mexico, Albuquerque.

Rice, Glen E.

1987a   The Marana Community Complex: A Twelfth Century Hohokam Chiefdom. In *Studies in the Hohokam Community of Marana,* ed. Glen E. Rice, pp. 249–54. Anthropological Field Studies 15. Office of Cultural Resource Management, Arizona State University, Tempe.

1987b   *A Spatial Analysis of the Hohokam Community of La Ciudad.* Arizona State University Anthropological Field Studies 16. Tempe.

1990   Variability in the Development of Classic Period Elites. In *A Design for Salado Research,* ed. Glen E. Rice, pp. 31–40. Roosevelt Monograph Series 1, Anthropological Field Studies 22. Office of Cultural Resource Management, Arizona State University, Tempe.

1998   War and Water: An Ecological Perspective on Hohokam Irrigation. *Kiva* 63:263–301.

——, ed.

1987c   *Studies in the Hohokam Community of Marana.* Anthropological Field Studies no. 15. Arizona State University, Tempe.

Riley, Carroll L.

1995   *Rio del Norte: People of the Upper Rio Grande from Earliest Times to the Pueblo Revolt.* Salt Lake City: University of Utah Press.

Rohn, Arthur

1989   Northern San Juan Prehistory. In *Dynamics of Southwestern Prehistory,* ed. Linda S. Cordell and George J. Gumerman, pp. 149–78. Washington, D.C.: Smithsonian Institution Press.

Rollefson, Gary

1983   Ritual and Ceremony at Neolithic Ain Ghazal. *Paleorient* 9:29–38.

Roney, John

1992   Prehistoric Roads and Regional Interaction in the Chacoan System. In *Anasazi Regional Organization and the Chaco System,* ed. David E. Doyel, pp. 123–32. Maxwell Museum of Anthropology Anthropological Paper no. 5. University of New Mexico, Albuquerque.

Root, Matthew J., and D. R. Harro

1992   Stone Artifacts from Casa del Rito and Burnt Mesa Pueblo. In *Bandelier Archaeological Excavation Project: Summer 1990 Excavations at Burnt Mesa Pueblo and Casa del Rito,* ed. Timothy A. Kohler and Matthew J. Root, pp. 107–34. Department of Anthropology Reports of Investigations 64. Washington State University, Pullman.

Roscoe, Paul B.

1993   Practice and Political Centralization. *Current Anthropology* 34:111–40.

Runciman, W. G.

1982   Origins of States: The Case of Archaic Greece. *Comparative Studies in Society and History* 24:351–77.

Russell, Frank

1975   *The Pima Indians.* Tucson: University of Arizona Press. (Originally published as the Annual Report of the Bureau of American Ethnology, 1904–5, Washington, D.C.: Smithsonian Institution Press.)

Sahlins, Marshall D.

1968   *Tribesmen.* New York: Prentice-Hall.
1972   *Stone Age Economics.* Chicago: Aldine-Atherton.

Saitta, Dean J.

1991   Room Use and Community Organization at the Pettit Site, West Central New Mexico. *Kiva* 56:385–409.
1994   Class and Community in the Prehistoric Southwest. In *The Ancient Southwestern Community: Models and Methods for the Study of Prehistoric Social Organization,* ed. W. H. Wills and Robert D. Leonard, pp. 25–44. Albuquerque: University of New Mexico Press.
1997   Power, Labor, and the Dynamics of Change in Chacoan Political Economy. *American Antiquity* 62:7–26.

Sandefur, James T.

1990   *Discrete Dynamical Systems: Theory and Applications.* Oxford: Clarendon Press.

Santley, Robert S., Michael J. Berman, and Rani T. Alexander

1991   The Politicization of the Mesoamerican Ballgame and Its Implications for the Interpretation of the Distribution of Ball Courts in Central Mexico. In *The Mesoamerican Ballgame,* ed. Vernon L. Scarborough and David R. Wilcox, pp. 3–24. Tucson: University of Arizona Press.

Scarborough, Vernon L., and David R. Wilcox, eds.

1991   *The Mesoamerican Ballgame.* Tucson: University of Arizona Press.

Schelberg, John D.

1984   Analogy, Complexity and Regionally-Based Perspectives. In *Recent Research on Chaco Prehistory,* ed. W. James Judge and John D. Schelberg, pp. 5–24. Reports of the Chaco Center no. 8. Albuquerque: National Park Service.

1992   Hierarchical Organization as a Short-Term Buffering Strategy in Chaco Canyon. In *Anasazi Regional Organization and the Chaco System,* ed. David E. Doyel, pp. 59–74. Maxwell Museum of Anthropology Anthropological Paper no. 5. University of New Mexico, Albuquerque.

Schieffelin, Edward

1985   Performance and the Cultural Construction of Reality. *American Ethnologist* 12:707–24.

Schlanger, Sarah H., William Lipe, and William Robinson

1993   An Atlas of Occupation and Abandonment across the Northern Southwest. Paper presented at the 58th Annual Meeting of the Society for American Archaeology, St. Louis.

Schlanger, Sarah H., and Richard H. Wilshusen

1993   Local Abandonments and Regional Conditions in the North American Southwest. In *Abandonments of Settlements and Regions: Ethnoarchaeological and Archaeological Approaches,* ed. Catherine M. Cameron and Steve A. Tomka, pp. 85–98. New York: Cambridge University Press.

Schmidt, Robert H., and Rex E. Gerald

1988   The Distribution of Conservation-type Water Control Systems in the Northern Sierra Madre Occidental. *Kiva* 53:165–80.

Schneider, Peter, Jane Schneider, and Edward Hansen

1972   Modernization and Development: The Role of Regional Elites and Noncorporate Groups in the European Mediterranean. *Comparative Studies in Society and History* 14:328–50.

Schroeder, Albert H.

1979a   Pecos Pueblo. In *Handbook of North American Indians.* Vol. 9: *Southwest,* ed. Alfonso Ortiz, pp. 430–37. Washington, D.C.: Smithsonian Institution Press.

1979b   Pueblos Abandoned in Historic Times. In *Handbook of North American Indians.* Vol. 9: *Southwest,* ed. Alfonso Ortiz, pp. 236–54. Washington, D.C.: Smithsonian Institution Press.

Sebastian, Lynne

1991   Sociopolitical Complexity and the Chaco System. In *Chaco and Hohokam: Prehistoric Regional Systems in the American Southwest,* ed. Patricia L. Crown and W. James Judge, pp. 109–34. Santa Fe, N.M.: School of American Research Press.

1992a   *The Chaco Anasazi: Sociopolitical Evolution in the Prehistoric Southwest.* New York: Cambridge University Press.

1992b   Chaco Canyon and the Anasazi Southwest: Changing Views of Sociopolitical Organization. In *Anasazi Regional Organization and the Chaco System,* ed. David E. Doyel, pp. 23–34. Maxwell Museum of Anthropology Anthropological Paper no. 5. University of New Mexico, Albuquerque.

Sempowski, Martha L., and Michael W. Spence

1994   *Mortuary Practices and Skeletal Remains at Teotihuacan.* Salt Lake City: University of Utah Press.

Senior, Louise

1995   The Estimation of Prehistoric Values: Cracked Pot Ideas in Archaeology. In *Expanding Archaeology,* ed. James M. Skibo, William H. Walker, and Axel E. Nielson, pp. 92–110. Salt Lake City: University of Utah Press.

Service, Elman R.

1962   *Primitive Social Organization.* New York: Random House.

1971   *Primitive Social Organization: An Evolutionary Perspective.* 2nd ed. New York: Random House.

Shelby, Charmion, trans.

1993   La Florida by the Inca. In *The De Soto Chronicles: The Expedition of Hernando de Soto to North America in 1539–1543,* ed. Lawrence A. Clayton, Vernon Knight, and Edward Moore, pp. 25–559. Tuscaloosa: University of Alabama Press.

Shepard, Anna O.

1936   The Technology of Pecos Pottery. In *The Pottery of Pecos,* by Alfred V. Kidder, pp. 389–587. Papers of the Southwest Expedition 7. Phillips Academy, Yale University, New Haven, Conn.

1942   Rio Grande Glaze Paint Ware. *Contributions to American Anthropology and History* 39. Carnegie Institution, Washington, D.C.

Simmons, Alan H., Ann Bulin, Carol Butler, Zeidan Kafai, and Gary Rollefson
1990   A Plastered Human Skull from Neolithic Ain Ghazal, Jordan. *Journal of Field Archaeology* 17:107–10.

Sires, Earl W.
1985   Hohokam Architecture and Site Structure. In *Hohokam Archaeology along the Salt-Gila Aqueduct, Central Arizona Project.* Vol. 9: *Synthesis,* ed. Lynn S. Teague and Patricia L. Crown, pp. 115–39. Arizona State Museum Archaeological Series 150. University of Arizona, Tucson.
1987   Hohokam Architectural Variability and Site Structure during the Sedentary-Classic Transition. In *The Hohokam Village: Site Structure and Organization,* ed. David E. Doyel, pp. 171–82. Glenwood Springs, Colo.: American Association for the Advancement of Science.

Smith, Carol A.
1976   Regional Economic Systems: Linking Geographic Models and Socio-economic Problems. In *Regional Analysis,* vol. 1, ed. Carol A. Smith, pp. 3–63. New York: Academic Press.

Smith, Watson, Richard B. Woodbury, and Nathalie F. S. Woodbury
1966   *The Excavation of Hawikuh by Frederick Webb Hodge: Report of the Hendricks-Hodge Expedition.* Contributions from the Museum of the American Indian, Heye Foundation, vol. 20. New York: Museum of the American Indian.

Snow, David H.
1981   Protohistoric Rio Grande Pueblo Economics: A Review of the Trends. In *The Protohistoric Period in the North American Southwest,* A.D. 1450–1700, ed. David R. Wilcox and W. Bruce Masse, pp. 354–77. Arizona State University Anthropological Research Paper no. 24. Tempe.

Sober, Elliott, and David Sloan Wilson
1998   *Unto Others: The Evolution and Psychology of Unselfish Behavior.* Cambridge, Mass.: Harvard University Press.

Sofaer, Anna
1997   The Primary Architecture of the Chacoan Culture: A Cosmological Expression. In *Anasazi Architecture and American Design,* ed. Baker H. Morrow and V. B. Price, pp. 88–132. Albuquerque: University of New Mexico Press.

Soltis, Joseph, Robert Boyd, and Peter J. Richerson
1995   Can Group-Functional Behaviors Evolve by Cultural Group Selection? An Empirical Test. *Current Anthropology* 36:473–94.

Spencer, Charles S.
1993   Human Agency, Biased Transmission, and the Cultural Evolution of Chiefly Authority. *Journal of Anthropological Archaeology* 12:41–74.

Speth, John, and Susan Scott

1989   Horticulture and Large Mammal Hunting: The Role of Resource Deple-
        tion and the Constraints of Time and Labor. In *Farmers as Hunters: Implica-
        tions of Sedentism,* ed. Susan Kent, pp. 71–79. New York: Cambridge
        University Press.

Spielmann, Katherine A.

1988   Changing Faunal Procurement Strategies at Gran Quivira Pueblo, New
        Mexico. Paper presented at the symposium "Rio Grande Chronology
        and Adaptations," 53rd Annual Meeting of the Society for American
        Archaeology, Phoenix.

1991a   Interaction among Nonhierarchical Societies. In *Farmers, Hunters, and
        Colonists: Interactions between the Southwest and the Southern Plains,* ed. Kath-
        erine A. Spielmann, pp. 1–17. Tucson: University of Arizona Press.

1991b   *Subsistence and Exchange at Gran Quivira Pueblo, New Mexico,* pt. 1. Report
        submitted to the National Park Service, Southwestern Regional Office,
        Santa Fe, N.M.

1992   *Subsistence and Exchange at Gran Quivira Pueblo, New Mexico,* pt. 2. Report
        submitted to the National Park Service, Southwestern Regional Office,
        Santa Fe, N.M.

1994   Clustered Confederacies: Sociopolitical Organization in the Protohistoric
        Rio Grande. In *The Ancient Southwestern Community: Models and Methods
        for the Study of Prehistoric Social Organization,* ed. W. H. Wills and Rob-
        ert D. Leonard, pp. 45–54. Albuquerque: University of New Mexico
        Press.

1996   Impressions of Pueblo III Settlement Trends among the Rio Abajo and
        Eastern Border Pueblos. In *The Prehistoric Pueblo World,* A.D. 1150–1350,
        ed. Michael A. Adler, pp. 177–87. Tucson: University of Arizona Press.

1998a   Aggregation in the Salinas Province: Excavations at Pueblo Colorado,
        New Mexico. Report submitted to the USDA Forest Service, Cibola Of-
        fice, Albuquerque.

1998b   Ritual Influences on the Development of Rio Grande Glaze A Ceramics.
        In *Migration and Reorganization: The Pueblo IV Period in the American South-
        west,* ed. Katherine A. Spielmann, pp. 253–61. Arizona State University
        Anthropological Research Paper no. 51. Tempe.

Spielmann, Katherine A., and David C. Eshbaugh

1988   Summary Report: Salinas Archaeological Survey May–June 1988. Report
        for the USDA Forest Service, Cibola Office, Albuquerque. Manuscript on
        file, Department of Anthropology, Arizona State University, Tempe.

Spores, Ronald

1967   *The Mixtec Kings and Their People.* Norman: University of Oklahoma Press.

Stark, Miriam T.

1993   *Pottery Economics: A Kalinga Ethnoarchaeological Study.* Ph.D. dissertation, University of Arizona, Tucson. Ann Arbor, Mich.: University Microfilms International.

1995   Commodities and Interaction in the Prehistoric Tonto Basin. In *The Roosevelt Community Development Study: New Perspectives on Tonto Basin Prehistory,* ed. Mark D. Elson, Miriam T. Stark, and David A. Gregory, pp. 307–42. Anthropological Paper no. 15. Tucson: Center for Desert Archaeology.

——, ed.

1998   *The Archaeology of Social Boundaries.* Washington, D.C.: Smithsonian Institution Press.

Stein, John R., and Stephen H. Lekson

1992   Anasazi Ritual Landscapes. In *Anasazi Regional Organization and the Chaco System,* ed. David E. Doyel, pp. 87–100. Maxwell Museum of Anthropology Anthropological Paper no. 5. University of New Mexico, Albuquerque.

Stein, John R., Judith E. Suiter, and Dabney Ford

1997   High Noon in Old Bonito: Sun, Shadow, and the Geometry of the Chaco Complex. In *Anasazi Architecture and American Design,* ed. Baker H. Morrow and V. B. Price, pp. 133–48. Albuquerque: University of New Mexico Press.

Steiner, Christopher B.

1990   Body Personal and Body Politic: Adornment and Leadership in Cross-Cultural Perspective. *Anthropos* 85:431–45.

Stevenson, Matilda C.

1894   *The Sia.* 11th Annual Report of the Bureau of American Ethnology, 1899–90. Washington, D.C.: Smithsonian Institution Press.

1904   *The Zuni Indians: Their Mythology, Esoteric Fraternities, and Ceremonies.* 23rd Annual Report of the Bureau of American Ethnology, 1901–2. Washington, D.C.: Smithsonian Institution Press.

Steward, Julian

1937   Ecological Aspects of Southwestern Society. *Anthropos* 32:87–104.

Stinson, Susan L.

1996   Roosevelt Red Ware and the Organization of Ceramic Production in the Silver Creek Drainage. M.A. thesis, Department of Anthropology, University of Arizona.

Stodder, Ann Lucy

1990   Paleoepidemiology of Eastern and Western Pueblo Communities in
        Protohistoric New Mexico. Ph.D. dissertation, Department of Anthro-
        pology, University of Colorado, Boulder.

Strathern, Andrew

1969   Finance and Production: Two Strategies in New Guinea Highlands Ex-
        change Systems. *Oceania* 40:42–67.

———, ed.

1982   *Inequality in the New Guinea Highlands.* New York: Cambridge University
        Press.

Strathern, Marilyn

1988   *The Gender of Gift: Problems with Women and Problems with Society in Mela-
        nesia.* Berkeley: University of California Press.

Stuart, David E.

1997   Power and Efficiency in Eastern Anasazi Architecture: A Case of Multiple
        Evolutionary Trajectories. In *Anasazi Architecture and American Design,* ed.
        Baker H. Morrow and V. B. Price, pp. 36–52. Albuquerque: University of
        New Mexico Press.

Stuart, David E., and Rory P. Gauthier

1981   *Prehistoric New Mexico: Background for Survey.* Santa Fe, N.M.: Historic
        Preservation Bureau.

Swanton, John R.

1946   *The Indians of the Southeastern United States.* Bureau of American Ethnol-
        ogy Bulletin 137. Washington, D.C.: Smithsonian Institution Press.

Tainter, Joseph A., and David "A" Gillio

1980   *Cultural Resources Overview, Mt. Taylor Area, New Mexico.* USDA Forest Ser-
        vice and Bureau of Land Management, Albuquerque and Santa Fe, N.M.

Teague, Lynn S.

1984   The Organization of Hohokam Economy. In *Part 2 of Hohokam Archaeol-
        ogy along the Salt-Gila Aqueduct, Central Arizona Project: Synthesis and Con-
        clusions,* vol. 9, ed. Lynn S. Teague and Patricia L. Crown, pp. 187–250.
        Arizona State Museum Archaeological Series 150. University of Arizona,
        Tucson.

1985   The Organization of Hohokam Exchange. In *Proceedings of the 1983 Hoho-
        kam Symposium,* pt. 2, ed. Alfred E. Dittert Jr. and Donald E. Dove,
        pp. 397–418. Arizona Archaeological Society Occasional Paper no. 2.
        Phoenix.

1989a   Local and Regional Organization and Interaction. In *Hohokam Archaeology along Phase B of the Tucson Aqueduct Central Arizona Project: Synthesis and Interpretations,* vol. 1, ed. Jon S. Czaplicki and John C. Ravesloot, pp. 277–340. Arizona State Museum Archaeological Series 178. University of Arizona, Tucson.

1989b   Production and Distribution at Las Colinas. In *The 1982–1984 Excavations at Las Colinas: Synthesis and Conclusions,* vol. 6, by Lynn S. Teague, pp. 89–131. Arizona State Museum Archaeological Series 162. University of Arizona, Tucson.

Tedlock, Dennis

1979   Zuni Religion and World View. In *Handbook of North American Indians.* Vol. 9: *Southwest,* ed. Alfonso Ortiz, pp. 499–508. Washington, D.C.: Smithsonian Institution Press.

Titiev, Mischa

1944   *Old Oraibi.* Papers of the Peabody Museum of American Archaeology and Ethnology, vol. 22, no. 1. Harvard University, Cambridge, Mass.

Toll, H. Wolcott

1984   Material Aspects of Pueblo Ritual with Regard to Goods Distribution in Chaco. Paper presented at the 49th Annual Meeting of the Society for American Archaeology, Portland.

1985   Pottery, Production, Public Architecture and the Chaco Anasazi System. Ph.D. dissertation, Department of Anthropology, University of Colorado, Boulder.

Toll, H. Wolcott, and Peter J. McKenna

1987   The Ceramography of Pueblo Alto. In *Investigations at the Pueblo Alto Complex, Chaco Canyon,* ed. Frances Joan Mathien and Thomas C. Windes. Vol. 3, pt. 1: *Artifactual and Biological Analyses,* pp. 19–230. Publications in Archeology 18F. Santa Fe, N.M.: National Park Service.

1997   Chaco Ceramics. In *Ceramics, Lithics, and Ornaments of Chaco Canyon,* ed. Frances Joan Mathien. Vol. 1: *Ceramics.* Publications in Archeology 18G. Santa Fe, N.M.: National Park Service.

Triadan, Daniela

1989   Defining Local Ceramic Production at Grasshopper Pueblo, Arizona. M.A. thesis, Lateinamerikainstitut, Freie Universität Berlin, Germany.

1997   *Ceramic Commodities and Common Containers: Production and Distribution of White Mountain Red Ware in the Grasshopper Region, Arizona.* University of Arizona Anthropological Paper no. 61. Tucson: University of Arizona Press.

Triadan, Daniela, Barbara J. Mills, and Andrew Duff

1997   From Analytical to Anthropological: 14th Century Red Ware Circula-
        tion and Its Implications for Pueblo Reorganization. Paper presented at
        the symposium "Chemical Sourcing of Ceramics in the Greater South-
        west," 62nd Annual Meeting of the Society for American Archaeology,
        Nashville.

Trigger, Bruce G.

1990   Monumental Architecture: A Thermodynamic Explanation of Symbolic
        Behavior. *World Archaeology* 22:119–32.

Turner, James

1992   Ritual, Habitus, and Hierarchy in Fiji. *Ethnology* 31(4):291–302.

Turner, Victor

1969   *The Ritual Process: Structure and Anti-Structure.* Ithaca, N.Y.: Cornell Uni-
        versity Press.

1974   *Dramas, Fields and Metaphors: Symbolic Action in Human Society.* Ithaca,
        N.Y.: Cornell University Press.

1977   Variations on a Theme of Liminality. In *Secular Ritual,* ed. Sally F. Moore
        and Barbara G. Myerhoff, pp. 36–52. Amsterdam: Van Gorcum.

Underhill, Ruth M.

1939   *Social Organization of the Papago Indians.* Columbia University Contribu-
        tions to Anthropology 30. New York.

Upham, Steadman

1982   *Polities and Power: An Economic and Political History of the Western Pueblo.*
        New York: Academic Press.

1987   The Tyranny of Ethnographic Analogy in Southwestern Archaeology. In
        Coasts, Plains and Deserts: Papers in Honor of Reynold J. Ruppé, ed. Sylvia W.
        Gaines, pp. 265–81. Arizona State University Anthropological Research
        Paper no. 38. Tempe.

1989   East Meets West: Hierarchy and Elites in Pueblo Society. In *The Socio-
        political Structure of Prehistoric Southwestern Societies,* ed. Steadman Upham,
        Kent G. Lightfoot, and Roberta A. Jewett, pp. 77–102. Boulder, Colo.:
        Westview Press.

1990   Decoupling the Process of Political Evolution. In *The Evolution of Political
        Systems, Sociopolitics in Small-Scale Sedentary Societies,* ed. Steadman Up-
        ham, pp. 1–17. New York: Cambridge University Press.

Upham, Steadman, Kent G. Lightfoot, and Gary M. Feinman

1981   Explaining Socially Determined Ceramic Distributions in the Prehistoric
        Plateau Southwest. *American Antiquity* 46:822–33.

Upham, Steadman, and Lori Stephens Reed

1989   Regional Systems in the Central and Northern Southwest: Demography, Economy, and Sociopolitics Preceding Contact. In *Columbian Consequences,* vol. 1, ed. David H. Thomas, pp. 57–76. Washington, D.C.: Smithsonian Institution Press.

Van Keuren, Scott

1998a   Breaking the Rules: White Mountain Red Ware Production at Grasshopper Pueblo. Paper presented at the 10th Mogollon Archaeology Conference, Silver City, N.M. Manuscript on file, Department of Anthropology, University of Arizona, Tucson.

1998b   14th-Century Ceramic Design Change and Community Reorganization in East-Central Arizona. Dissertation Improvement Grant funded by the National Science Foundation. Manuscript on file, Department of Anthropology, University of Arizona, Tucson.

1999   *Ceramic Design Structure and the Organization of Cibola White Ware Production in the Grasshopper Region, Arizona.* Arizona State Museum Archaeological Series 191. University of Arizona, Tucson.

Van Keuren, Scott, and J. Jefferson Reid

1996   Homage to Hieronymus Bosch: Linking Ceramic Design to Style. Paper presented at the 61st Annual Meeting of the Society for American Archaeology, New Orleans.

Varien, Mark

1997   New Perspectives on Settlement Patterns: Sedentism and Mobility in a Social Landscape. Ph.D. dissertation, Department of Anthropology, Arizona State University, Tempe.

Varien, Mark D., and Barbara J. Mills

1997   Accumulations Research: Problems and Prospects for Estimating Site Occupation Span. *Journal of Archaeological Method and Theory* 4:141–91.

Vivian, Gordon, and Tom W. Matthews

1964   *Kin Kletso: A Pueblo III Community in Chaco Canyon, New Mexico.* Southwest Parks and Monuments Association Technical Series, vol. 6, pt. 1. Globe, Ariz.

Vivian, R. Gwinn

1970   An Inquiry into Prehistoric Social Organization in Chaco Canyon, New Mexico. In *Reconstructing Prehistoric Pueblo Societies,* ed. William A. Longacre, pp. 59–83. Albuquerque: University of New Mexico Press.

1974   Conservation and Diversion: Water-Control Systems in the Anasazi Southwest. In *Irrigation's Impact on Society,* ed. T. Downing and M. Gibson, pp. 95–83. University of Arizona Anthropological Paper no. 25. Tucson: University of Arizona Press.

1989   Kluckhohn Reappraised: The Chacoan System as an Egalitarian Enterprise. *Journal of Anthropological Research* 45:101–13.

1990   *The Chacoan Prehistory of the San Juan Basin.* New York: Academic Press.

1991   Chacoan Subsistence. In *Chaco and Hohokam: Prehistoric Regional Systems in the American Southwest,* ed. Patricia L. Crown and W. James Judge, pp. 57–76. Santa Fe, N.M.: School of American Research Press.

1992   Chacoan Water Use and Managerial Decision Making. In *Anasazi Regional Organization and the Chaco System,* ed. David E. Doyel, pp. 45–58. Maxwell Museum of Anthropology Anthropological Paper no. 5. University of New Mexico, Albuquerque.

1997   Chacoan Roads: Function. *Kiva* 63:35–68.

Vivian, R. Gwinn, Dulce N. Dodgen, and Gayle H. Hartmann

1978   *Wooden Ritual Artifacts from Chaco Canyon, New Mexico: The Chetro Ketl Collection.* University of Arizona Anthropological Paper no. 32. Tucson: University of Arizona Press.

Wallace, Henry D.

1995   *Archaeological Investigations at Los Morteros, a Prehistoric Settlement in the Northern Tucson Basin.* Anthropological Paper no. 17. Tucson: Center for Desert Archaeology.

Ware, John A., and Eric Blinman

1996   Cultural Collapse and Reorganization: The Origin and Spread of Ritual Sodalities. Paper presented at the 5th Southwest Symposium, Tempe.

Warren, A. Helene

1969   Tonque: One Pueblo's Glaze Pottery Industry Dominated Middle Rio Grande Commerce. *El Palacio* 76:36–42.

1970   Notes on the Manufacture and Trade of Rio Grande Glazes. *Artifact* 8(4):1–7.

1979   The Glaze Paint Wares of the Upper Middle Rio Grande. In *Archaeological Investigations in Cochiti Reservoir, New Mexico.* Vol. 4: *Adaptive Change in the Northern Rio Grande Valley,* ed. Jan V. Biella and Richard C. Chapman, pp. 187–216. Office of Contract Archeology, Department of Anthropology, University of New Mexico, Albuquerque.

1981a   Appendix I: Description of Pottery Tempering Materials of Gran Quivira. In *Excavations at Mound 7,* by Alden C. Hayes, pp. 179–82. National Park Service Publications in Archaeology 16, Washington, D.C.

1981b   A Petrographic Study of the Pottery of Gran Quivira. In *Contributions to*

Gran Quivira Archaeology, by Alden C. Hayes, pp. 67–73, 182–83. National Park Service Publications in Archaeology 17, Washington, D.C.

Wason, Paul K.
1994   *The Archaeology of Rank.* New York: Cambridge University Press.

Watson, Patty Jo, Steven LeBlanc, and Charles Redman
1980   Aspects of Zuni Prehistory: Preliminary Report on Excavations and Survey in the El Morro Valley of New Mexico. *Journal of Field Archaeology* 7:201–18.

Watts, D. J., and S. H. Strogatz
1998   Collective Dynamics of "Small World" Networks. *Nature* 393:442.

Watts, Linda K.
1997   Zuni Family Ties and Household-Group Values: A Revisionist Cultural Model of Zuni Social Organization. *Journal of Anthropological Research* 53:17–29.

Weber, Max
1978   *Economy and Society: An Outline of Interpretive Sociology,* vols. 1 and 2, ed. G. Roth and C. Wittich. Berkeley: University of California Press. (Originally published in 1922.)

Webster, Laurie D.
1997   Effects of European Contact on Textile Production and Exchange in the North American Southwest. Ph.D. dissertation, Department of Anthropology, University of Arizona, Tucson.

Weiner, Annette B.
1994   *Inalienable Possessions: The Paradox of Keeping While Giving.* Berkeley: University of California Press.

Welbourn, Alice
1984   Endo Ceramics and Power Strategies. In *Ideology, Power, and Prehistory,* ed. Daniel Miller and Christopher Y. Tilley, pp. 17–25. New York: Cambridge University Press.

Whalen, Michael E., and Paul E. Minnis
1996a   Ballcourts and Political Complexity in the Casas Grandes Region. *American Antiquity* 61:732–46.
1996b   The Context of Production in and around Paquimé, Chihuahua, Mexico. In *Interpreting Southwestern Diversity: Underlying Principles and Overarching Patterns,* ed. Paul R. Fish and J. Jefferson Reid, pp. 173–84. Arizona State University Anthropological Research Paper no. 48. Tempe.
1996c   Studying Complexity in Northern Mexico: The Paquimé Regional Sys-

tem. In *Debating Complexity: Proceedings of the 26th Annual Chacmool Conference,* ed. Daniel A. Meyer, Peter C. Dawson, and Donald T. Hanna, pp. 282–89. Archaeological Association and the Department of Archaeology, University of Calgary, Alberta.

1997   Investigaciones especializadas sobre el sistema regional de Paquimé, Chihuahua, México. Report submitted to the National Institute of Anthropology and History of Mexico. Manuscript on file at the Universities of Tulsa and Oklahoma.

White, Leslie

1974   *Zia—The Sun Symbol Pueblo.* Albuquerque: University of New Mexico Press. (Originally published as *The Pueblo of Sia, New Mexico,* Bureau of American Ethnology Bulletin 184, Washington, D.C.: Smithsonian Institution, 1962.)

Whitecotton, Joseph

1977   *The Zapotecs: Princes, Priests, and Peasants.* Norman: University of Oklahoma Press.

Whiteley, Peter M.

1985   Unpacking Hopi "Clans": Another Vintage Model out of Africa? *Journal of Anthropological Research* 41:359–76.

1988   *Deliberate Acts: Changing Hopi Culture through the Oraibi Split.* Tucson: University of Arizona Press.

Whittle, Alasdair

1985   *Neolithic Europe: A Survey.* New York: Cambridge University Press.

Whittlesey, Stephanie M., and Richard Ciolek-Torrello

1992   A Revolt against Rampant Elites: Toward an Alternative Paradigm. In *Proceedings of the Second Salado Conference, Globe, Arizona, 1992,* ed. Richard C. Lange and Stephen Germick, pp. 312–24. Arizona Archaeological Society Occasional Paper. Phoenix.

Wiessner, Polly, and Wulf Schiefenhövel, eds.

1996   *Food and the Status Quest: An Interdisciplinary Perspective.* Providence, R.I.: Berghahn Books.

Wilcox, David R.

1981   Changing Perspectives on the Protohistoric Pueblos, A.D. 1450–1700. In *The Protohistoric Period in the North American Southwest, A.D. 1450–1700,* ed. David R. Wilcox and W. Bruce Masse, pp. 378–409. Arizona State University Anthropological Research Paper no. 24. Tempe.

1987a   *Frank Midvale's Investigation of the Site of La Ciudad.* Anthropological Field

Studies 19. Office of Cultural Resource Management, Arizona State University, Tempe.

1987b New Models of Social Structure at the Palo Parado Site. In *The Hohokam Village: Site Structure and Organization,* ed. David E. Doyel, pp. 211–22. Glenwood Springs, Colo.: American Association for the Advancement of Science.

1991 Changing Context of Pueblo Adaptations, A.D. 1250–1600. In *Farmers, Hunters, and Colonists: Interactions between the Southwest and the Southern Plains,* ed. Katherine A. Spielmann, pp. 128–54. Tucson: University of Arizona Press.

1993 The Evolution of the Chacoan Polity. In *The Chimney Rock Archaeological Symposium,* ed. James Malville and Gary Matlock, pp. 76–90. USDA Forest Service General Technical Report RM-227. Fort Collins, Colo.: Rocky Mountain Forest and Range Experiment Station.

1995 A Processual Model of Charles C. Di Peso's Babocomari Site and Related Systems. In *The Gran Chichimeca: Essays on the Archaeology and Ethnohistory of Northern Mesoamerica,* ed. Jonathan E. Reyman, pp. 281–319. London: Avebury.

Wilcox, David R., and Jonathan Haas
1994 The Scream of the Butterfly: Competition and Conflict in the Prehistoric Southwest. In *Themes in Southwest Prehistory,* ed. George J. Gumerman, pp. 211–38. Santa Fe, N.M.: School of American Research Press.

Wilcox, David R., Thomas R. McGuire, and Charles Sternberg
1981 *Snaketown Revisited.* Arizona State Museum Archaeological Series 155. University of Arizona, Tucson.

Wilcox, David R., and Charles Sternberg
1983 *Hohokam Ballcourts and Their Interpretation.* Arizona State Museum Archaeological Series 160. University of Arizona, Tucson.

Wilk, Richard
1998 Comment on *The Distributional Approach: A New Way to Identify Marketplace Exchange in the Archaeological Record,* by Kenneth G. Hirth. *Current Anthropology* 39:469.

Wills, Wirt H., Patricia L. Crown, Jeffrey S. Dean, and Christopher G. Langdon
1994 Complex Adaptive Systems and Southwestern Prehistory. In *Understanding Complexity in the Prehistoric Southwest,* ed. George J. Gumerman and Murray Gell-Mann, pp. 297–339. SFI Studies in the Sciences of Complexity Proceedings 16. Reading, Mass.: Addison-Wesley.

Wilshusen, Richard H.
1989 Unstuffing the Estufa: Ritual Floor Features in Anasazi Pit Structures and

Pueblo Kivas. In *The Architecture of Social Integration in Prehistoric Pueblos,* ed. William D. Lipe and Michelle Hegmon, pp. 89–112. Crow Canyon Archaeological Center Occasional Paper no. 1. Cortez, Colo.

Wilshusen, Richard H., and Sarah H. Schlanger
1993   Late Pueblo I Population Movement in the Northern Southwest: The Big Picture. Paper presented at the 5th Anasazi Symposium, San Juan College, Farmington, N.M.

Windes, Thomas C.
1984   A New Look at Population in Chaco Canyon. In *Recent Research on Chaco Prehistory,* ed. W. James Judge and John D. Schelberg, pp. 75–88. Reports of the Chaco Center no. 8. Albuquerque: National Park Service.
1987   Architecture and Stratigraphy. In *Investigations at the Pueblo Alto Complex, Chaco Canyon, New Mexico, 1975–1979,* vol. 11, pt. 2. Publications in Archeology 18F. Santa Fe, N.M.: National Park Service.
1992   Blue Notes: The Chacoan Turquoise Industry in the San Juan Basin. In *Anasazi Regional Organization and the Chaco System,* ed. David E. Doyel, pp. 159–68. Maxwell Museum of Anthropology Anthropological Paper no. 5. University of New Mexico, Albuquerque.

Windes, Thomas C., and Dabney Ford
1996   The Chaco Wood Project: The Chronometric Reappraisal of Pueblo Bonito. *American Antiquity* 61:295–310.

Winter, Joseph C.
1983   A Comparative Study of Prehistoric, Historic and Contemporary Agriculture along the Lower Chaco: I—The Anasazi. In *Economy and Interaction along the Lower Chaco River,* ed. Patrick Hogan and Joseph C. Winter, pp. 421–43. Office of Contract Archeology, Department of Anthropology, University of New Mexico, Albuquerque.
1988   The Casamero-Pierre's Outlier Community Survey and the Chacoan System. In *The Casamero and Pierre's Outliers Survey: An Archaeological Class III Inventory of the BLM Lands Surrounding the Outliers,* by Randy A. Harper, Marilyn K. Swift, Barbara Mills, and Joseph C. Winter, pp. 115–30. Office of Contract Archeology, Department of Anthropology, University of New Mexico, Albuquerque.
1994   Conclusions and Synthesis. In *Across the Colorado Plateau: Anthropological Studies for the Transwestern Pipeline Expansion Project,* vol. 20. Office of Contract Archeology, Department of Anthropology, University of New Mexico, Albuquerque.

Wobst, H. Martin
1977   Stylistic Behavior and Information Exchange. In *For the Director: Research*

Essays in Honor of James B. Griffen, ed. Charles E. Cleland, pp. 317–42. Museum of Anthropology Anthropological Paper no. 61. University of Michigan, Ann Arbor.

Wolf, Eric R.

1982   *Europe and the People without History.* Berkeley: University of California Press.

Wonderley, Anthony

1986   Material Symbolics in Pre-Columbian Households: The Painted Pottery of Naco, Honduras. *Journal of Anthropological Research* 42:497–534.

Wood, J. Scott

1989   *Vale of Tiers, Too: Late Classic Period Salado Settlement Patterns and Organizational Models for Tonto Basin.* Cultural Resources Inventory Report 89-12-280. Tonto National Forest, Phoenix.

1995   Vale of Tiers Palimpsest: Salado Settlement and Internal Relationships in the Tonto Basin Area. Paper prepared for the advanced seminar "Prehistoric Salado Culture of the American Southwest," Amerind Foundation, Dragoon, Ariz.

Woodbury, Richard B., and Nathalie F. S. Woodbury

1966   Decorated Pottery of the Zuni Area. In *The Excavation of Hawikuh by Frederick Webb Hodge: Report of the Hendricks-Hodge Expedition,* by Watson Smith, Richard B. Woodbury, and Nathalie F. S. Woodbury, pp. 302–36. Contributions from the Museum of the American Indian, Heye Foundation, vol. 20. New York: Museum of the American Indian.

Wuensche, Andrew

1994   The Ghost in the Machine: Basins of Attraction of Random Boolean Networks. In *Artificial Life III: Proceedings of the Workshop on Artificial Life Held June, 1992, in Santa Fe, New Mexico,* ed. C. G. Langton, pp. 465–501. SFI Studies in the Sciences of Complexity Proceedings 17. Reading, Mass.: Addison-Wesley.

1998   Discrete Dynamical Networks and Their Attractor Basins. Paper presented at Complex Systems '98, University of New South Wales, Sydney, Australia. (http://www.santafe.edu/w̃uensch/complex98—ab.html)

Yoffee, Norman

1993   Too Many Chiefs? Or, Safe Texts for the 90s. In *Archaeological Theory: Who Sets the Agenda?* ed. Norman Yoffee and Andrew Sherratt, pp. 60–78. New York: Cambridge University Press.

1994   Memorandum to Murray Gell-Mann Concerning: The Complications of Complexity in the Prehistoric Southwest. In *Understanding Complexity in the Prehistoric Southwest,* ed. George J. Gumerman and Murray Gell-

Mann, pp. 341–58. SFI Studies in the Sciences of Complexity Proceedings 16. Reading, Mass.: Addison-Wesley.

Yoffee, Norman, and George Cowgill
1987   *The Collapse of Ancient States and Civilizations.* Tucson: University of Arizona Press.

Yoffee, Norman, Suzanne K. Fish, and Gerald R. Milner
1999   Comunidades, Ritualities, Chiefdoms: Social Evolution in the American Southwest. In *Great Towns and Regional Polities in the Southwest and Southeast,* ed. Jill E. Neitzel, pp. 261–71. Albuquerque: University of New Mexico Press.

Zedeño, Maria Nieves
1994   *Sourcing Prehistoric Ceramics at Chodistaas Pueblo, Arizona: The Circulation of People and Pots in the Grasshopper Region.* University of Arizona Anthropological Paper no. 58. Tucson: University of Arizona Press.
1995   The Role of Population Movement and Technology Transfer in the Manufacture of Prehistoric Southwestern Ceramics. In *Ceramic Production in the American Southwest,* ed. Barbara J. Mills and Patricia L. Crown, pp. 115–41. Tucson: University of Arizona Press.

About the Contributors

DAVID R. ABBOTT has designed and is conducting a long-term research program focused on the ancient pottery of central and southern Arizona. His work is dedicated to modeling the exchange and social networks that composed the Hohokam regional system, investigating the impact of large-scale irrigation on sociocultural evolution, and developing the unique contribution that ceramic research can make to the study of prehistoric communities. He enthusiastically devotes 100 percent of his workday to research as a CRM consultant and a research associate at the Arizona State Museum. He earned his Ph.D. in anthropology at Arizona State University in 1994.

JAMES M. BAYMAN received his Ph.D. at Arizona State University in 1994 and is currently an assistant professor of anthropology at the University of Hawai'i. He held a Smithsonian Institution Post-Doctoral Fellowship in 1994–95, and his archaeological research has been funded by the National Science Foundation, the Wenner-Gren Foundation, and Sigma Xi. He has conducted archaeological fieldwork in North America, Southeast Asia, and the Hawaiian Islands. His current research interests include political economy and craft production in the North American Southwest and the Hawaiian Islands and traditional water management in the Sonoran Desert.

MARK D. ELSON is a senior research archaeologist with Desert Archaeology, Inc., in Tucson. He received his Ph.D. from the University of Arizona in 1996. His research interests include social organization and kinship systems, monumental architecture, economic systems, and the formation of social boundaries. Recent publications include *Expanding the View of Hohokam Platform Mounds: An Ethnographic Perspective* (Anthropological Papers No. 63, University of Arizona Press, 1998).

GARY M. FEINMAN is the chair of anthropology at the Field Museum. He has degrees from the University of Michigan and the City University of New York, Graduate School, and has taught at Arizona State University,

Bloomsburg State University, and the University of Wisconsin–Madison. Feinman has directed regional surveys, intensive site surveys, and excavation projects in Oaxaca, Mexico, as well as regional surveys in eastern Shandong, China. He also has participated in field studies in the American Southwest. Feinman has authored or edited twelve books and more than eighty-five journal articles or book chapters.

PAUL R. FISH received his Ph.D. in anthropology from Arizona State University. He is currently curator of archaeology and head of the Archaeology Division at the Arizona State Museum and professor of anthropology at the University of Arizona. Fish has conducted research on a variety of archaeological cultures in the Southwestern United States and northwestern Mexico. His current research focuses on the political and social organization of the Hohokam in southern Arizona. He publishes widely on archaeological methodology as well as research in the Southwest, northern Mexico, and Brazil.

SUZANNE K. FISH combines archaeological investigations in the Southwest and northwestern Mexico with studies of the region's ethnobotany and traditional agriculture. She received her Ph.D. from the Arid Lands Interdisciplinary Program at the University of Arizona, where she is now a museum curator and associate professor of anthropology. She codirects a long-term Arizona State Museum research program on the Hohokam of southern Arizona. Her current research includes the Trincheras Culture of Sonora, Mexico, and shell mound builders of coastal southern Brazil. Publications include books, monographs, and articles on Hohokam settlement and social organization, prehistoric and traditional Southwestern farming, and archaeological survey methodology.

WILLIAM M. GRAVES is a Ph.D. student at Arizona State University. His research interests include the development of social inequality and status differentiation in middle-range societies and the social and political organization of late prehistoric and protohistoric Pueblo communities in the Southwestern United States. His current research is an examination of intercommunity sociopolitical relationships among the late prehistoric Jumanos pueblos in the Salinas district of the Rio Grande region.

KAREN G. HARRY is the director of cultural resources for the Texas Parks and Wildlife Department in Austin, Texas. She received her doctoral degree in anthropology from the University of Arizona in 1997. Her research interests include prehistoric economic organization, craft specialization, compositional analysis, and ceramic technology.

KEITH W. KINTIGH is professor of anthropology at Arizona State University and has held appointments at the University of California at Santa Barbara and the University of Arizona. His research focuses on the social, political, and economic organization of middle-range societies. Over the last twenty-five years, he has concentrated his fieldwork in the Cíbola area near Zuni, New Mexico, and along the upper Little Colorado River in Arizona. Kintigh is also known for his publications concerning the development and use of quantitative and formal methods in archaeology. He earned his Ph.D. in anthropology at the University of Michigan in 1982.

TIMOTHY A. KOHLER is professor and the current chair of anthropology at Washington State University. He graduated from New College (Sarasota, Florida) in 1972 with an A.B. in general studies and received his M.A. (1975) and Ph.D. (1978) in anthropology from the University of Florida. He recently served as the Fulbright–University of Calgary chair in North American studies and is an external faculty member at the Santa Fe Institute. Recent publications include *Dynamics in Human and Primate Societies: Agent-Based Modeling of Social and Spatial Processes* (Santa Fe Institute and Oxford University Press, 1999), coedited with George Gumerman.

BARBARA J. MILLS is associate professor of anthropology and director of the Archaeological Field School at the University of Arizona. She received her A.B. from the University of Pennsylvania in 1976 and her M.A. (1982) and Ph.D. degrees (1989) from the University of New Mexico. She has directed field and laboratory projects in the Zuni, Eastern Mimbres, Chaco, Rio Grande, and Mogollon Rim areas of the American Southwest. Her interests include the social contexts of craft economies, ceramic analysis, gender and archaeology, and the archaeology of inequality. She is currently investigating Western Pueblo social, economic, and political organization in the Silver Creek area of eastern Arizona.

PAUL E. MINNIS is an associate professor of anthropology at the University of Oklahoma. He received his Ph.D. from the University of Michigan in 1981. He has conducted fieldwork in the Four Corners, Mimbres, and Chihuahua areas of the Southwest. His interests include ethnobotany, famine foods, sociopolitical evolution, ecological anthropology, biodiversity, and indigenous ecology. He is a frequent contributor to works on the ethnobotany of the Greater Southwest and the sociopolitical organization of the Casas Grandes region.

ELIZABETH M. PERRY received a B.A. in anthropology from Arizona State University in 1996. Currently she is a graduate student in anthropology at the University of Arizona. She has worked in the Zuni area, the Four Corners region, the Hopi area, and the Silver Creek area. Her interests include Southwestern prehistory, social theory, gender and sexuality, bio-archaeology, and health and status differentiation in small-scale societies.

JAMES M. POTTER received a B.A. in anthropology and Near Eastern studies at the University of California–Berkeley in 1987 and an M.A. and Ph.D. in anthropology at Arizona State University in 1991 and 1997, respectively. His M.A. research focused on the effects of settlement mobility on Pleistocene lithic assemblage variability in the southern Levant. His Ph.D. research, upon which this essay is based, investigated the Pueblo III to Pueblo IV transition in the Zuni region of the American Southwest. His interests include ritual and social organization in middle-range societies, faunal and lithic analysis, and quantitative methods, especially computer simulation and spatial analyses.

KATHERINE A. SPIELMANN is an associate professor in the Department of Anthropology at Arizona State University. She received her Ph.D. in anthropology at the University of Michigan in 1982 and has conducted archaeological fieldwork in the Southeastern and Southwestern United States. Recent publications have focused on craft specialization in middle-range societies, gender in archaeology, and political organization in the late prehistoric Southwest.

SCOTT VAN KEUREN is currently completing his dissertation at the University of Arizona. His research focuses on the social context of production and use of Pueblo IV period polychromes in eastern Arizona. He is interested in the social correlates of ceramic design, the role of painted pottery in human societies, and the reorganization of pueblo communities in the fourteenth-century upland Southwest. He recently published *Ceramic Design Structure and the Organization of Cibola White Ware Production in the Grasshopper Region, Arizona* (Arizona State Museum Archaeological Series, 1999).

MATTHEW W. VAN PELT is a Ph.D. student in anthropology at Washington State University. His B.A. and M.A. in anthropology were from the

University of Cincinnati in 1995 and 1997, respectively. He has recently worked with the Osaka City Cultural Properties Association in Japan and has been associated with the Upper Basin Archaeological Research Project in northern Arizona for a number of years. His dissertation research focuses on new techniques for interpreting the spatial patterning of prehistoric land use on the South Rim of the Grand Canyon. Recent publications include a contribution to Koukogaku Kenkyu (Archaeological Research) in Japan.

MICHAEL E. WHALEN is a professor of anthropology at the University of Tulsa. He received his Ph.D. in 1976 from the University of Michigan. He has conducted fieldwork in Mesoamerica and the Southwest, including the Casas Grandes, El Paso, and Oaxaca areas. His interests include cultural ecology, settlement patterns, and ceramic analysis. He is codirector (with Paul E. Minnis) of the Paquimé Regional Survey project in northern Chihuahua.

W. H. WILLS is an associate professor of anthropology at the University of New Mexico. He received his B.A. from the University of New Mexico in 1977 and his Ph.D. from the University of Michigan in 1985. He has done fieldwork in several portions of the Southwest, including Chaco Canyon. Most recently he has been directing fieldwork near Cochiti, New Mexico. His interests include social and economic organization.

LORENE Y. L. YAP is a visiting professor in the Department of Anthropology, Washington State University, Pullman. She holds an A.B. in economics from Stanford University and an M.A. and Ph.D. in economics from Harvard University. A specialist in microeconomics, economic development, demography, and migration, Yap is retired from a position as a manager and economist for the World Bank and has also served as a senior research associate at the Urban Institute and professor in economics at SUNY–Binghamton. Her publications include contributions to the *Journal of Development Economics,* the *Quarterly Review of Economics,* and the *Journal of Human Resources.*

Index

145–47; of utilitarian, 127, 129. *See also* exchange

Chaco Canyon, 19–44, 219

Chaco Phenomenon, 201; described, 19; and Southwestern Cult, 40–41

Chalowa, 102

Chetro Ketl, 25–29, 30, 34

Chicken Ranch, 138, 141, 145–47, 149, 151, 152

chiefdoms: described, 208–209; Hawaiian, 25; in Hohokam society, 159; Mississippian societies as, 154; in prehistoric Southwest, 154–55, 208, 209–11; protohistoric Zuni as, 97; and redistributive economies, 195; variability in, 155. *See also* neo-evolutionary theory

Choctaw, 123–27

Cíbola, 97, 100

Cibola White Ware, 86

Cienega, 72, 112

Civano phase, 122, 129, 131–32, 134

civic-territorial, 156, 160–64

complex adaptive systems theory, 4, 12, 180

complexity theory, 5; and protohistoric Pueblos, 114

comunidad, 164–65

Coronado, 97, 98, 102. *See also* Spanish accounts

corporate strategy. *See* dual-processual theory

craft specialization, 7; at Casas Grandes, 170–71, 175, 223; and markets, 199

cremation: distribution of, 115n. 3; at Hawikuh, 109; in historic Zuni, 109, 115n. 3; at Los Muertos, 115n. 3; at Pueblo Grande, 115n. 3

Cushing, Frank, 63, 97

dialectics, 136

direct historical approach, 95, 216

dual-processual theory, 4, 136; as applied to Casas Grandes, 174, 223–24; as applied to Classic Hohokam, 132–35; as applied to ethnographic mound-building groups, 132–33; as applied to Marana community, 150–52; as applied to protohistoric Rio Grande, 57–58; as applied to proto-historic Zuni, 98–100, 113; described, 10–11, 47–48, 81, 150, 155, 211–16, 220–24; and reciprocity, 193

East Community, 44n. 3

Eggan, Fred, 217

elite, defined, 174–75

elite status, cross-cultural data on, 174–75

embedded specialization, 7

exchange: as balanced reciprocity, 182; in dual-processual theory, 214, 221–22; of glazed ceramics, 51–54; long-distance, 197, 201; in protohistoric Rio Grande, 47; Pueblo-Plains, 49–50, 197, 203; among pueblos, 50; role of, 58; of utilitarian ceramics, 127, 129. *See also* reciprocity

feasting: around Casas Grandes, 176; ceremonial, 54; competitive, 18, 56; function of, 176; at Gran Quivira, 54–55, 57, 201; in historic Pueblos, 22; intercommunity, 56; in northern Southwest, 8; as "pathway to power," 114; and platform mound construction, 126; on platform mounds, 120; and prestige in middle-range societies, 47, 48; in protohistoric Rio Grande, 14; at Pueblo Colorado, 54–55; in Pueblo IV Zuni, 116n. 7; and religious events, 56–57; and roasting pits, 176

Fourmile Polychrome, 87, 89, 90, 92; compositional analysis of, 89; use-wear on, 90
Fourmile Ruin, 84
Fourmile style, 85–94; significance of, 93
Fried, Morton, 208, 215
Frijoles Canyon, 196

Galisteo Basin glaze ware, 47
Galisteo Basin pueblos, 47
Gila phase, 122
Gila Polychrome, 87, 107, 108–109
Gila River, platform mound cluster, 129–30
Gran Quivira, 49–58, 72, 201
Grasshopper Polychrome, 90, 91, 92
Grasshopper Pueblo, 68, 84, 87, 90, 92–93; migration to, 91
great houses, Chacoan: construction histories of, 24–31; described, 19; outside of Chaco Canyon, 22; residential function of, 31–32

Hawikku, 8. See also Hawikuh
Hawikuh: excavations at, 97; glazed Zuni ceramics at, 103; historic ceramic types, 103, 107; importance in Zuni system of, 111; mortuary data from, 15, 97, 104–11; polity at, 102; Salado polychromes at, 108–109; Spanish accounts of, 98, 104
Heshotauthla, 112
Heshotauthla ceramic types, 103
heterarchy, 4, 211; at Casas Grandes, 179; defined, 11–12, 48; in proto-historic Zuni, 100, 112; in South-west, 12
hierarchy: at Casas Grandes, 170–72; and centralization, 211; at Chaco, 23; and communication, 37; cross-cultural identification of, 220; in

dual-processual theory, 223; in Marana community, 140, 149–50; in prehistoric and protohistoric Pueblos, 96, 100; in protohistoric Zuni, 101; ritual basis for, 60–66; simultaneous vs. sequential, 136, 214; in Southwest, 207
Hillside Ruin, 44n. 3
Hohokam, Classic period, 219; embedded specialization in, 7; labor recruitment in, 10; mortuary data from, 164, 167; Phoenix area, 127–35; platform mounds in, 117, 162, 163; residential structure in, 157–58; social power in, 165–66. See also Marana community; Marana platform mound
Hohokam, Preclassic: ball courts in, 162, 163; and corporate leadership, 151; cremation rituals in, 163; in Marana area, 138, 151; residential structure in, 157–58; ritual artifacts in, 159
Homolovi, Salado polychromes from, 108
Homol'ovi II, 72
Hopewell, 202
Hopi, historic: factionalism, 21; land, 22; leadership, 8; organization, 100–101; and Totonteac, 100
Hopi, protohistoric: ceramics at Hawikuh and Kechipawan, 107; exchange in, 197; markets in, 202
Hopi Yellow Ware, 87
Hungo Pavi, 30
hunting: communal strategy, 70; and ritual, 70–72, 77
Huntington, 138, 141, 145–47, 149, 151, 152

Ifaluk, 123–27
irrigation: control in historic Pueblos,

22; and leadership, 165; management and Hohokam platform
mounds, 121; Piman, 165; along
Rio Grande, 203. *See also* canal networks; canal system

Kachina Cult, 68
kachinas, 112, 200
Kechipawan: excavation at, 97; glazed
Zuni ceramics at, 103; importance in
Zuni system of, 111; mortuary data
from, 15, 103–11; in settlement system, 102; Spanish accounts of, 104
Kechipawan Polychrome, 103
Kinishba, 84
Kin Nahasbas, 44n. 3
kinship: vs. descent-based strategies,
222; in dual-processual theory, 221;
Hohokam patterns of, 158–60; and
inequality, 9; and kivas, 160; and
labor recruitment, 10
kivas: change in use over time, 77; in
great houses, 29; investment in, 32;
in protohistoric Rio Grande, 46;
ratio to rooms in Pueblo IV, 69; as
ritual architecture, 85, 147. *See also*
ritual architecture
kivas, great, 160; near Chacoan great
houses, 31; at Chetro Ketl, 29; and
ritual activity, 67
kivas, small: ethnographic view of, 161;
Hohokam equivalents of, 160
Kluckhohn site, 67, 72
Kwakina Polychrome, 103

labor estimates: for Chacoan great
houses, 25, 26, 29–30; for Hawaiian
temples, 25; in Southwest, 9
labor organization, in dual-processual
theory, 213
Laguna Pueblo, 161
Las Colinas, 127

La Vaca Enferma, 138, 144, 146
Los Morteros, 138, 140, 141, 142, 143,
145–47, 149, 151, 152
Los Muertos, 115n. 3

macaws, 170, 176, 177, 178
Mapuche, 123–27, 131
Marana community, 15–16, 137–52
Marana platform mound, 134, 138,
140–52
markets: and aggregation, 199; antiquity in Americas of, 194; archaeological identification of, 194–95; and
craft specialization, 199; defined,
194, 206n. 6; at Gran Quivira, 201–
202; and kinship, 203; and migration,
199, 203; in northern Rio Grande,
199, 203; origin of, 199, 203–204;
and states, 195; traits of, *198*
Marquesa, 123–27, 131
masks: in ritual, 9; at Teotihuacan, 218
Matsaki, 102; in Spanish accounts, 98,
104
Matsaki Brown-on-buff, 107–108
Matsaki Polychrome, 107–108
Maya, 216
McElmo phase, 30
Medio period, 168
Mesa Grande, 119
Mesoamerica: ball courts in, 163; connection with Casas Grandes, 170,
171; ethnographic data from late
Postclassic, 170; iconography and
power, 82
Mexico, northern, ball game, 163
middle-range society: Casas Grandes
as, 176–77; defined, 176; inequality
in, 79; and platform mounds, 122–
27; variability in, 47
migration: and collective ritual at
Chaco, 39–40; and corporate formations, 224; and cremation at

Zuni, 115n. 3; cross-cultural patterns, 7; explanation of, 199; to Grasshopper Pueblo, 91; and leadership, 18; into Little Colorado River drainage, 85; into Marana community, 151–52; and markets, 199–200, 203; into Mogollon Rim area, 85; onto Pajarito Plateau, 196; and platform mound construction, 131–32; of protohistoric Zuni, 111–12; in Pueblo histories, 111; in Pueblo IV period, 112; at Pueblo III to IV transition, 84; into San Juan Basin, 38; and social inequality, 91; into Tonto Basin, 85

Mirabal, 72–73

Mississippian societies: as chiefdoms, 154; iconography and power, 82; mortuary data from, 173; social components of, 160

monumental architecture: at Casas Grandes, 169; defined, 120; in Egypt, 38; great houses as, 19; in Marana community, 140–41; in Neolithic Europe, 38; in prehistoric Pueblos, 211; at Teotihuacan, 218. *See also* great houses; platform mounds

mortuary data: from Casas Grandes, 172–73; from Classic period Hohokam, 164, 167; from Hawikuh, 15, 97, 104–11; from Kechipawan, 15, 103–11; from Mississippian societies, 173; from Teotihuacan, 218

Muchas Casas, 138, 143–44, 146

Natchez, 123–27, 131

National Museum of the American Indian, 97, 116n. 6

neo-Darwinian theory, 5

neo-evolutionary theory, 3; as applied

to protohistoric Pueblos, 95–96; as applied to Southwest, 88, 136, 154–55, 207, 209–11; described, 208–209; and hierarchy, 211

neo-Marxist theory, 5, 9

network strategy. *See* dual-processual theory

obsidian, compositional analysis, 143–44

Pajarito Plateau, 195–96

Papaguería, platform mound cluster, 129

Paquimé, 7, 168. *See also* Casas Grandes

Pecos, 197

Peñasco Blanco, 30

Peru, 82

Pescado, 112

Phoenix area, platform mounds, 15, 17, 121–22, 127, 129–32, 133–34, 162

Picacho Peak, platform mound cluster, 129

Pimans: ball game, 163; irrigation, 165; kinship, 158–59

Pinedale Black-on-red, 86

Pinedale Black-on-white, 86

Pinedale Polychrome, 86

Pinedale Ruin, 84

Pinedale style, 85–94

Pinnawa, 102

Pinnawa Red-on-white, 107

Pinto Polychrome, 86

Plains. *See* exchange, Pueblo-Plains

platform mounds: appearance of, 117, 162; at Casas Grandes, 171; clusters in Southwest, 129; cross-cultural data on, 122–27; defined, 117; description of Southwestern, 118–20, 129–30; distribution of, 118, *118;* function of, 15, 120–22, 163–

64; and irrigation management, 121; in Marana community, 140–41, 147; at Mesa Grande, 119–20; as monumental architecture, 120; in Phoenix Basin, 15, 17, 121–22, 127, 129–32, 133–34, 162; at Pueblo Grande, 119–20; in Tonto Basin, 15, 17, 121, 129–30, 134; in Tucson Basin, 15–16, 129–30, 134, 162

plazas: function of, 76, 90; in Pueblo IV, 67, 76, 84; and ritual activity, 67–69

pochteca, 170–71

Point of Pines Pueblo, 84, 87

power, defined, 61

prestige goods: at Casas Grandes, 171, 175; Classic period Hohokam, 165, 167; in dual-processual theory, 48, 214, 221–22; iconography and leadership, 81–82; in Marana community, 141–42, 148; in Phoenix Basin, 17; Pinedale-style ceramics as, 89, 91; and political strategies, 48, 174; in protohistoric Rio Grande, 46, 58; in protohistoric Zuni, 113; in Southwest, 17; in Tonto Basin, 17; in Tucson Basin, 17

public architecture. *See* ball courts; kivas; platform mounds; plazas; ritual architecture

Pueblo Alto, 30, 32, 36

Pueblo Bonito, 25, 30, 36, 38

Pueblo Colorado, 49–58, 201

Pueblo del Arroyo, 30

Pueblo de los Muertos, 67, 70, 72, 74, 112, 202

Pueblo IV period: described, 67, 76; ritual practice in, 67–70; settlement pattern in, 84

Pueblo Grande, 115n. 3, 119, 127, 129, 134, 164

Pueblo Revolt, 97, 101

Pueblo III to IV transition, 84, 89

Pueblos, Classic period. *See* Pueblos, protohistoric

Pueblos, historic: dual organization in, 75; game animals in, 71, 75; kinship and lineage in, 158, 159–60; labor in, 217; leadership and architecture in, 22; organization in, 21–22, 216–18; reciprocity in, 191–92; ritual in, 63, 217; social power in, 83

Pueblos, prehistoric, traits of, 209–11

Pueblos, protohistoric: as tribes, 95; hierarchy in, 96

Q-Ranch Pueblo, 84

Rancho Bajo, 138, 143–44

Rancho Derrio, 138, 143–44

reciprocity: cross-cultural patterns of, *182;* defined, 205n. 1; explanations of, 181–83; in historic Pueblos, 192; origin and maintenance of, 204; in prehistoric Pueblos, 200; traits of, *198,* 201

religious architecture. *See* ritual architecture

ritual: and Chacoan great house construction, 23–24, 33–36, 37–38; in Classic period Hohokam, 147, 148, 163; communal, 64, 69; cremation, 163; in dual-processual theory, 213; ethnographic examples of, 62–66; exclusionary, 147, 148, 163; knowledge and ceramic style, 85–86, 91, 93; masking in, 9; and migration at Chaco, 39–40; performance, 64–66; on platform mounds, 121, 133–34, 164; and power, 8–9, 14, 62–63, 75–76, 83; Pueblo IV, 67–70; secular, 42; and style, 14

ritual architecture: ball courts as, 148; kivas as, 67, 85, 147; platform